THE
PEOPLE'S
BUSINESS

THE REPORT OF THE CITIZEN WORKS CORPORATE REFORM COMMISSION

THE
PEOPLE'S
BUSINESS

CONTROLLING CORPORATIONS AND RESTORING DEMOCRACY

LEE DRUTMAN AND CHARLIE CRAY

FOREWORD BY RALPH NADER

BK
BERRETT-KOEHLER PUBLISHERS, INC.
San Francisco

Berrett-Koehler Publishers, Inc.
235 Montgomery Street, Suite 650
San Francisco, CA 94104-2916
Tel: (415) 288-0260 Fax: (415) 362-2512 www.bkconnection.com

ORDERING INFORMATION

Quantity sales. Special discounts are available on quantity purchases by corporations, associations, and others. For details, contact the "Special Sales Department" at the Berrett-Koehler address above.

Individual sales. Berrett-Koehler publications are available through most bookstores. They can also be ordered direct from Berrett-Koehler: Tel: (800) 929-2929; Fax: (802) 864-7626; www.bkconnection.com

Orders for college textbook/course adoption use. Please contact Berrett-Koehler: Tel: (800) 929-2929; Fax: (802) 864-7626.

Orders by U.S. trade bookstores and wholesalers. Please contact Publishers Group West, 1700 Fourth Street, Berkeley, CA 94710. Tel: (510) 528-1444; Fax (510) 528-3444.

Berrett-Koehler and the BK logo are registered trademarks of Berrett-Koehler Publishers, Inc.

Printed in the United States of America

Berrett-Koehler books are printed on long-lasting acid-free paper. When it is available, we choose paper that has been manufactured by environmentally responsible processes. These may include using trees grown in sustainable forests, incorporating recycled paper, minimizing chlorine in bleaching, or recycling the energy produced at the paper mill.

Library of Congress Cataloging-in-Publication Data

Drutman, Lee, 1961–
    The people's business : controlling corporations and restoring democracy /
by Lee Drutman and Charlie Cray.
        p. cm.
    Includes bibliographical references and index.
    ISBN 1-57675-309-3
    1. Corporations—Social aspects—United States. 2. Corporations—Corrupt practices—United States. 3. Corporate governance—United States. 4. Social responsibility of business—United States. I. Cray, Charlie, 1976– II. Title.

HD2785.D78 2004
333.6′0973—dc22   2004048604

First Edition
09 08 07 06 05 04   10 9 8 7 6 5 4 3 2 1

CONTENTS

FOREWORD

By Ralph Nader

The corporate supremacists of early-twenty-first-century America are at the pinnacle of their domination over our political economy, our culture, our educational institutions, our choice of technologies, and our foreign and military policies. At no time in our history—not even in the Gilded Age of the Robber Barons— have the floodgates of commercialism been flung open in so many directions to subordinate, suppress, destroy, or distort those values that so informed our Declaration of Independence.

The more myopic of these corporate barons, still riding the crest of the recent crime wave that provoked little in the way of institutional change or shifts of power, can look over their globalized domains with avaricious satisfaction. Their concentrated power over all levels of government, their centralized control of the mass media, and their penetration of the minds of youngsters, with daily brain-shredding entertainment by violence and addiction, has made them both the financiers and practitioners of oligarchy and plutocracy.

Yet, the residual stamina of our weakened democracy still contains the seeds of its own regeneration. Like nature abused by polluters until a tipping point is crossed at which time it turns against its abusers with a ferocity known as the collapse of ecosystems, the citizenry can take and take and take only so much of the humiliating abuses of their work, their dignity. Eventually there must come a point when they will reassert their own sovereignty against the soulless control of those artificial entities that our state governments charter without responsibility or accountability—large corporations.

When that time will come, no one knows, just as no one knows when the repressed poor in our country will be heard from.

Certainly, even the more thoughtful corporatists must marvel at how far their more pernicious counterparts have been able to push the envelope without retribution. Indeed, so entrenched has corporate power grown that it has become almost immune from mainstream media muckraking, which dutifully produces its exposés to little avail.

Yet what goes around comes around. Warnings about excessive greed have increasingly come from inside the business community—from the Buffetts, the Druckers, the Soroses, and the Monks—and have been denounced on the front cover of leading business magazines, including *Business Week* and *Fortune*. Moreover, the secular shift of economic activity and dynamism is away from responding to human necessities to focusing on wants and whims. This has allowed enormous statistical productivity gains in our economy to expand hand in hand with endemic poverty, a widening disparity of wealth, and the downward drift of the middle class in the midst of crumbling infrastructures and public institutions. In his prescient book, *The Affluent Society* (1958), John Kenneth Galbraith wrote of a public squalor and private affluence that looks quaint compared to the expansion of those contrasts in contemporary America.

Just as every oak tree began as an acorn, so too the coming systematic drive for *corporate reform*—let that phrase ring throughout the land—may be seen in the acorn planted by the Citizen Works Corporate Reform Commission and its product, *The People's Business*. Other fine books have been written over the past decade about various dimensions of commercial rampage. They are largely descriptive with some recommendations in later chapters. *The People's Business* is entirely about approaches that confront corporate crime, fraud, and abuses at the level of their poisoned fruit and their roots. These structural and prosecutorial remedies strive not for sporadic law enforcement that leaves the roots able to ply their nefarious trades and controls, but for the deterrence and the sanctions that reshape economic power as servants, not masters, of the people and their supposed democratic institutions.

Sporadic law enforcement—against the Enrons, WorldComs, HCAs, Merrill Lynches, and Pfizers—is just that, and quantitatively

FOREWORD | ix

comes nowhere near the trillions of dollars looted or drained from investors, workers, and pension holders over the past four years. But it preserves the appearances of government and political leadership as if something enduring is occurring. But it is not. Forty years ago, a comparable corporate crime wave, headlined by the mainstream press and television networks repeatedly, would have produced tougher laws, stronger penalties, and larger enforcement budgets. Today, the crime wave only produced the Sarbanes-Oxley Act, a limited, modest piece of legislation that only addressed a small sliver of the problem (accounting fraud). Yet members of Congress, unwilling to rock the corporate money boat upon which their political fortunes float, touted the bill as if it would put the whole mess behind us.

The People's Business addresses the "mess" with a wide range of integrated reforms that complement each other and make it difficult for omnipresent corporate attorneys to slide around, below, or above their vigilance. These reforms provide more effective public enforcement and more enabling private enforcement, more criminal and civil remedies and deterrence and restitution. This report is intended to be a catalytic provocation for thoughtful citizen engagement of the question: How do we organize a proactive offensive to take our country back from corporations and restore democracy?

Corporations are different from you or me; they are artificial persons under the law, not real persons. Unless their rights and roles as business institutions are subordinated to those of the people, there cannot be a semblance of "equal justice under the law." Corporatism, as businessman and corporate governance leader Robert Monks points out, is the major power menace in our country. It is why investors have been stripped of control over the corporations they own. It is why tens of millions of workers and individuals do not earn a living wage or do not have health insurance. It is why we have a tax system that has disgraced our politics and economy with its waste, unfairness, and perverse incentives. It is why our elections are for sale, our many politicians are for sale, our government is for sale. It is why giant corporations dominating one industry and area of commerce after another are strategically planning our global futures—our economic, political, military, environmental, educational, worker, consumer, taxpayer, even our genetic futures. That is what they do: amass power behind their strategic planning. That is what we the people do not do.

This report by the Corporate Reform Commission lights and paves the way for this great and needed initiative by enough committed people from all backgrounds who want to shape the future as if the children of the world today and their posterity matter first and foremost.

Ralph Nader
Washington, D.C.
May 2004

ABOUT THE CITIZEN WORKS CORPORATE REFORM COMMISSION

The Citizen Works Corporate Reform Commission is an advisory commission of academics, activists, authors, professionals, and others concerned with questions of corporate power. Though this book is the Report of the Corporate Reform Commission, individual commission members bear no responsibility for the specific conclusions of the report.

The members of the commission who have endorsed the report are as follows:

Theresa Amato, Former President, Citizen Works

Nicholas A. Ashford, Professor of Technology and Policy, Director, Technology and Law Program, Massachusetts Institute of Technology

Medea Benjamin, Founding Director, Global Exchange

Steve Conn, Retired Professor of Justice, University of Alaska

Charlie Cray, Director, Center for Corporate Policy; Former Director of the Campaign for Corporate Reform, Citizen Works

David Crowther, Professor of Corporate Social Responsibility, London Metropolitan University

Herman Daly, School of Public Affairs, University of Maryland

Kevin Danaher, Co-Founder, Global Exchange

Charles Derber, Professor of Sociology and Political Economy, Boston College

Tom Devine, Legal Director, Government Accountability Project

Jesse Dillard, KPMG Professor of Accounting, University of Central Florida

Lee Drutman, Former Communications Director, Citizen Works

Ralph Estes, Professor Emeritus of Accounting, American University

Bill Fletcher, President, TransAfrica Forum

Frances Fox Piven, Professor of Public Policy and Public Administration, CUNY Graduate Center

Martin Freedman, Professor of Accounting, Towson University

Bishop Thomas J. Gumbleton, Auxiliary Bishop, Archdiocese of Detroit

Rev. Graylan S. Hagler, Plymouth Congregational Church

Wenonah Hauter, Director, Public Citizen/Critical Mass Energy & Environment Program

Hazel Henderson, Evolutionary Economist; Columnist, Interpress Service; Co-creator, the Calvert-Henderson Quality of Life Indicators

Robert Jensen, Professor, Department of Journalism, University of Texas

Nicholas Johnson, Professor, College of Law, University of Iowa

Marjorie Kelly, Co-Founder and Editor, Business Ethics

Charles Kernaghan, National Labor Committee

David Korten, President, People Centered Development Forum

Marc J. Lane, President, The Law Offices of Marc J. Lane, P.C., and of its Financial Services Affiliates

Robert McChesney, Institute of Communications Research, University of Illinois

Lawrence E. Mitchell, Professor, George Washington University Law School

Robert A.G. Monks, Publisher

Ted Nace, founder, Peachpit Press

Ralph Nader, Consumer Advocate; Founder, Citizen Works

Jan Pierce, former Vice-President, Communications Workers of America

Mark Ritchie, Institute for Agriculture and Trade Policy

Anita Roddick, Founder and Co-Chair, The Body Shop; Board Director, Ruckus Society

Linda Ruchala, Associate Professor of Accountancy, University of Nebraska Lincoln

Alice Slater, attorney and board member, of the Nuclear Policy Research Institute, the Global Network Against Weapons

and Nuclear Power in Space, and the New York City Bar
   Ass'n Committee for International Security Affairs
Tony Tinker, Professor of Accountancy, Baruch College—City
   University of New York
Chris Townsend, Political Action Director, United Electrical
   Workers Union (UE)
Judy Wicks, Co-founder/Co-Chair, Business Alliance for Local
   Living Economies; President and Founder, White Dog Café
Cynthia Williams, Professor, University of Illinois College of Law
Paul Williams, Professor of Accounting, North Carolina State
   University

ACKNOWLEDGMENTS

We'd like to begin by thanking the Citizen Works Corporate Reform Commission, whose ideas and insight are the basis of this report. Without their tireless probing of the tough questions about corporations over many years, none of this would have been possible.

Among the commission members, there are several who have proven to be an especially invaluable resource. We want to especially thank David Korten and Ted Nace for spending much valuable time pushing us to think harder and smarter. Robert Hinkley, Larry Mitchell, and Ralph Estes also deserve thanks for their advice and assistance.

We also owe a special thanks to Robert Weissman, whose thorough reading of our entire manuscript proved an invaluable part of the always-difficult editing process. We also want to thank Tom Curren, David DeRosa, Jeff Kaplan, Gail Martin, Carl Mayer, Jim McNeill, James McRitchie, Jeff Milchen, Russell Mokhiber, John Richard, and Tyson Slocum for their valuable feedback along the way.

Finally, we'd like to thank Citizen Works, and especially Ralph Nader and Theresa Amato, for allowing us to devote so much of our time to gathering and honing the ideas presented in this book over the course of two and a half years. In addition to Theresa Amato and Ralph Nader, we'd like to thank all of our former colleagues at Citizen Works for their support, insight, and camaraderie: Ali Arace, Heidi Grube, Jacob Harold, Laila Hlass, Katie Selenski, Jennifer Tucker, and R. Peter Wolf. We would also like to thank the Unilever Fund of the Ben and Jerry's Foundation, whose generous grants helped to make this work possible.

INTRODUCTION

*"The citizens of the United States must effectively
control the mighty commercial forces which they have
themselves called into being."*

—Teddy Roosevelt, Speech to Union Army Veterans,
Osawatomie, Kansas, 1910

This is a book about the dominant power that large corporations[1] have over our society and how we can begin to control
them and restore our democracy. We write based on the premise that the increasingly dominant power of large corporations
over virtually every dimension of our lives—economic, political, cultural, even spiritual—poses a fundamental threat to the
well-being of our society. More than ever before, large corporations wield an excessive influence over most aspects of our
lives.

There are many reasons to be concerned. The vast political
influence of large corporations has imperiled the notion of a
democracy "of the people, by the people, and for the people."
The polarization of wealth that corporations have fostered has
undermined our faith in a shared sense of prosperity, raising
the frightening prospects of class warfare. A corporate-driven
consumer culture has driven millions of Americans into personal debt and alienated millions more by convincing them
that the only path to happiness is through the purchase and
consumption of ever increasing quantities of material goods.
The damage to the earth's life-supporting systems caused by the

accelerating extraction of natural resources and the continued production, use, and disposal of life-threatening chemicals and greenhouse gases is large and, in some respects, irreversible. And as corporations become more and more powerful, the problems associated with their dominant position will only grow more acute.

In recent years, many insightful and important books have been written about how and why the intensifying dominance of large corporations threatens most of our ideals of the good life. It is not our intention to duplicate that work in this report, though we will borrow from it frequently.[2] Our goal is to present a variety of approaches to the problem in a way that we hope will encourage people to take up and advance the difficult challenge of organizing an effective response.

This book has its genesis in the aftermath of Enron's December 2001 collapse. Realizing that the factors which led to Enron and other scandals that shook our economy were numerous and complex, Citizen Works, a national nonprofit concerned with the dominant power of corporations, pulled together a diverse group of policymakers, lawyers, scholars, accountants, activists, and others with a variety of expertise in many issues (deregulation, corporate influence over politics, corporate governance, corporate crime, etc.) to share their analysis. This group became the basis of our Corporate Reform Commission, an advisory board of experts that helped us develop this report.[3]

In doing our autopsy on Enron and other corporate scandals, it became clear that no single factor could explain a problem that was so obviously systemic and multidimensional. And yet, as we pushed our own analysis further, we concluded that though the immediate causes were varied, the fundamental cause was not. At the root of Enron and other scandals lay a problem of too much corporate power (over both the economy and the government) and too few limits and restraints on what corporations could do in their relentless pursuit of profit. Answering the frequently posed question, "How can we prevent another Enron?" we responded: "Curb the power of large corporations." That is what this book is about.

THE PROBLEM OF CORPORATE POWER

Today's giant corporations spend billions of dollars a year to project a positive, friendly, and caring image, promoting themselves as "responsible citizens" and "good neighbors." They have large marketing budgets and public relations experts skilled at neutralizing their critics and diverting attention from any controversy. By 2004, corporate advertising expenditures were expected to top $250 billion,[4] enough to bring the average American more than 2,000 commercial messages a day. [5]

Corporations, however, are not the inherently benevolent institutions that they would have us believe that they are. And although we will not deny that corporations can serve certain useful purposes, they are also very dangerous institutions, capable of causing great harm to society, particularly when left largely unregulated.

The problem of the corporation is at root one of design. Corporations are not structured to be benevolent institutions. They are structured to make money. Under the prevailing interpretation of corporate law, corporations have one primary duty: to make money for shareholders. This is a task that corporations have become very, very good at accomplishing. In the pursuit of this one goal, they will freely cast aside concerns about the societies and ecological systems in which they operate.

"The difficulty with the corporate entity," explains corporate governance expert Robert Monks, "is that it has a dynamic that doesn't take into account the concerns of flesh-and-blood human people who form the world in which it exists. . . . In our search for wealth and prosperity, we created a thing that's going to destroy us."[6]

When corporations are reasonably sized, these problems can be dealt with through good rules and limits on corporate behavior—through a well-regulated market system that can channel the enterprise of business into serving the public good. But when corporations reach the size that they have reached today, they begin to overwhelm the political institutions that can keep them in check, eroding key limitations on their destructive capacities. Internationally, of the one hundred largest economies in the world, fifty-one are corporations and forty-nine are nations, and the combined sales of the world's top two hundred corporations are far greater than a quarter of the world's economic activity.[7] Domestically, few would dispute that large corporations are the dominant economic institutions in our society and wield overwhelming influence over the political, legal, and cultural spheres.

HOW BIG BUSINESS GOT TO BE SO BIG

As we will explore in the pages to come, corporations in the United States began as quasi-governmental institutions, business organizations created by deliberate acts of state governments for distinct public purposes such as building canals or turnpikes. These corporations were limited in size and had only those rights and privileges directly written into their charters. Over the course of the nineteenth century, however, with unforeseen consequences, states began to grant increasing independence and freedom to the corporate form. They gradually shifted from special charters to a loose system of general incorporation, allowing anybody to incorporate. They reduced the rules and limits written directly into corporate charters until such rules and limits became virtually nonexistent. Meanwhile, as corporations grew bigger and more independent, their legal status changed from creatures of the state to independent entities, from mere business organizations to "persons" with constitutional rights. By the end of the nineteenth century, corporations had become the dominant institutions in society.

Although the power of large corporations has steadily increased over the course of the twentieth century (despite various attempts to keep their power in check), the last three decades have represented the most sustained pro-business period in U.S. history.

The corporate sector's game plan for fortifying its power in America over the last three decades was outlined in a memo written by soon-to-be Supreme Court Justice Lewis F. Powell Jr. in

August 1971 at the behest of the U.S. Chamber of Commerce. The "Powell Memorandum," drafted in response to rising popular skepticism about the role of big business and the unprecedented growth of consumer and environmental protection laws, was intended as a catalytic plan to spur big business into action.[8] Starting from the premise that "the American economic system is under broad attack," Powell argued that corporate leaders should "study and analyze possible courses of action and activities, weighing the risks against the probable effectiveness and feasibility of each," singling out the campuses, the courts, and the media as key battlegrounds.[9]

Powell also reminded the nation's corporate leaders that "strength lies in organization, in careful long-range planning and implementation, in consistency of action over an indefinite period of years, in the scale of financing available only through joint effort, and in the political power available only through united action and national organizations." Powell's point was simple: develop a multifront plan of attack and patiently implement it.

The business community's response to Powell's call to action was impressive. Marshalling their resources through the Chamber of Commerce and a slew of front groups, think tanks, and foundations, the business sector began to plan and unroll a long-term campaign that has been central in advancing a broad ideological program. At the same time, corporate America's critics have been divided into issue-specific movements and increasingly marginalized.

One of the most significant developments that followed Powell's memo was the formation of the Business Roundtable in 1972 by Frederick Borch of General Electric and John Harper of Alcoa.[10] As author Ted Nace has explained, "the Business Roundtable occupied a position of unique prestige and leverage. It functioned as a sort of senate for the corporate elite, allowing big business as a whole to set priorities and deploy its resources in a more effective way than ever before."[11] Most importantly, the Roundtable was "remarkably successful in imposing a modicum of discipline of 'class solidarity'" among business leaders.[12]

Corporate America's newfound passion for political, legal, and cultural organizing, however, went far beyond the Business Roundtable. As Nace has written, "the 1970s saw the creation of institutions to support the corporate agenda, including foundations, think tanks, litigation centers, publications, and increasingly sophisticated public relations and lobbying agencies."[13] For example, moved by Powell's memo, beer magnate Joseph Coors donated a quarter of a million dollars to the Analysis and Research Association, the forerunner of the massive font of pro-business and conservative propaganda known today as the Heritage Foundation.[14] Meanwhile, existing but tiny conservative think tanks, like the Hoover Institute and the American Enterprise Institute for Public Policy Research grew dramatically in the 1970s. [15] Today, they are key players in the pro-business policy apparatus that dominates state and federal policymaking.

Corporations also funded legal societies like the Washington Legal Foundation, the National Chamber Litigation Center, and about twenty other "free-enterprise" law firms devoted to fostering a system of jurisprudence that supports the rights of corporations to make money above the rights of citizens to govern themselves and enjoy such basic human dignities as clean air, privacy, or decent working conditions.

Meanwhile, as Powell suggested they do, corporations have also established a stronghold in both education and the media. Today, corporate ties to universities run deep, and their designs on our system of public education are growing daily. Meanwhile, the news media are primarily in the control of a handful of corporate conglomerates, all of which largely provide a pro-business filter for anyone who wants to know what's going on in the world.

The money for the business community's ideological vanguard—the nonprofit front groups and think tanks that were formed in the early 1970s—continues to pour in. According to a recent study by the National Committee for Responsive Philanthropy (NCRP), between 1999 and 2001, seventy-nine conservative foundations made more than $252 million in grants to 350 "archconservative policy nonprofit organizations." Atop that list were the Sara Scaife Foundation ($44.8 million), the Lynde and Henry Bradley Foundation ($38.9 million), and the John M. Olin Foundation ($17.4 million), all of which have actively funded many of the groups described above since the early 1970s.[16]

"Unlike most foundations, these conservative foundations are confident and aggressive in making grants available to non-profits that will actively lobby lawmakers, challenge laws and regulations in the courts, and broadcast conservative ideas and ideologies."[17] By contrast, the few timid foundations that have funded liberal causes seem to act as a "drag anchor" on the progressive movement, moving from issue to issue like trust fund children with a serious case of attention-deficit disorder.[18]

Add it all up, and we begin to understand how large corporations have managed to be so successful in establishing such a ubiquitous stranglehold over our economy, politics, and culture.

THE IMPETUS FOR CHANGE

Looking at the unprecedented advance of corporate power over the last three decades, it should be clear that challenging corporate power and changing the course of our political economy is going to be hard work.

Still, the simple fact is that most people do not want the kind of society in which large corporations control everything for their own profit. The vast majority of people, when asked, believe that corporations have too much power and that corporations are too focused on making a profit. "Business has gained too much power over too many aspects of American life," agreed 82 percent of respondents in a June 2000 *Business Week* poll, a year and a half before Enron's collapse. In the same poll, 95 percent of people said that corporations should do more than just make profits and, in fact, "should sometimes sacrifice some profit for the sake of making things better for their workers and communities."[19] A 2004 Harris poll found that three-quarters of respondents said that the image of large corporations was either "not good" or "terrible."[20]

The vast majority of people want to live in a world where they can earn a decent living, reside in a pleasant and safe community, and provide a good life for their children. They want a world where they can enjoy basic freedoms and basic privacies, where they are financially independent and spiritually fulfilled. And the more they begin to understand how these aspirations are imperiled by the growth of unaccountable corporate power, the more popular support there will be for organized resistance.

Perhaps we are approaching a turning point. The corporate scandals at Enron, WorldCom, Tyco, HealthSouth, and many other companies offered ample evidence of much that has gone wrong in the corporate world: disregard for the law, overwhelming political influence, the destructive consequences of blind deregulation, excessive greed, and frenetic profit and growth at all costs, even at the expense of shareholders or the company's own future. The underlying motivation driving the companies involved in the recent scandals—to make money first and foremost (even if it sometimes means manipulating governments and markets and ripping off millions of pensioners, consumers, workers, and investors)—is written into the DNA of all publicly traded corporations. The destructive impulses inherent in the for-profit corporations have led corporate governance experts like Robert Monks to regard them as "doom machines." [21] Meanwhile, the continuous stream of stories about corporate crime, job and industry outsourcing, corporate tax dodging, and war profiteering reinforces a growing sense that We, The People have let corporations get out of control.

FROM ANALYSIS TO ACTION

As we have mentioned, there are many books about the dangerous consequences of corporate power. There are also a number of books that focus on specific approaches to keeping corporations under control. But, as far as we can tell, there are few books that attempt a comprehensive look at the vast array of reforms and approaches that will be necessary if we are truly serious about restoring democracy and controlling corporations here in the United States.

The reason that a multifaceted approach is so important is that corporations have achieved their dominant role in society through a complex power grab that spans the economic, political, legal, and cultural spheres. Any attempt to challenge their power must take all these areas into account.

This book is meant to serve both as a starting point for those who want to understand corporate power and what to do about it and as a general guide for activists who want a fresh perspective.

Our approach is to address the corporation within the framework of domestic U.S. politics. We believe that there is a great need to cohere a domestic strategy for challenging corporate power in the United States, where 185 of the world's 500 largest corporations are headquartered.[22] Since American companies largely set the agenda for the international business world, any changes here will have a far-reaching effect globally.

We do not address many questions related to corporate globalization, such as international trade and development policies. Others have looked at many of these questions from a global perspective. For example, we see no need to duplicate the excellent work of the International Forum on Globalization, which recently re-released *Alternatives to Economic Globalization*.[23] That document, along with others, serves as an important template for those interested in questions concerning global corporate rule, along with the many discussions that are happening at places like the World Social Forum. Indeed, we believe that the emerging global justice movement (as expressed through the protests against the World Trade Organization in Seattle in 1999 and the annual World Social Forum meetings) poses perhaps the strongest challenge to global corporate rule. Although our efforts to challenge corporations here in the U.S. are inevitably bound up in the global justice movement, we have left the broader context for others. We believe there is much to do here in the United States that can have a profoundly important effect on the global situation.

Additionally, this book is not intended as a guide for those interested in organizing campaigns that target specific corporations, even though corporate campaigns are an important way of directly confronting the many egregious abuses and injustices committed by corporations.[24]

Though we recognize that this is not an exhaustive study, we believe that the ideas included in the pages to follow represent much of what needs to be done domestically if we hope to challenge corporate domination and create a sustainable, life-respecting society where people feel empowered to act in their role as citizens. Ultimately, it is our hope that this report will help stimulate further debate and propel those interested in this issue to organize the movement that will be necessary to confront the crisis of unaccountable corporate power in the United States.

WHAT'S INSIDE

As we have said, our focus is primarily on political and legal challenges to corporations and their role in government and society.

In the first three chapters we establish a framework for understanding corporations by first asking questions about what corporations actually are, how they operate, and what legal rights they should have.

In Chapter 1, we look at how corporations are formed and for what reasons. Taking a historical approach, we explore how the corporation evolved from a quasi-public extension of the state with few rights and privileges into a much more private entity with many rights and privileges. By understanding the origin of the corporation as a creature of the state, we believe that we can better understand how we, as citizens with sovereignty over our government, ultimately can and must assert our right to hold corporations accountable.

In Chapter 2, we look at how corporations have come to claim constitutional protections, which were originally intended only for real human beings, in order to undermine laws enacted by citizens. We also look at how corporate legal societies have been successful in promoting the idea of "business civil rights."

In Chapter 3, we examine the system of corporate governance and evaluate whether and how it can be used or changed to force the corporation to respect and reflect the broader public interest. We examine the problem of "shareholder primacy" (the unyielding corporate focus on maximizing shareholder value, at the expense of the public interest) and explore whether it is possible to reform the system of corporate governance in a way that will mitigate these pressures.

In the next two chapters, we look at ways that we can better utilize existing government power to control corporations. In Chapter 4, we explore the importance of stopping deregulation and recommend stronger antitrust enforcement, recognizing that keeping corporations smaller and more competitive is important to our ability to control them and hold them accountable. In Chapter 5, we look at what it will take to bring about a real government crackdown on corporate crime.

Chapter 6 turns to one of the main obstacles we face in implementing many of the specific reforms discussed in this book: corporate domination of our political processes. We explore the fundamental problem of corporate control of our government and discuss strategies for reducing and eliminating corporate influence over the political process.

Finally, we conclude by examining some of the ways we can organize the kind of movement that will be necessary to fundamentally challenge corporate power.

Though the approaches are diverse, they all rest on a fundamental understanding that the best way to control corporations is to reestablish a government "of the people, by the people, and for the people." Democracy means rule by the people, not by corporations or their proxies. Therefore, the task that we set out to accomplish in this book is to understand how we can begin to reestablish true citizen sovereignty in a country where corporations currently have almost all the power. This, we believe, is the people's business.

1 | Reclaiming the Public Purpose of the Corporation

"The State need not permit its own creation to consume it."

—Justices White, Brennan, and Marshall, 1978

In March 2003, a new tobacco company called "Licensed to Kill, Inc." was incorporated by the state of Virginia. The company's purpose, as stated in its articles of incorporation, was "the manufacture and marketing of tobacco products in a way that each year kills over 400,000 Americans and 4.5 million other persons worldwide." The Virginia Secretary of State's office didn't ask any questions. It simply collected the incorporation fee, filed some paperwork, and Licensed to Kill, Inc. was free to conduct business.[1]

Though Licensed to Kill was incorporated by antitobacco activists as a parody, it proved a useful point: that anybody can get a charter to do business, even if the stated purpose of that business is to kill 4.5 million people. In a press release announcing the formation of the company, Director Gary Vastone publicly thanked the Commonwealth of Virginia's State Corporation

Commission for "granting us permission to exist. If a person were to ask the state for authorization to go on a serial killing rampage, he would surely be locked up in a jail or a mental institution. Luckily, such moral standards do not apply to corporations."[2]

Licensed to Kill's charter granted the new corporation all kinds of privileges as defined by the state's corporate laws: unlimited size and scope, unlimited lifespan, and limited liability, among other privileges. All Licensed to Kill had to do was file some paperwork and pay a small fee ($130).

While Licensed to Kill is obviously a parody, real tobacco corporations like Altria (formerly Philip Morris) and RJ Reynolds with actual track records of selling deadly products to consumers also hold corporate charters granted by state governments (Altria is incorporated in Virginia; RJ Reynolds is incorporated in Delaware). Yet, despite evidence that they have violated tobacco control laws around the world,[3] these corporations continue to enjoy all the rights and privileges granted in their corporate charters. Neither the state of Virginia nor the state of Delaware, which so generously granted these charters, has ever proposed revoking the charters of these corporations, even though they have the right to and many tobacco industry critics would argue that there is just cause for doing so.

In fact, thousands of corporations responsible for major social, ecological, and economic crimes continue to exist and prosper, enjoying state-granted powers in spite of their criminal records. If these corporations were ordinary persons, they would probably be locked up and put away for life for what they had done. In some states, they would even be executed. But corporations are not ordinary persons. In fact, they are not persons at all.

Yet what is a corporation? In essence, the corporation is one of many ways to conduct business and organize money and property. It is a legal form, an abstraction that gives incorporators certain rights and privileges they would not normally enjoy on their own. "Corporations are constructs of the law," explains legal scholar Harry Glasbeek. "They are not natural phenomena. No one has ever seen a corporation, smelled a corporation, touched a corporation, lifted a corporation, or made love to a corporation."[4]

The corporate form of business organization essentially allows a bunch of investors to pool their capital together into one shared enterprise—the corporation—in exchange for ownership shares. The owners, in turn, set up a governance structure to carry out the business of the corporation, and, if the company makes money, they traditionally enjoy a share of the profits.

There are millions of corporations in America and around the world. Corporations exist in all forms and sizes. There are publicly traded corporations and privately held corporations, widely held corporations and closely held corporations. There are corporations that are wholly owned subsidiaries of other corporations. There are nonprofit corporations, such as charities, churches, and universities. The list goes on.

Among these variations on the corporate form, however, some are more dangerous than others. The form of the corporation that is of principal concern to us is the large, limited-liability, publicly traded corporation. This is the form of the corporation that dominates our economy and our society.

By "limited-liability, publicly traded corporation," we mean a corporation whose stock certificates of ownership are publicly traded on open markets, such as the New York Stock Exchange, and whose investors are only responsible for their initial investment (limited liability). These companies also enjoy a host of other privileges that we will explore, such as unlimited size, perpetual life, and the ability to own other companies, among others. This is the form of the corporation of which we speak when we refer to corporations throughout this book. Every *Fortune* 500 company is a large, limited-liability, publicly traded corporation.

Though the corporate form that dominates our economy today is one with virtually no inherent limits on behavior and virtually no liability for investors (other than the initial investment), this was not always the case. In a little bit we will take a look at how this current corporate form evolved in American history from a limited and tightly controlled entity to a sprawling and seemingly uncontrollable conglomerate.

However, before we do, we want to be clear that there was nothing inevitable about the corporation evolving the way it did. Early Americans understood both the dangers and benefits of corporations, and they controlled them accordingly, utilizing corporations only for distinct public purposes—to deal with such public matters as bridges, roads, canals, banking, and insurance—tasks that could be considered the people's business. Gradually, however, America began to embrace the corporate form while downplaying its dangers, unleashing a wave of corporations while weakening the mechanisms for controlling them. As a result, today we have a system in which large corporations are the dominant institutions in our society. They maintain incredible power over our lives and can be responsible for devastating social, ecological, and financial harms. And yet, despite their dominant position in society, they have very little accountability to the public, and the ability of the people to use public institutions, such as governments, to control corporations is largely circumscribed.

To understand how we might effectively control corporations today, it makes sense to review the history of corporations and the public's attempts to control them.

A HISTORY LESSON

Although it is possible to trace the roots of the modern corporation back to medieval guilds and towns and churches and universities, perhaps the most logical starting point is the seventeenth-century trading companies of the British Empire, such as the famous East India Company. These companies were different from modern corporations in that they were quasi-governmental institutions chartered by the crown for specific purposes, such as grabbing as much wealth as possible from the East Indies and bringing it back to England. But the basic premise was essentially the same: a bunch of investors pooled their money into a "joint-stock" company, and then, if the enterprise was a success, they shared in the financial rewards. As author Ted Nace notes, "With pooled capital, the corporation for the first time became a single unified entity rather than a federation of independent merchants. The internal consolidation made the joint-stock corporation ideally suited for the emergence of a key defining principle of the corporate form: the idea that a corporation represents a separate legal entity from the owners."[5]

The United States itself began partly as a series of British colonial companies, such as the Virginia Company, chartered by the crown for the purposes of exploring the New World, extracting its wealth and developing its markets. As corporate historian John D. Davis has explained, "The strongest particular motive for the formation of colonial companies was doubtless the economic purpose of establishing and extending English commerce."[6] As these corporations set up shop running the colonies, they employed colonists to develop natural resources for the British crown. Additionally, other British corporations, such as the powerful British East India Company, saw the colonies as markets for their goods.

This exploitive relationship between the colonists and the British corporations would ultimately prove unsustainable. British companies were granted exclusive "monopoly" rights to sell commodities to colonists, which meant high prices and dissatisfied colonists. Things came to a boil with the Tea Act of 1773, which was designed to prop up the fortunes of the East India Company by raising the taxes on non–East India tea and expanding the company's exclusive access to American markets. Local businessmen responded by dumping 90,000 pounds of East India Company tea into Boston Harbor, helping to catalyze a revolution in which the fight for economic independence from British corporations and political independence from the British crown were thoroughly intertwined.

Once the Revolution had been won and the Founding Fathers set upon the task of forming a new government, one of the questions they faced was what role corporations should play in society. As sociologist Charles Perrow has written, "What we take for granted today was hotly debated as the eighteenth century turned into the nineteenth. Citizens and elites recognized at the time that permitting the existence of large organizations that were primarily responsive only to owners, and not to the public, was a fateful act."[7]

The memory of exploitation by British corporations and of European feudalism in general made the Founding Fathers wary of any large concentrations of wealth and power because they knew where such concentrations could lead. And they knew that the corporate form, with its unique capacity to combine the wealth of many parties into one single entity, could pose such a threat if not properly regulated in the public interest. As historian Louis Hartz has written, wariness toward corporations was "one of the most powerful, repetitious and exaggerated themes in popular literature" during the first few decades of the nineteenth century.[8]

Economist Adam Smith, a contemporary and friend of some of America's early leaders, also issued a strong warning against the corporate form. His concern was that the separation of owners and managers inherent in the corporation was a recipe for irresponsible behavior. In his famous 1776 work *Wealth of Nations,* he wrote that "the directors of such companies . . . being the managers rather of other people's money than their own, it cannot well be expected that they should watch over it with the same anxious vigilance with which the partners in a private guild frequently watch over their own. . . . Negligence and profusion, therefore, must always prevail, more or less, in the management of the affairs of such a company."[9] Smith was also generally opposed to corporations because he believed that their tendencies toward monopoly interfered with the workings of the free market's "invisible hand."[10]

Despite these fears and concerns, however, there was also a recognition that the corporation, as a way to organize business, could offer many benefits. After all, a new nation needed turnpikes and banks and canals and insurance and other enterprises that were too massive and risky for individual businessmen to undertake themselves. And through the device of the corporation, individual investors could pool their funds together to form the kind of capital needed to build and maintain a turnpike or a bridge, which would presumably benefit society as a whole.

The balancing act, then, was controlling corporations in such a way that would guarantee that they served the public good, harnessing the ability of the corporate form to stimulate economic development while restraining the irresponsible and even destructive tendencies inherent in the corporate form. This was accomplished by close legislative control of the chartering process. Corporations were only chartered for specific public purposes with clear limits on what they could do. When a corporation caused harm or went beyond its mandate, its charter could be revoked.[11] As Richard Grossman and Frank Adams, co-founders of the Program on Corporations, Law and Democracy (POCLAD), have written, "For one hundred years after the American Revolution, citizens and legislators fashioned the nation's economy by directing the chartering process."[12] Put another way, the early chartering process recognized the public nature of corporations and established that the very legitimacy of the corporation came from the privileges that the sovereign people bestowed on it.

To keep corporations under control, strict limits were placed on corporate enterprises through rules on capitalization, debt, land-holdings, and sometimes even profits. States also limited corporate charters to a set number of years, forcing their review and renewal when the charter expired. Unless a legislature renewed an expiring charter, the corporation was dissolved and its assets divided among shareholders. Strict rules also limited the issuance of stock, clarified shareholder voting rules, and determined procedures for record keeping and disclosure of corporate information. Owners were personally liable for losses incurred from corporate activities. Corporations were strictly prohibited from participating in politics.

Much of what we write into external financial regulations today was directly established in the charters governing a corporation's purpose. Specific rules were written into corporate charters to give equal voting rights to large and small investors, outlaw interlocking directorates, and limit capitalization and debts. A company's accounting books were also turned over to the state legislature upon request.

In 1800, 334 corporations existed in the United States, and the vast majority were chartered to accomplish tasks that could rightly be considered the public's business. Of these 334 corporations, 219 (65.4 percent) were involved in building turnpikes, bridges, and canals. Another 67 (20 percent) were involved in banking and insurance. Just 8 were involved in manufacturing.[13] As Henry Carter Adams described it, "Corporations originally were regarded as agencies of the state. They were created for the purpose of enabling the public to realize some social or national end without involving the necessity of direct government administration. They were in reality arms of the state."[14]

Of course, we shouldn't get too nostalgic for these early days of American corporations. Because legislatures controlled the granting of corporate charters, most of the charters went to politically well-connected and wealthy individuals, who became richer and more influential though their corporations. Many of these early-day corporations also received monopoly rights and government powers of eminent domain (the right to take private land) as part of their charter and pushed hard for other advantages that were not always in the public's interest.

Recognizing the threat from these early corporations, Thomas Jefferson wrote in 1816, "I hope we shall crush in its birth the aristocracy of our monied corporations which dare already to challenge our government to a trial of strength and bid defiance to the laws of our country."[15] Economist Daniel Raymond, meanwhile, wrote in his 1820 *Thoughts on Political Economy* that corporations "are always created for the benefit of the rich, and never for the poor. . . . The rich have money, and not being satisfied with the power which money itself gives them, in their private individual capacities, they seek for an artificial combination, or amalgamation of their power, so that its force may be augmented."[16]

Perhaps the most famous corporate confrontation during this period was President Andrew Jackson's "War on the Bank." At issue was the charter of the Second Bank of the United States, set to expire in 1836. The federally chartered bank had an impressive 35 million dollars in capital, one-fifth of which was government deposits. However, it could use those government deposits as it liked without paying any interest. The bank also enjoyed a monopoly and could not be taxed. In short, the bank possessed "unique and profitable relations with the government."[17]

But the bank was also privately owned, and its president, Philadelphia banker Nicholas Biddle, exhibited little but contempt for government oversight. In an 1824 letter to Washington, Biddle wrote that "no officer of the Government, from the President downwards, has the least right, the least authority, the least pretence, for interference in the concerns of the bank."[18]

Biddle's sentiment, however, was at odds with Andrew Jackson, a self-styled man of the people. Jackson's attorney general, Roger Taney, warned that "this powerful corporation and those who defend it, seem to regard it as an independent sovereignty, and to have forgotten that it owes any duties to the People, or is bound by any laws but its own will."[19] In 1832 Jackson vetoed an extension of the charter, noting that "every monopoly, and all exclusive privileges, are granted at the expense of the public, which ought to receive a fair equivalent."[20]

The War on the Bank went on for several years, and the debate spanned issues of currency and banking as well as corporate power. Still, at the root of the discussion was a strong sentiment that the power of corporations must be kept under control and that the Second Bank had gotten out of control. As Attorney General Taney put it, "It is a fixed principle of our political institutions to guard against the unnecessary accumulation of power over persons and property in any hands. And no hands are less worthy to be trusted with it than those of a moneyed corporation."[21]

Much critical sentiment of the era was directed at the way that corporations were being used as tools to advance the interests of the wealthy and politically well-connected, often through exclusive chartering agreements that allowed for monopolies. As historian Richard Hofstadter has explained it, "The prevalent method of granting corporation charters in the states was a source of enormous resentment. Very often the corporation charters granted by the legislatures were, or were construed to be, monopolies. Men whose capital and influence was too small to gain charters from the lawmakers were barred from such profitable and strategic lines of corporate enterprise as banks, bridges railroads, turnpikes, and ferries."[22]

One solution to the growing problem of corporate power was to open up the chartering process so that anyone, regardless of privilege, could get a corporate charter, thus eliminating the air of political privilege surrounding the process of incorporation. Jackson promoted this solution, and, as historian Arthur Schlesinger Jr. describes it, "sprinkled holy water on corporations, cleansing them of the legal status of monopoly and sending them forth as the benevolent agencies of free competition."[23] Of course, the idea behind general incorporation was to encourage commerce in such a way that would benefit the public at large, allowing anybody who wanted to go into business to enjoy the benefits of the corporate form. Yet, "the fate of Jacksonian economic legislation was that common historical irony: it on the whole promoted the very ends it was intended to defeat."[24]

Though several states, starting with North Carolina in 1795,[25] had passed general incorporation laws for specific types of businesses, it wasn't until 1837 that Connecticut passed the first general incorporation law for "any lawful business." Connecticut did, however, limit incorporation to enterprises with between $4,000 and $200,000 in capital. Other states enacted similar laws in the following decades, and by the end of the 1870s most states had free incorporation laws. However, many states continued to allow for special charters as well for businessmen who wanted something more that what the general incorporation rules offered.[26]

Another important blow to the ability of states to control corporations came in an 1819 legal decision, *Trustees of Dartmouth College v. Woodward.* At issue was a law passed by the state of New Hampshire to turn Dartmouth, a private college chartered by the King of England in 1769, into a public institution in order to "extend the opportunities and advantages of education."[27] The trustees of Dartmouth College, however, argued that the law was unconstitutional because it violated the United States Constitution clause that prohibits a state "from impairing the obligation of contracts." The Supreme Court agreed, establishing the sanctity of the corporate charter and striking a blow against the ability of states to repeal and revise corporate charters.

In response to this decision, many states took it upon themselves to assert tighter public control over corporations. In 1825, for example, Pennsylvania legislators gave themselves the power to "revoke, alter, or annull" the charter of any corporation at any time and then revoked the charters of ten banks in 1832. In 1831, Delaware voters adopted a constitutional amendment that would limit all corporate charters to twenty years. Louisiana and Michigan followed with similar limits. In the 1840s and 1850s, nineteen states amended their constitutions so that legislatures could revoke and alter charters. Rhode Island, for example, declared in 1857 that "the charter or acts of association of every corporation hereafter created may be amendable or repealed at the will of the general assembly."[28]

But despite the new laws, "the [*Dartmouth*] decision expanded the privileges of private property against the claims of the public interest, and it helped unleash capitalist enterprise in nineteenth-century America," as Louis Menand has written.[29] In short, it was the first step in defining the corporation as something beyond the realm of citizen sovereignty.

As the nineteenth century progressed, the economy changed. Agrarianism gave way to industrialization. People left the countryside for the cities. In an age of railroads and steel, of oil and manufacturing, corporations became significant, powerful, and, increasingly, national institutions. And as corporate lawyers increasingly perfected the use of holding companies and trusts to get around existing limits on the size and scope of corporations, state corporate law was about to hit a crisis point.

THE CORPORATE CHARTER RACE TO THE BOTTOM

In the 1870s, oil baron John D. Rockefeller was looking for a way to expand his Standard Oil Company without running afoul of state laws limiting corporate size. As it turned out, Rockefeller's lawyer, S.C.T. Dodd, had just the thing: the "trust" company. By organizing several separate legal companies through one common board of trustees, the "trust" would allow

Rockefeller to control 95 percent of all refined oil shipments by the 1880s.[30]

But Ohio attorney general David K. Watson was on to Rockefeller's tricks, and in 1890 he brought an antitrust suit against the Ohio-chartered Standard Oil Trust. In 1892, the Supreme Court of Ohio ruled that Rockefeller's Standard Oil Trust was "organized for a purpose contrary to the policy of our laws" and therefore "void." The Ohio court found that the Ohio-chartered company had gone beyond its charter by entering into a trust. "The act so done is *ultra vires* [beyond the powers] of the corporation and against public policy," the court held, and ordered a dissolution.[31]

Standard Oil, however, refused to comply and remained steadfast. In 1898, Ohio's attorney general responded by bringing a contempt action against Standard Oil to revoke the company's charter. But instead of sticking around to defend itself, Standard Oil simply picked up and reincorporated in New Jersey, where recent "reforms" in state corporate law had made it possible for a giant trust like Standard Oil to incorporate without any potential legal threat to its size, structure, or market power.

Beginning in 1891, New Jersey had become the first state to allow corporations to buy and sell stock or property in other corporations and issue their own stock as payment, creating "holding companies" that were crucial to the functioning of trusts. The state followed this up by repealing its antitrust law in 1892.[32]

But the real watershed came in 1896, when New Jersey enacted its General Revision Act, an embarrassingly permissive law that effectively signaled the end of states' ability to regulate and control corporations through their charters. The General Revision Act removed the fifty-year limit on corporate charters. It allowed corporations to conduct business in any state or any foreign country. It revised capitalization requirements to pave the way for easy concentration. It also permitted companies to issue nonvoting stock, which enabled certain owners of a corporation to easily retain control. It allowed directors to amend bylaws without the consent of the shareholders.[33]

The result was that a stampede of large companies like Standard Oil rushed to reincorporate in New Jersey. Between 1880 and 1896, 15 corporations with capital of $20 million or more were chartered in New Jersey. Between 1897 and 1904, 104 similarly sized companies were governed by New Jersey's lax laws. In 1896, New Jersey granted 854 charters. In 1906, it granted 2,093 charters. By 1900, 95 percent of the nation's major corporations were chartered in New Jersey.[34]

New Jersey did reap the intended financial rewards from this fire sale of its own sovereignty. In 1893, the state generated $434,000 in corporation fees. In 1896, it gained $857,000 in franchise tax revenues, and in 1906 it generated $3.2 million in tax revenues.[35] The cost to society, however, was dramatic. Because the vast majority of corporations flocked to incorporate in New Jersey, New Jersey's law became the nation's law, creating the legal opportunities for massive consolidation and combination into mergers and trusts. Between 1895 and 1904, 1,800 companies merged to form 137 megacorporations, thoroughly transforming the U.S. economy from a nation of small independent enterprises into the home of a handful of giant corporations. Between 1898 and 1902, 2,653 large firms disappeared in a wave of merger mania.[36]

Though other states initially expressed outrage at New Jersey's changes, when they realized they couldn't beat the Garden State, many of them joined it, removing almost all restrictions in corporate charters and doing away with the idea that corporations should be held directly accountable to the public and should be reasonably constrained in their quest to pursue private profits.

The epilogue to the charter-mongering game of the 1890s came in 1913, when New Jersey decided that maybe it had gone too far and that maybe it was not such a good idea after all to allow corporations to do whatever they wanted. So, under President-Elect Woodrow Wilson, then the governor of New Jersey, the Garden State decided to prohibit many previously allowed corporate privileges, such as combinations, monopolies, price fixing, and other laws that Wilson considered "manifestly inconsistent with the policy of the Federal Government."[37]

"A corporation exists, not of natural right, but only by license of law, and the law, if we look at the matter in good conscience, is responsible for what it creates," Wilson said. "If law is at liberty to adjust the general conditions of society itself, it is at liberty to control these great instrumentalities which nowadays, in so large part, determine the character of society."[38]

Despite Wilson's rousing rhetoric, New Jersey's efforts to tighten its rules had minimal effect. Many companies simply moved to Delaware, which in 1899 had adopted an even more permissive law than New Jersey—and offered even lower fees, to boot. Delaware's 1899 act essentially allowed the incorporators to insert any provisions they wanted in the charter regulating the powers of the corporation, the directors, and the stockholders.[39]

Today more than 308,000 companies, including 296 (59.2 percent) of the *Fortune* 500 largest corporations in the United States, are incorporated in Delaware, which is widely acknowledged as having the most management-friendly statutes of any state. Delaware's laws give executives of the corporation the most liberal control over the company versus minority shareholders and other stakeholders. Delaware has put a lot of effort into making itself the favored state of incorporation, keeping its fees low and its paperwork easy.[40] As a result, the corporate law of Delaware has been more or less the national corporate law for almost one hundred years now.

THE RISE OF LIMITED LIABILITY

Besides reducing their own ability to hold corporations directly accountable, states also fostered increased corporate irresponsibility by a widespread shift to limited liability for investors. What limited liability meant was that corporate investors were only responsible for their initial investment in the company. If a company went into debt, investors might lose everything they invested, but the creditors or unpaid employees couldn't go after the investors' personal assets.

The rise of limited liability in the nineteenth century was justified on the grounds that it was a necessary prod to generate investment because it reduced the risks associated with investing. However, the flip side to this was that it distanced owners from the companies they invested in and, on the whole, encouraged irresponsibility by removing owners from the consequences of their investments. As legal scholar William W. Cook wrote in 1891, "There is nothing in the corporate form itself to justify the exaggerated application of limited liability. This pernicious movement has decreased the personal responsibility on which the integrity of democratic institutions depends, and has introduced into both investments and social services a dangerous element of insecurity."[41]

Limited liability had been around since the early British corporations, and perhaps even earlier. But in early America, there was little consensus on limited liability. Some states granted it, some didn't, and some did for some companies and not for others. Massachusetts, the dominant industrial state in the early nineteenth century, was opposed to limited liability early on. In 1822, for example, the Massachusetts law read, "Every person who shall be a member of any manufacturing company . . . shall be liable, in his individual capacity, for all the debts contracted during the time of his continuing to be a member of such corporation."[42] But by 1839, facing competitive pressure from other states allowing limited liability, Massachusetts had changed its laws to allow for limited liability.[43]

Up until the 1840s, courts generally recognized that incorporators were responsible for outstanding corporate debts.[44] But over the remainder of the nineteenth century judges increasingly recognized limited liability, except when otherwise specified by the corporation's charter. Some states, like Ohio, maintained double liability (investors were liable for twice their original investment) for investors even at the end of the century. And up to the end of the century, nine states, including New York, New Jersey, and Pennsylvania, held stockholders individually responsible for debts owed to workers. It is important to note that even in states like Ohio, which maintained double liability, small and medium-sized corporations continued to incorporate. Indeed, there were many who felt that "full liability served as a check upon irresponsibility, that the more one had at stake, the more carefully one would conduct business affairs. Others felt that abrogating liability was not only bad business but perhaps immoral."[45]

Still, the big corporate money flooded to states with limited liability. Corporations were becoming much larger than ever before, ownership was growing increasingly diffuse, and shareholders were becoming more and more distant from the operations of the corporations they owned. Limited liability also had something to do with the separation of ownership and control. As sociologist William G. Roy has suggested, "One of the consequences of limited liability was that the corporation could to a much greater degree than otherwise act as an entity in itself, apart from its owners, both legally and practically. The conception that stockholders were not liable beyond the value of their stock subscription was closely connected to the concept that the corporation was an entity in itself."[46]

We will return to questions of who should be responsible when things go wrong within the corporation later in this report. In Chapter 3, for example, we will further examine problems of corporate governance. And in Chapter 5, which discusses corporate crime, we will also delve deeper into questions of responsibility at various levels of the corporate hierarchy. For now, however, what is important to understand is that by shifting risks from corporations and their investors onto society as a whole, the law changed the nature of the corporation. In short, these changes made the corporation much harder to control and much less responsible and hence less responsive to the public.

THE POWER OF THE CHARTER

Though today we have largely lost touch with the chartering process that creates corporations, that doesn't mean that we can't begin to take the incorporation process more seriously and recognize that incorporation is a privilege that the public offers to private investors and that the public ought to get something back in return. Indeed, any serious attempt to control corporations should be built on this point. We must recognize that every corporation, be it Wal-Mart, ExxonMobil, General Motors, Halliburton, or any other, exists because once upon a time a state granted a charter to it in exchange for a promise to obey the law. As the Temporary National Economic Committee (TNEC) of the U.S. Congress concluded in 1941, "The principal instrument of the concentration of economic power and wealth has been the corporate charter with unlimited power."[47]

Today, however, we rarely think about how we might place direct limits on corporations through their charters. Incorporation today is a routine, bureaucratic process. States ask very little in return for giving incorporators a whole host of privileges associated with the corporate form, including limited liability, the ability to accumulate unlimited capital and operate anywhere and everywhere at once, and the ability to own other companies, among countless other advantages that the modern corporation enjoys.

One way that states can begin to assert control over corporations using corporate charters is extremely simple: threaten to revoke them.[48] Every state except Alaska has a statute that provides for the revocation of corporate charters.[49] This authority, however, remains woefully underused. Even corporations that engage in repeated criminal activities are rarely threatened with charter revocation.

In 1998 a group of thirty citizens' organizations and individuals decided to test the state of California's willingness to exercise this authority. With the help of Loyola Law School professor Robert Benson, the group filed a 127-page petition asking the California attorney general to revoke the charter of the Union Oil Company of California (Unocal). The group cited ten counts against Unocal, charging that the company was responsible for eighty-two "Superfund" or similar toxic sites and a 1969 oil blowout in the Santa Barbara Channel and was complicit in "unspeakable" human rights violations by working with brutal governments in Afghanistan and Burma, among other crimes.[50] As the petition explained:

> Courts have consistently held that certain acts of wrong-doing clearly warrant charter revocation. Judges have upheld revocation as a remedy for "misuse" or "nonuse" of the corporate charter, "unlawful acts," "fraud," "willful abuse of chartered privileges," "usurpation of powers," "improper neglect of responsibility," "excess of power," "mistake in the exercise of an acknowledged power" and "failure to fulfill design and purpose."
>
> Corporations have been held dissolvable for failing to lay railroad tracks by a date promised, joining other companies to monopolize sugar, conducting fraudulent real estate practices, putting out false advertising, serving polluted water to customers, running baseball games on Sundays, paying members of the president's family excessive salaries, self-dealing, and for the corporate president being convicted four times in a year for illegally selling alcohol.[51]

Attorney General Dan Lungren rejected the petition three days later in a three-sentence letter, declining to act. As Benson described it:

> Lungren's office went into a comical panic when it got wind of the petition. His department called the California Highway Patrol the night before the coalition's press conference at the state office building in Los Angeles and had the CHP warn the group not to appear because a permit was needed to have a press conference on state property. Lungren's spokeswoman told the press first that the attorney general had no authority to revoke corporate charters; then—oops!—reversed herself hours later and said the department would take several months to study it. Three business days later, the refusal letter went out.[52]

Though the petition failed, the filers regrouped and in 2003 worked to introduce a Corporate Three Strikes bill in the California State Senate.[53] As originally drafted, the bill would require the state attorney general to revoke the charter of any corporation that is convicted of three major felonies (defined as felonies with a fine of $1 million or more or that result in a human death) within a ten-year period. For corporations not incorporated in the state, the attorney general would revoke the corporations' rights to conduct business in the state. The law also would require corporations to take out a full-page ad in the state's leading newspapers to publicize their crimes.

The bill met stiff resistance in committee, where it failed to get the support of two key Democrats. The critics' concern was that a third-strike conviction would be disastrous for workers and shareholders. However, the bill did state that in the case of a third-strike conviction, the court may appoint a receiver to take over and manage the affairs of the corporation "as justice and equity require . . . and shall issue orders to ensure that jobs and wages are not lost, to protect community interests and legitimate investor interests, and to maintain the entity's obligations to protect the health, safety, and environment of workers and the public."[54] California activists have vowed to reintroduce the legislation.

Although state attorneys general have shown little interest in going after large corporations by revoking their charters, they do occasionaly revoke the charters of small corporations. The state of California alone, for example, revoked the charters of 58,000 corporations in fiscal year 2001-2002 for failure to pay taxes or file proper statements (though it is likely that most of those corporations were not conducting any actual business anyway).[55]

More substantially, in 2001, the Texas secretary of state revoked the charter of Lionheart Newspapers Inc. (a publisher of more than seventy publications) for nonpayment of franchise taxes. And in 1998, New York attorney general Dennis Vacco revoked the charters of two tobacco industry front groups incorporated as nonprofits: The Council for Tobacco Research and the Tobacco Institute Inc. Though the groups were officially incorporated "to provide truthful information about the effects of smoking on public health," Vacco explained, "instead . . . these entities fed the public a pack of lies in an underhanded effort to promote smoking to addict America's kids."

When campaigning to replace Vacco in 1998, future New York attorney general Eliot Spitzer declared that "when a corporation is convicted of repeated felonies that harm or endanger the lives of human beings or destroy our environment, the corporation should be put to death, its corporate existence ended, and its assets taken and sold at public auction."[56]

Challenges to corporate charters reject the notion that corporations have any intrinsic right to exist in perpetuity without regard to their behavior. Instead, they recognize that people, through their elected officials in government, create corporations and grant corporations the privileges that they enjoy through their charters. The sovereign governments that create these corporations, however, should also have the right to dismantle these corporations when it becomes clear that a corporation is a danger to society.

As Benson explains it, "The people mistakenly assume that we have to try to control these giant corporate repeat offenders one toxic spill at a time, one layoff at a time, one human rights violation at a time. But the law has always allowed the attorney general to go to court to simply dissolve a corporation for wrongdoing and sell its assets to others who will operate in the public interest."[57]

Another way to control corporations through their charters is by writing specific limits directly into the charters, as governments once did. For example, there is nothing prohibiting any state from once again placing limits on how big corporations can grow to be or how long they can exist for or what kind of liability investors should enjoy. There is nothing inherent about the corporation that requires it to enjoy all the privileges it enjoys today, and if any state wanted to get serious about controlling corporations it could change its incorporation laws to ensure that proper limits were directly placed on corporate size, scope, and behavior.

Such a change would send a strong message that the state was serious about reasserting citizen control over corporations. But unfortunately, the only practical result it would likely have would be to effectively keep any business from ever incorporating in the state. That's because any corporation can choose to incorporate in any state it likes. And if one state decided to enact restrictive corporate laws, you can bet most corporations would flee for friendlier grounds, just as they did during the chartermongering battles of the 1890s.

THE PROBLEM OF STATE-BASED CORPORATE LAW

One of the oddities of our corporate law system is that though most of our large corporations conduct business on national and international levels, they are chartered at the state level, and state laws define their operating governance.

A state-based system of corporate law may have made sense two hundred years ago, when state economies were much more distinct and corporations generally only operated within the borders of a single state (often because their charters prevented them from doing otherwise). But today, when corporations can operate anywhere and be chartered anywhere, such a chartering system seems woefully anachronistic.

The consequence is that the state with the laws most favorable to incorporators attracts the vast majority of incorporation activity. And, as we noted earlier, that state is Delaware, home to 308,000 corporations, including almost sixty percent of *Fortune* 500 companies, and recipient of $500 million a year in incorporation fees (which accounts for roughly one-quarter of state revenue).[58] The state with the second-most *Fortune* 500 incorporations (New York) has just 25.

As a result, Delaware, "a pygmy among the 50 states, prescribes, interprets, and indeed denigrates national corporation policy as an incentive to encourage incorporation within its borders, thereby increasing its revenue."[59] Delaware offers the most pro-management statutes available, essentially allowing incorporators to do whatever they would like as long as it is not otherwise illegal.

This situation presents a troubling obstacle to holding corporations democratically accountable. If tiny Delaware (population: 783,600) effectively sets the corporate law for the entire nation (population: approximately 290 million), and in some cases, the whole word, it means that more than 99 percent of Americans (and more than 99.9% of the world) have essentially been cut out of having a claim to deciding how corporations should be governed. As law professor Daniel J. H. Greenwood has written:

> Citizens, acting through the political process as presently constituted, have effectively no say in constituting corporate law. The law, and the corporations formed under it, are rather products of a market that, by historical accident, has freed itself from political control.
>
> Our corporate law is chosen by the very corporate managers who ought to be controlled by it, and created by lawyers, legislatures and judges unanswerable to the people whose lives are affected by it. Large corporations and Delaware determine the nation's corporate law, and the rest of us are not even "virtually represented." Under the Delaware system, corporate managers are entrusted with stewardship of enormous concentrations of wealth and power—in many instances both larger and more important in our daily lives than most governmental units—with little supervision or answerability to the political process. These autonomous power concentrations, in turn, are granted the strikingly unusual right to choose the law that governs them, thus guaranteeing that corporate law will continue to respect their independence from the will of the people. In short, we have created institutions of major importance and power and then set them on their way to do good or ill with little control or influence by the citizens whom, ultimately, they should serve.[60]

Corporations are subject to the environmental, labor, securities, and other laws of each state in which they operate. Why should governance laws be any different? If state legislatures want to make sure that employees or shareholders of corporations that primarily operate within their state enjoy more rights than Delaware corporate law grants them, why should they be prohibited from doing so? There is simply no good reason. But the fact that this is so, that Delaware effectively sets the corporate law of the land, creates a troubling obstacle for the ability of states to regulate and control corporations that operate within their borders.

One possible way to deal with this problem would be for a state (say, for example, New York) to challenge the ability of Delaware to set corporate governance rules for corporations that operate primarily in New York. Law professor Kent Greenfield suggests that "Delaware's dominance is illegitimate because its ability to define the rules of corporate governance depends on the so-called 'internal affairs' doctrine, which says that the internal affairs of corporations (i.e. the rules of corporate governance) are provided by the state where the corporation is chartered."[61]

Greenfield argues that "the state that has the greatest interest in regulating the internal affairs of a corporation should provide for the rules of corporate governance."[62] In practice, this would mean that individual states would write their own corporate governance laws designed to apply to corporations whose business is primarily carried on within that state, regardless of where they are incorporated. And when these laws come in conflict with Delaware law (as they inevitably would), it would ultimately be up to a judge to decide which law should prevail. As Greenfield concludes: "A state may not always be able to convince a judge that its interests are the most significant and that its law should apply. But if usual conflict of law rules were to apply, a state would win sometimes. This would be more often than such a state wins now, which is never. In relaxing the constraints on the internal affairs doctrine, corporate law would become more democratic."[63]

Another approach to solving this problem is to establish a system of federal chartering for national businesses. Instead of a system where states compete to offer the most pro-corporate standards, a federal chartering system could require businesses above a certain size or businesses that plan to conduct business in more than one state to get a federal charter. If a corporation is going to operate on a national level, it should be accountable to the whole nation, not just the people in the state in which it happens to be incorporated.

Proposals to charter corporations at the federal level have been raised periodically in our nation's history, as Ralph Nader,

Mark Green, and Joel Seligman point out in *Taming the Giant Corporation*, their examination of federal chartering. But "whenever federal chartering was considered a vehicle of corporate law reform, an alternative remedy became public policy."[64]

Between 1903 and 1914, for example, Presidents Roosevelt, Taft, and Wilson all voiced strong support for a federal incorporation or licensing scheme in their annual messages to Congress. President Taft had his attorney general, George Wickersham, draft a federal licensing bill and propose it to Congress in 1910. The *Wall Street Journal* supported a federal licensing bill in 1908: "Why should not the Federal Government . . . embody this underlying principle in a statement under which the development of corporations in general may proceed?"[65] Even Elbert H. Gary of U.S. Steel supported the idea: "The only regulation in scope and power to deal with these aggregations of capital is regulation by the Federal Government, because the subject matter of regulation is largely interstate commerce with which the states may not interfere, and the size and extent of the organizations involved is such as to require uniform and national regulation."[66]

Some form of federal corporate law was part of the 1904 Democratic Platform, the 1908 Republican Platform, and the 1912 Democratic Platform. Between 1915 and 1932, at least eight congressional bills related to federal chartering or licensing were introduced. In the late 1930s, Joseph O'Mahoney, a populist senator from Wyoming, promoted the idea of "National Charters for National Business." In his statement to the Temporal National Economic Committee (TNEC) at its closing session in March 11, 1941, O'Mahoney said, "It is idle to think that huge collective institutions which carry on our modern business can continue to operate without more definite responsibility toward all the people of the Nation than they now have. To do this it will be necessary, in my judgment, to have a national charter system for all national corporations."[67]

O'Mahoney's proposal required corporations whose assets exceeded $100,000 to obtain a federal license to engage in interstate business and forbade both the ownership of stock by one corporation in another and the diversification of a corporation's business to areas "incidental to the business in which it is authorized to engage." O'Mahoney also threatened corporations that violated child labor and collective bargaining laws that they would lose their license to do interstate business. His proposal also provided significant penalties for violations of the company's license. The effort, however, was derailed by the gathering storm surrounding World War II, and the TNEC that O'Mahoney had convened to ask tough questions about excessive corporate power was unfortunately pushed aside and largely forgotten.

The idea of federal chartering was revived again in 1976, when Nader, Green, and Seligman published *Taming the Giant Corporation.* The authors proposed a dual chartering system, by which national businesses with more than $250 million in annual sales or more than 10,000 employees would be required to obtain federal charters. These federal charters would require such things as a full-time outside board of directors, more detailed disclosure about workplace conditions, prohibitions against monopoly concentration, and full disclosure of lobbying activities and tax returns, among other provisions designed to protect shareholders, employees, consumers, taxpayers, and communities.

"The problem is ultimately one of power," Nader, Green, and Seligman wrote. "How can we limit unaccountable power and how can we ensure that those who do exercise managerial power are the best managers feasible?"[68] The answer, they proposed, was a system of federal chartering that laid down specific rules of operation for corporations that required them to pay attention to a broad range of concerns beyond profit.

There are a handful of federally chartered companies today. Amtrak, for example, is federally chartered, as are mortgage lenders Freddie Mac and Fannie Mae, both of which were created for the worthwhile public purpose of increasing homeownership. However, as we saw with the recent accounting fraud at Freddie Mac, federally chartered companies are prone to many of the same problems as state-chartered companies, absent proper oversight.

Certainly, from a logical standpoint, it makes sense to have a national system of corporate law to match with what has become a national system of business. But until we can restore meaningful citizen control over the federal government, there are legitimate reasons to question whether federal chartering would make much of a difference.

Still, as we will see again in our discussions of corporate governance in Chapter 3, the state-based system of corporate law can present a formidable obstacle to reform, because it means that using the chartering process to bring serious accountability to corporations will be very difficult unless all fifty states are willing to adopt the same reform at once (and even then, there is the threat that corporations will reincorporate offshore). Ultimately, federal charters do make sense, but only in a context where we have wrestled control of the federal government from the corporations and restored a vigorous citizen democracy.

For now, the ideas presented in this chapter may be most useful as framing devices. As soon as we can begin to see corporations as institutions that are essentially chartered on the premise that they will serve the public good and understand that the people have certain inherent rights to place proper limits on what corporations can and cannot do, we will more clearly see the legitimate basis that we have for regulating corporations in the public interest and holding their interests subordinate to the interests of living, breathing people.

As Justices Byron White, William Brennan, and Thurgood Marshall noted in 1978:

> Corporations are artificial entities created by law for the purpose of furthering certain economic goals. In order to facilitate the achievement of such ends, special rules relating to such matters as limited liability, perpetual life, and the accumulation, distribution, and taxation of assets are normally applied to them. States have provided corporations with such attributes in order to increase their economic viability and thus strengthen the economy generally. It has long been recognized, however, that the special status of corporations has placed them in a position to control vast amounts of economic power which may, if not regulated, dominate not

only the economy but also the very heart of our democracy, the electoral process. . . . The State need not permit its own creation to consume it.[69]

Indeed. The state need not permit its own creation to consume it. And if we can remember the simple fact that corporations are creatures of the state and that We The People, acting through our democratic governments, have the power to control corporations, we will be on the right track.

Returning to the tobacco example with which we began this chapter, it is worth considering what David Kessler, head of the Food and Drug Administration from 1990 to 1997, concluded about the tobacco industry in his memoir, *A Question of Intent*. "My understanding of the industry's power finally forced me to see that, in the long term, the solution to the smoking problem rests with the bottom line, prohibiting the tobacco companies from continuing to profit from the sale of a deadly, addictive drug," Kessler wrote. "These products are inevitably used to promote that same addictive product and to generate more sales. If public health is to be the centerpiece of tobacco control—if our goal is to halt this manmade epidemic—the tobacco industry, as currently configured, needs to be dismantled. . . . The industry cannot be left to peacefully reap billions of dollars in profits."[70]

After attempting to regulate the industry for seven years, Kessler felt there was no other solution to deal with this public-health menace than to dismantle the industry. He suggested forcing tobacco companies to be spun off from their corporate parents and that Congress should "charter a tightly regulated corporation, one from which no one profits, to take over manufacturing and sales."[71]

Kessler's solutions to the tobacco problem resonate closely with what we have been saying in this chapter (and a theme that we will repeat throughout the book)—that the public needs to take control of the corporations it has created, and that corporations that consistently harm the public should not enjoy government charters that allow them to continue to conduct business. Kessler's suggestion remains a useful one in imagining how we might rein in corporations that pose a direct threat to our collective well-being.

As we proceed through this book, we will encounter numerous other examples of corporations behaving badly. We will also explore many remedies to prevent them from behaving badly in the future. As we explore these remedies, however, we must remain fully aware that our ability to control corporations comes from a very powerful starting point: the simple fact that we create corporations and endow them with rights and privileges for one and only one ultimate purpose—to serve the public good. Upon this basic framework, much follows.

2 | Challenging the Corporate Claim to Constitutional Rights

"The judiciary may be the most important instrument for social, economic and political change."

—Former Supreme Court Justice Lewis F. Powell Jr.

One of the most significant protest movements in the late 1990s was the antisweatshop movement. Across the country, activists on college campuses, armed with documentation of young women working in subhuman conditions to make shoes and shirts for third world sweatshops under contract to major brand-name American companies, began to pressure university officials, apparel manufacturers, and consumers to do something about the problem.

After much hard work, the activists succeeded in publicly airing the dirty laundry about how Nike was making its shoes, how the Gap was making its pants, how Kathie Lee Gifford's line of clothing was making its shirts. Apparel manufacturers responded in various ways. Some tried to improve the awful conditions at the factories where the clothes and shoes were being made. But others worked to neutralize their critics through sophisticated public relations campaigns.

Among the companies that tried to pave over the situation with public relations was the Nike Corporation, which responded to sweatshop allegations by claiming it had fixed the problems and was now treating its workers in far-flung factories with decency. In various statements, Nike claimed that workers "are paid in accordance with applicable local laws and regulations governing wages and hours" and receive "free meals and health care"; that workers "are protected from physical and sexual abuse"; and that "working conditions are in compliance with applicable local laws and regulations governing occupational health and safety."[1] As a $10-billion-a-year corporation, Nike was able to inundate members of the media with pamphlets, send out copious press releases, and orchestrate mass mailings to athletic directors at every major university in an extensive attempt to convince potential sneaker buyers that it had cleaned up its act. Though activists had reports and documents that they said demonstrated Nike was lying, they simply did not have the financial resources to wage a comparable public relations campaign to rebut the company wherever it spread its propaganda.

Still, one San Francisco activist, Marc Kasky, realized that under California state law, individual citizens could serve as watchdogs against false and misleading advertising and public statements by bringing suit. In 1998 Kasky did just that, arguing that the Nike corporation had violated California law by issuing false statements in its public relations campaign and misleading consumers into thinking that they were buying sneakers and other apparel produced under humane conditions.

Nike responded to the suit not by defending the veracity of its statements, but by arguing that applying California's law to its public relations campaign amounted to an unconstitutional infringement upon the company's right to speak freely on political issues.

Much of the legal discussion surrounding the case focused on whether Nike's public relations campaign was commercial speech (speech intended to sell a product, and thus not afforded much protection under the First Amendment and subject to California's law) or political speech (speech intended to contribute to a robust political debate, and thus afforded full protection under the First Amendment and outside the scope of California's law).

Ultimately, the Supreme Court decided it had made a mistake in taking on the case in the first place, sending it back to the California court that had ruled Nike's speech was commercial and could be regulated under the state law. Shortly thereafter, Nike settled with Kasky out of court, which meant that it avoided the ordeal of having to defend its labor practices in court, where details about the conditions in the sweatshops where Nike-brand clothing is produced would become part of the public record.

For some observers, however, the Nike case posed a set of questions that went far beyond the specific details of the case. How was it that any corporation could even argue that it was entitled to First Amendment protections at all? After all, aren't Bill of Rights protections, such as the freedom of speech, meant to apply to living, breathing citizens, whose ability to express themselves fully is essential to the functioning of a democracy? Corporations are organizations, forms of doing business. How can they claim constitutional protections? They aren't people.

The sad truth is that corporations have been claiming Bill of Rights protections for more than one hundred years now, using these protections to undermine and subvert laws designed to regulate their behavior.

We believe that it is essential that we have a system of jurisprudence that supports the ability of We The People, to govern ourselves, rather than serve as a sort of backdoor way for corporations to get around the laws that they don't like. If citizens are to be able to effectively set the rules by which they want to live, including the rules by which corporations operate, it does not make much sense to allow corporations to undermine those rules by legitimizing their claims to Bill of Rights protections originally intended to protect the rights of real persons.

Thus, the question that we as a sovereign people should ask ourselves is, What constitutional rights should corporations, who are mentioned nowhere in the Constitution, have in our democracy?

Ask the corporations and their lawyers, and they will say plenty. As legal scholar Carl Mayer has written, "Today, the corporation boasts a panoply of Bill of Rights protections: first amendment guarantees of political speech, commercial speech, and negative free speech rights; fourth amendment safeguards against unreasonable regulatory searches; fifth amendment double jeopardy and liberty rights; and sixth and seventh amendment entitlements to trial by jury."[2]

But do all of these rights make sense for corporations? After all, as we discussed in Chapter 1, corporations are essentially creatures of the state. In theory, they are granted charters based on the premise that their existence will serve the public good. And to ensure that corporations serve the public good, citizens must be empowered to set the rules governing corporations. Giving corporations constitutional protections that they can turn around and use to overturn those rules will make it extremely difficult for citizens to effectively control corporations.

Such thinking was more or less the prevailing legal theory for most of the nineteenth century. Under this "artificial entity" theory, the law viewed the corporation "as nothing more than an artificial creature of the state, subject to government imposed limitations and restrictions. . . . Under this view, corporations cannot assert constitutional rights against the state, their creator."[3]

Gradually, however, the "artificial entity" theory of corporations was replaced by the "natural entity" or person theory. As Mayer has explained it, "This theory regards the corporation not as artificial, but as real, with a separate existence and independent rights. . . . This understanding of the corporation most favors corporate constitutional rights."[4]

Corporations were first recognized as having legal status as persons in an 1886 Supreme Court Decision, *Santa Clara v. Southern Pacific Railroad*, and the doctrine that recognizes their status as legal persons has stood ever since.

Viewing corporations as legal "persons" and natural entities had powerful effects on the law and jurisprudence. As David Millon has suggested, if the corporation "was to be viewed in the same light as natural persons, there was a basis for arguing that the corporation should be exempt from special efforts to regulate its conduct that did not apply to natural persons."[5] Such a view of the corporation as an independent individual gave it a new set of rights that seemed more consistent with the rights of real persons. These rights included the ability of corporations to challenge laws they felt were unfairly discriminatory or otherwise violated their rights as legal "persons."

Though corporate claims of constitutional protections date back to the late nineteenth century, in the last three decades the business community has become particularly aggressive in asserting that the Constitution should apply to corporations in increasingly creative ways. These efforts have been carried out by corporate lawyers with support from conservative, corporate-funded legal societies, particularly the National Chamber Litigation Center and the Washington Legal Foundation, which even has a program designed exclusively to promote "business civil liberties."[6]

Today, corporations enjoy a wide range of constitutional protections that by and large help them undermine regulations and other laws that citizens have enacted to protect themselves. Corporations have successfully claimed a constitutional right to participate in initiative elections, to advertise tobacco within 1,000 feet of schools and playgrounds, and to turn away surprise OSHA health and safety inspections, among other things.

In this chapter, we will explore some of the specific ways that corporations have undermined citizen-enacted laws by wielding the Constitution and ask whether these rights make sense for corporations. We will take a look at corporate-funded legal societies that have been extremely effective in fostering a jurisprudence that is excessively friendly to the rights of corporations and property at the expense of other concerns, and have been aggressive in pushing Bill of Rights protections for corporations. And finally, we will examine the significance of the doctrine of corporate personhood as the basis for these constitutional protections.

Though the cases we discuss are varied and rely on different reasoning by different courts, we believe that what they all have in common is an interpretation of the law that sees the rights of business and property as more important than the rights of citizens to govern themselves. It is this interpretation of the law that we believe poses a major threat to citizen democracy, and it is this interpretation that, ultimately, we must challenge.

FIRST AMENDMENT (FREEDOM OF SPEECH)

Congress shall make no law respecting an establishment of religion, or prohibiting the free exercise thereof; or abridging the freedom of speech, or of the press; or the right of the people peaceably to assemble, and to petition the government for a redress of grievances.

The First Amendment guarantees freedom of speech. This is, in many ways, the most fundamental guarantee of any political democracy. In fact, without guaranteeing the ability to speak one's mind freely and fearlessly, it is difficult to imagine how any government can claim to be a democracy.

Freedom of speech, however, is not an absolute. The Supreme Court has traditionally imposed various "time, place, and manner" restrictions on speech. For example, somebody shouting epithets about your mother through a megaphone into your window at 3 A.M. is not engaging in constitutionally protected free speech. The First Amendment has generally been interpreted to afford the highest protection to political speech, while allowing restrictions on other kinds of speech, such as "fighting words" and commercial speech (including advertising,[7] and corporate communications associated with securities or shareholder proxy statements,[8] where certain forms of corporate speech are either mandated or prohibited).

What makes applying the law difficult is that the boundaries between political speech and commercial speech can be extremely fuzzy, as we saw in the *Nike* case.

When applied to advertising, the question becomes: Is the advertisement conveying information that could conceivably contribute something to public discourse? If it does, then the Court says that states should not have much ability to regulate it. Yet, what counts as important information, and who decides? Is advertising, generally designed with the goal of manipulating its audience into buying a particular product, really conveying important information? As law professor Bruce Ledewitz has written, "The Court's current view is that advertising primarily provides information and that consumers, as rational actors, use this information to make decisions that improve their lives. Assuming that the information in the advertising is true, or assuming that the consumer will have enough time to find out for herself whether the information is true or not, one simply cannot have 'too much' speech as far as the Court is concerned."[9]

Yet, it is widely understood by cultural critics and even advertisers themselves that their efforts are primarily geared toward demand-side management and manipulation of consumer desires: to ensure that people buy what is produced rather than to provide information to make people better-informed consumers. As economist John Kenneth Galbraith observed in 1971, "A vast advertising and sales effort employing elaborate science and art to influence the customer" had created a system wherein "the individual . . . is increasingly subordinate to the goals of the producing organization."[10] Few ads today provide information that is geared to helping people make rational decisions; instead they manipulate people's emotional desires and create artificial needs directed toward the purchase of a specific product, often providing as little meaningful information as possible.

Ledewitz, for example, argues that the Court has understood advertising in the wrong way, viewing it as merely a source of information, as opposed to "a stealthy impediment to democratic outcomes, completely manipulative, achieving political ends only by disguising its message. . . . The Court's current view fails to take account of the power of advertising."[11]

One of the first key modern commercial speech cases came out of New York during the 1970s energy crisis, when the state enacted a ban on electricity advertisements in order to promote conservation. The Central Hudson Gas & Electric Corporation, an electricity monopoly whose profits were based on electrical consumption, didn't like that regulation one bit. So it sued the Public Service Commission of New York. The case made its way up to the Supreme Court, and in 1980 Justice Lewis F. Powell Jr.

delivered a fervent defense of commercial speech in writing the majority opinion: "Commercial expression not only serves the economic interest of the speaker, but also assists consumers and furthers the societal interest in the fullest possible dissemination of information."[12]

In ruling in favor of Central Hudson, the Court argued that as long as New York couldn't prove why an advertising ban was necessary (or why conservation couldn't be accomplished by other means that didn't involve restricting speech), it didn't have a convincing enough argument to enact one: "Administrative bodies empowered to regulate electric utilities have the authority—and indeed the duty—to take appropriate action to further [energy conservation]," wrote the court. "When, however, such action involves the suppression of speech, the First and Fourteenth Amendments require that the restriction be no more extensive than is necessary to serve the state interest. In this case, the record before us fails to show that the total ban on promotional advertising meets this requirement."[13]

This case effectively set the bar extremely high for regulating commercial speech. The ruling was based on an underlying value judgment that more speech is invariably useful and more information is always better. The courts have used this reasoning over and over.

In *44 Liquormart v. Rhode Island* (1996), for example, the Court used this logic to declare a state ban on advertising alcohol prices unconstitutional. The state had argued that banning advertising would discourage bargain hunting and keep prices high, which would discourage liquor consumption. But the Court felt that there were other ways to discourage alcohol consumption that didn't restrict free speech. "The First Amendment directs us to be especially skeptical of regulations that seek to keep people in the dark for what the Government perceives to be their own good," wrote Justice John Paul Stevens for the Court.[14]

News reports described how the ruling chilled the Clinton administration's plans to regulate tobacco advertising, including "a ban on outdoor displays of cigarette advertising within 1,000 yards of a school or playground, a ban on the use of color advertising in media likely to be seen by young people and restrictions on the use of cigarette brand names and logos on caps and other items."[15]

The Clinton administration's fears were well founded, because in 2001 the Supreme Court ruled that a Massachusetts law that prohibited tobacco advertising within 1,000 feet of any school or playground was indeed a violation of the First Amendment. "The First Amendment . . . constrains state efforts to limit advertising of tobacco products, because so long as the sale and use of tobacco is lawful for adults, the tobacco industry has a protected interest in communicating information about its products and adult customers have an interest in receiving that information," Justice Sandra Day O'Connor wrote for the majority in *Lorillard Tobacco Company v. Reilly*.[16] Again, the ability of states to legislate in the public interest failed to triumph over the rights of a corporation to advertise freely.

Though the logic of the Court may appear to be that more speech is better, the 1986 *Pacific Gas & Electric v. Public Utilities Commission*[17] case turns this logic on its side to accommodate the corporate point of view. In this case, state regulators were requiring Pacific Gas & Electric to include a consumer newsletter in its billing envelope four times a year. But the utility company argued that such a law violated its First Amendment speech right of association because it was being forced to associate with speech with which it did not agree. The Court supported this argument, creating a sort of negative free speech right that seemed to undermine its prior assertions that more speech was better.

At issue in most of these cases is an attempt by a state government to serve the public interest by regulating advertising. The courts have responded by saying that states must be extremely careful in restricting speech, even if it is commercial speech (as long as the speech is not dishonest). Although a certain level of advertising is essential to promoting commerce, the idea that corporations should have a First Amendment trump card over advertising regulations is exceedingly troublesome. As we have noted, states allow for the creation of corporations and grant certain privileges and rights to corporations, ostensibly to promote commerce and economic development. Defining these privileges and rights should be up to the states that create these corporations. If state legislatures want to restrict corporate advertising, that should be their prerogative.

Managers and employees of corporations, as real citizens, should enjoy full rights of freedom of speech, just like every other citizen. But the claim that the corporation itself should enjoy freedom of speech is both dubious and dangerous. Corporations are not persons. While individual managers and employees may have thoughts and opinions that form the basis for speech, the assertion that the corporation itself, which has no mind of its own, can have such thoughts and opinions makes little sense.

The rationale behind the First Amendment is to promote a robust public debate in which a diversity of opinions can be heard. This is fundamental to a functioning democracy. But if corporate voices are allowed to drown out all other voices (as is increasingly the case), our democracy is in serious trouble. The truth is that corporate advertising has incredible sway over our daily lives; it informs many of our thoughts and desires in both subtle and obvious ways with little apparent contribution to the marketplace of ideas other than the promotion of mindless materialism. In 2004, annual U.S. spending on advertising was projected to reach \$266.4 billion[18] (enough to expose the average American to an estimated 2,000 commercial messages in a single day, or more than 100 per waking hour[19]). If our elected legislatures are limited in their power to regulate this, then the marketplace of ideas will eventually become just a marketplace.

We should also note that while corporations claim that more speech is always better, they regularly restrict the free speech of employees, or anyone else who might want to say something on the company's premises. The lack of employee free speech in workplaces is a tremendous obstacle to the ability of employees to organize into labor unions (employees are sometimes even fired for talking about unions in the workplace). For corporations to claim speech rights when it comes to their own communications but in turn to claim the right to restrict the freedom of speech of individuals on their premises seems, on its face, the height of hypocrisy.

Even in shopping centers and malls, which are the closest things to public spaces in many communities these days, corporate owners have had people arrested for handing out leaflets and other acts of free speech. As professor Lawrence Solely has argued, "Businesses and corporations now pose a greater threat to free speech than does government."[20] For example, in 2000, the Minnesota Supreme Court ruled that the Mall of America, the nation's largest mall, was private property and that there was "no compelling reason" to extend free-speech rights to those who would want to protest there, even though the mall was partially built with public money.[21]

CORPORATE POLITICAL SPEECH

As we noted, the Court has historically afforded less protection for commercial speech than for political speech. So what happens when it comes to political speech?

Perhaps the most important modern corporate political speech case is *First National Bank of Boston v. Bellotti*, which was brought by a group of major corporations (led by First National Bank of Boston) that wanted to spend money to publicize their views on a November 1976 state ballot question on whether the legislature could impose a graduated income tax on individuals. Since a Massachusetts law prohibited corporations from buying advocacy advertisements on citizen initiatives, the corporations sued. The Court found in their favor, saying the Massachusetts law was indeed in violation of the First Amendment.

In deciding the case, the Court was essentially forced to answer the question of whether Massachusetts had a compelling interest in restricting certain speech—that is, the speech of corporations. The state of Massachusetts argued that it did indeed have a compelling reason: it wanted to ensure that individual citizens, not big corporations, played the most active roles in the electoral process.

Writing for the majority, Justice Powell recognized citizen control over elections as an important consideration, but then dismissed the concern, saying, "There has been no showing that the relative voice of corporations has been overwhelming or even significant in influencing referenda in Massachusetts."[22]

But considering that corporations were banned from participating in the first place, it is perhaps not particularly surprising that their relative voice was not "overwhelming." Certainly, the last twenty-five years have shown that when corporations are allowed to participate in elections, their voice is indeed "overwhelming."

Powell went on to suggest (contradicting himself) that even if corporations did influence the election, it still wouldn't be a problem: "The fact that advocacy may persuade the electorate is hardly a reason to suppress it . . . the people in our democracy are entrusted with the responsibility for judging and evaluating the relative merits of conflicting arguments." So perhaps what he really meant to say is that he didn't have a problem with corporations "overwhelmingly" influencing elections.

Note the deceptive two-step logic: first he says that while states should ensure that individual citizens control their referenda, there's no worry, because there's no evidence corporations would overwhelm the process (though one has to wonder where he found the evidence for this conclusion, since at the time of the ruling corporations had not been allowed to participate in the referenda). Then he turns around and says it doesn't matter if corporations do overwhelm the process—individual voters are smart enough to sort out good and bad arguments and come to their own conclusions.

Ultimately, *Bellotti* was decided on the grounds that the statute is underinclusive because it discriminated unfairly based on who the speaker is. As Powell wrote:

> The question must be whether [the law] abridges expression that the First Amendment was meant to protect. We hold it does. . . . The inherent worth of the speech in terms of its capacity for informing the public does not depend upon the identity of its sources, whether corporation, association, union, or individual.[23]

The precedent has stood ever since. In 1998, for example, opponents of a 1996 Montana initiative that banned corporate money from citizen ballot initiatives successfully invoked the *Bellotti* precedent in getting the U.S. 9th Circuit Court of Appeals to declare the Montana initiative unconstitutional.[24]

Few could dispute today that corporations have an "overwhelming" voice in the political process. Yet so long as the courts choose to abide by *Bellotti*, any law to silence that voice would be considered unconstitutional. As long as this precedent is in force, corporations will continue to hide behind the Constitution in their attempts to influence elections.

However, it is worth noting a few key points from future chief justice William Rehnquist's dissent in the *Bellotti* case:

> Legislatures of 30 other States of this Republic have considered the matter, and have concluded that restrictions upon the political activity of business corporations are both politically desirable and constitutionally permissible. The judgment of such a broad consensus over a period of many decades is entitled to considerable deference from this Court.
>
> Although the Court has never explicitly recognized a corporation's right of commercial speech, such a right might be considered necessarily incidental to the business. It cannot be so readily concluded that the right of political expression is equally necessary to carry out the functions of a corporation organized for commercial purposes.[25]

Rehnquist also quotes Chief Justice Marshall's 1819 *Dartmouth* decision to show that the law proscribes a very limited corporate purpose: "Being a mere creature of the law, [the corporation] possesses only those properties which the charter of creation confers to it, either expressly, or as incidental to its very existence."[26]

Essentially, Rehnquist is saying that corporations are chartered for specific purposes, and since participating in the political process is not one of them, corporations have no inherent right to do so. Furthermore, states should be able to judge for themselves whether these "creatures of the law" should participate in politics.

On a related note, however, the Court did uphold the constitutionality of a Michigan law that placed limits on corporate campaign expenditures in *Austin v. Michigan State Chamber of Commerce* (1990). As the Court wrote:

> State law grants corporations special advantages—such as limited liability, perpetual life, and favorable treatment of the accumulation and distribution of assets—that enhance their ability to attract capital and to deploy their resources in ways that maximize the return on their shareholders' investments. These state-created advantages not only allow corporations to play a dominant role in the Nation's economy, but also permit them to use "resources amassed in the economic marketplace" to obtain "an unfair advantage in the political marketplace."[27]

The court has also upheld limits on corporate donations for federal elections, as it has for all political donors.

In approaching corporate political speech cases, we would again say that corporations should not enjoy First Amendment rights that were intended to protect people, since corporations are not people and do not vote in elections. Individual stockholders, managers, and employees, all of whom are indeed people, should be free to participate in the political process however they choose. But allowing corporations to participate in the political processes that create them and determine how they are regulated makes little sense. As law professor Daniel Greenwood has argued, "In a democracy, citizens are the only legitimate sources of the law. . . . Like the government itself, corporations are mere tools of the citizenry, political objects rather than political subjects, to be given just as much respect as the citizens deem useful and no more. To grant a tool a right against the citizens who use it is a form of political idolatry that ought to be abhorrent to any democratic regime. Rights are for people, not for their instruments."[28]

Political scientist Charles Lindblom has written, "The rationale for democracy is rights and powers for living, hurting, and aspiring persons whose assigned rights and powers give them protections as well as opportunities to pursue their aspirations. It would make no sense, on democratic grounds, to assign such rights and powers to fire hydrants or computers—they neither suffer nor aspire. Neither does a corporation suffer or aspire. Only the people in it do. To them alone would a democratic state assign the rights and powers of persons."[29]

In Chapter 6 we will take a more comprehensive look at the role of corporate money in politics. For now, however, it is important to understand how the corporate claim to First Amendment protections both undermines the ability of sovereign governments to limit the political process to citizens and only citizens and also empowers corporations to overwhelm the very states that created them in the first place. Put simply, if We The People hope to effectively control corporations through democratic processes, we must make sure that corporations cannot participate in these processes in the same way that citizens can. If corporations are allowed to participate in the same way as citizens, they will use their overwhelming economic power to effectively cut citizens off from the very mechanisms that were originally intended to allow citizens to guard against abuses of concentrated power.

In addressing issues of corporate free speech, however, we need to be careful. Though we would say in general that corporations should not enjoy constitutional free speech protections, we believe there must be exceptions. For example, we believe that freedom of the press is essential to a functioning democracy. That means that media corporations must enjoy a good deal of freedom in what they print, broadcast, or otherwise disseminate in their capacity as media providers. (Though there are obviously limits to this freedom. Libel laws, for example, make reckless disregard for the truth illegal). Additionally, nonprofit corporations organized for political and issue advocacy should also enjoy First Amendment rights. We realize that these issues are slippery, and the boundaries are blurry (for example, what do we say about NBC's right to speak on behalf of its parent company, General Electric?).[30] Yet we think there is a way to carve out space for media and issue groups organized as corporations to enjoy free speech that has a very clear purpose of contributing to a diversity of ideas without extending it to all for-profit business corporations, which are first and foremost organized to make money.

FOURTH AMENDMENT (PRIVACY)

The right of the people to be secure in their persons, houses, papers, and effects, against unreasonable searches and seizures, shall not be violated, and no warrants shall issue, but upon probable cause, supported by oath or affirmation, and particularly describing the place to be searched, and the persons or things to be seized.

The Fourth Amendment protects citizens from unreasonable searches and seizures and is the closest thing we have to an outright protection of privacy in the Constitution.

But since the Fourth Amendment only applies to government action, a troubling inconsistency arises in the world of the corporation. On corporate property, employees lose their rights to privacy: employers can read personal e-mails without a warrant, request a drug test as a condition of employment, or install hidden spy cameras without permission. But when a government safety inspector wants to enter corporate property to make sure working conditions are adequate, he or she needs the permission of the company or a court-granted search warrant. This is because corporations have claimed that the Fourth Amendment protects them from searches and seizures.

The key ruling here came in 1977, when the Court ruled in *Marshall v. Barlow's Inc.* that an Occupational Health and Safety Administration (OSHA) inspector needed a warrant to enter the premises of an Idaho electrical and plumbing corporation.

"The Warrant Clause of the Fourth Amendment protects commercial buildings as well as private homes," the Court wrote. "To hold otherwise would belie the origin of that Amendment, and the American colonial experience. . . . The general warrant was a recurring point of contention in the Colonies immediately preceding the Revolution. The particular offensiveness it engendered was acutely felt by the merchants and businessmen whose premises and products were inspected for compliance with the several parliamentary revenue measures that most irritated the colonists. Against this background, it is untenable that the ban on warrantless searches was not intended to shield places of business as well as of residence."[31]

In 1986, Dow Chemical attempted to convince the Supreme Court that EPA planes shouldn't even be allowed to fly over Dow's manufacturing facilities and take photos. Though the Court agreed that Dow had legitimate privacy expectations, it found that Dow's facility was "open fields" subject to public viewing and thus taking photos was not a "search." But though the decision was not in Dow's favor, the case did solidify the corporate right to protection from searches and seizures.[32]

The effect of this jurisprudence is that corporations are able to refuse surprise warrant-less inspections from federal and state regulators. If OSHA inspectors are required to obtain a warrant to search for safety violations, how likely is it that they will catch a safety violation? Or if EPA inspectors need a warrant, how likely is it that they will catch a company violating toxic waste regulations? Or if USDA inspectors can be prohibited from inspecting meat plants unless they have evidence of health violations, how likely is it they will find those violations?

The mission of agencies like OSHA, USDA, and EPA is, of course, to protect people from workplace, food, and environmental hazards. These agencies serve an important function: to protect our health and safety. But when corporations use their Fourth Amendment rights to obstruct the actions of those charged with protecting worker safety and public health, it is not clear how the public is benefiting.

It seems one effect of corporations claiming constitutional protections is that it undermines the ability of citizens to enact laws to protect themselves from such threats as unsafe food, toxic waste, and dangerous working conditions. Though such recent developments as the Patriot Act continue to remind us how important privacy rights can be, we must also recognize that there is a crucial difference between the privacy rights of individual citizens and of corporations. The privacy rights of individual citizens should be sacrosanct. But the privacy rights of a corporation make little sense because corporations are forms of business organization, not people. Citizens should have a right to know what's in their food or what the brown stuff coming out of the local power plant is.

Yet, the way we have it now, corporations can monitor employees as they like: read their e-mails, listen to their phone conversations, keep hidden cameras in the bathroom, and require surprise drug tests. But if OSHA agents want to show up for a surprise inspection at a manufacturing plant to make sure that worker safety standards are up to par, they can be turned away.

It seems upside down. The very invasions of privacy that corporations subject their own employees to, if done to the corporations themselves, would be decried as unconstitutional. When it comes to the Fourth Amendment, we have a situation where the purported rights of the corporation have become more important than our rights as people.

FIFTH AMENDMENT

No person shall be held to answer for a capital, or otherwise infamous crime, unless on a presentment or indictment of a grand jury, except in cases arising in the land or naval forces, or in the militia, when in actual service in time of war or public danger; nor shall any person be subject for the same offense to be twice put in jeopardy of life or limb; nor shall be compelled in any criminal case to be a witness against himself, nor be deprived of life, liberty, or property, without due process of law; nor shall private property be taken for public use, without just compensation.

When it comes to undermining regulations, corporations have taken the concept to a whole new level with a rather creative use of the Fifth Amendment's due process and takings clauses, which, among other things, protect citizens from having their private property taken away for public purposes "without just compensation."

In practice, what the Fifth Amendment means is that if the state wants to seize your property for a public purpose (e.g., to build a highway), it has to offer you "just compensation." (Of course, plenty of battles have been fought over the definition of "just compensation.")

But while the Fifth Amendment requires compensation for takings of physical possessions, such as property, does it also apply to "hidden takings," such as regulations that render private property less profitable than it has the potential to be? Corporations have argued that it does, and that it should apply to them as well. They have argued that regulations that reduce their profitability can, in certain cases, be construed as violations of the Fifth Amendment.[33]

This interpretation of the Fifth Amendment has had resonance in the courts for more than eighty years—since 1922, to be exact, when the Supreme Court ruled that a state law that prohibited below-ground mining in areas where homeowners could be harmed amounted to an unconstitutional taking of the property of the Pennsylvania Coal Co. The case established the principle that "'if regulation goes too far it will be recognized as a taking."[34] Prior to that ruling, the courts held that no one could claim damages due to a police regulation on behalf of the common welfare, particularly in the area of health and safety regulations.[35]

One of the most famous corporate Fifth Amendment cases is *Penn Central Transportation Co. v. City of New York* (1978), in which Penn Central claimed that the city's denial of Penn Central's wish to build a 53-story office building above Grand Central Terminal, a denial based on the city's landmark preservation law, was an unconstitutional taking. Though the Court upheld the city's law, it established a takings test that was favorable to property owners: "'The economic impact of the regulation on the claimant and, particularly, the extent to which the regulation has interfered with reasonable investment-backed expectations are . . . relevant considerations."[36]

A particularly egregious corporate abuse of this principle came in the 2002 First Circuit Court of Appeals case of *Philip Morris Inc. v. Reilly*, in which Philip Morris successfully claimed that a Massachusetts law that required tobacco manufacturers to disclose their product ingredients amounted to an unconstitutional taking of a valuable trade secret—the company's "secret" ingredient list. Though Massachusetts claimed its Disclosure Act was a public interest law designed to help consumers make informed choices about the products they wished to consume, the court of appeals would have none of it. The court argued that the economic impact was "potentially tremendous" and "essentially destroys the tobacco companies' trade secrets. . . . Frankly, for a state to be able to completely destroy valuable trade secrets, it should be required to show more than a possible beneficial effect."[37]

The Philip Morris case offers a particularly stark conflict between the public's right to know what is in the products it is consuming and a corporation's right to keep those ingredients secret because to do otherwise might impair the corporation's ability to maximize profit. But it boils down to the same fundamental problem: a corporation claiming a constitutional protection for behavior that is potentially quite harmful to the public at large.

In the case of this creative use of the Fifth Amendment, the contrast between corporate rights and citizen sovereignty is starker than in prior examples. Instead of just serving to undermine one type of government regulation, this interpretation of the takings clause undermines the entire idea of regulation, arguing that any government regulation that interferes with the ability of corporations to make expected profits is somehow a potentially unconstitutional taking of private property if not properly compensated.

To assume that corporations are somehow entitled to a certain amount of profit is a gross misunderstanding of the basic tenets of competitive capitalism. And placing the rights of corporations to make a profit above the rights of citizens to enact laws to protect themselves against corporate excess, when taken to its logical conclusion, means that citizens will never be able to control corporations and that property rights will always trump human rights.

Unfortunately, such an understanding of the law is not as extreme as we would like it to be. Already, this principle of law is finding its way into many international trade agreements, which often place the rights of investors to make money above all other rights. Consider, for example, Chapter 11 of the North American

Free Trade Agreement (NAFTA), which allows investors of foreign corporations to sue governments when local laws, such as environmental regulations, interfere with a corporation's ability to make a profit. As journalist William Greider has explained, "NAFTA's new investor protections actually mimic a radical revision of constitutional law that the American right has been pushing for years—redefining public regulation as a government 'taking' of private property that requires compensation to the owners."[38]

FOURTEENTH AMENDMENT (DUE PROCESS)

Section 1. All persons born or naturalized in the United States, and subject to the jurisdiction thereof, are citizens of the United States and of the state wherein they reside. No state shall make or enforce any law which shall abridge the privileges or immunities of citizens of the United States; nor shall any state deprive any person of life, liberty, or property, without due process of law; nor deny to any person within its jurisdiction the equal protection of the laws.

The Fourteenth Amendment, enacted in 1868, was written to guarantee the rights of citizenship to recently freed slaves. The amendment sets forth the simple premise that the state should not "deprive any person of life, liberty, or property, without due process of law; nor deny to any person within its jurisdiction the equal protection of the laws," thus prohibiting any sort of unfairly discriminatory treatment.

Yet, the very first case brought under the Fourteenth Amendment had very little to do with the rights of freed slaves. Instead, the case, brought in 1873, concerned a Louisiana law that granted a monopoly to a slaughterhouse. The plaintiffs in the case claimed that this law had destroyed their right to pursue their business and thus deprived them of property without due process, a violation of the Fourteenth Amendment. Though the Court ruled against them, the case set in motion a debate about property rights under the Fourteenth Amendment.[39]

In the 1870s and 1880s, corporate lawyers (particularly those from the giant railroad companies) began fashioning arguments that the Fourteenth Amendment should apply to corporations, too, and that corporations should be considered persons. They recognized that if such protections were to extend to corporations, then corporations would have a powerful tool to challenge various state regulations that deprived them of property without due process or otherwise unfairly discriminated against them.

The corporations got their wish in 1886, in a case that involved a Southern Pacific Railroad challenge to a California tax. In *Santa Clara v. Southern Pacific Railroad* the Court for the first time, said that corporations were indeed "persons" and were thus entitled to the Fourteenth Amendment protections they claimed in the case.

However, the decision itself is shrouded in a bit of mystery and confusion. As author Thom Hartmann explains in *Unequal Protection*, the Court never actually ruled that corporations were persons in *Santa Clara*. As Hartmann notes, the defining personhood statement attributed to Chief Justice Morrison Waite— "The court does not wish to hear arguments on the question of whether the provision in the Fourteenth Amendment . . . applies to these corporations. We are of the opinion that it does."—was never actually part of the official decision. It was part of the headnotes, or commentary that has no legal standing. And it was put there by court reporter J. C. Bancroft Davis, a former railroad board member.[40]

Despite the dubious origins of corporate "personhood," corporate lawyers happily took this ruling and ran with it, citing it in numerous cases to object to a wide array of regulations. In a 1912 book entitled *The Fourteenth Amendment and the States*, Charles Wallace Collins summarized the first forty-four years of the Fourteenth Amendment, concluding that of the 604 cases that had brought the amendment into question, 28 involved African Americans as the principal party and 312 concerned the corporation as the principal party.[41]

The Court even ruled that "property" could include expected profits, and in 1890 it determined that a Minnesota regulation that did not allow railroads to appeal decisions of the state's rate-setting commission to state courts amounted to an unconstitutional deprivation of property because it deprived the Chicago, Milwaukee, and St. Paul R.R. Co. of expected profits.[42]

One of the most famous Fourteenth Amendment cases is *Louis K. Liggett Company v. Lee* (1933). In this case, the Court struck down a Florida state law designed to protect small businesses by enacting special taxes on chain stores, finding that it violated chain stores' equal protection rights under the Fourteenth Amendment.

Though corporate claims to Fourteenth Amendment protections have largely disappeared since the late 1930s, when the doctrine of substantive due process fell out of fashion, they still pop up sometimes. For example, in January 2004, the city of Turlock, California (population 60,000), decided that it would ban most new or expanding discount stores that exceed 100,000 square feet and devote at least 5 percent of the space to groceries and other nontaxable items. A month later, Wal-Mart, which planned to build a store twice that size in Turlock, filed a lawsuit in U.S. District Court in Fresno, claiming that the ban was a violation of Wal-Mart Inc.'s equal protection rights. "They cannot discriminate against Wal-Mart as opposed to other businesses in the area," a Wal-Mart attorney told a local newspaper. "Certainly, our belief is that Wal-Mart was the subject of the ordinance." The retail giant claimed that the law also violated the Commerce Clause of the Constitution.[43] Wal-Mart also sued over similar laws in Alameda County and Bakersfield, California.[44]

According to Turlock mayor Curt Andre, "The overwhelming majority of people that have talked to me have been fervent in their desire to keep any kind of superstore out of Turlock."[45] Yet, Wal-Mart's claim to such constitutional protections is in blatant defiance of what the citizens of Turlock have chosen for themselves. Now, the city is being forced to spend up to $80,000 to defend its ability to make its own rules regarding how big stores should be within its own city limits.[46]

RECLAIMING THE COURTS

As we have seen, the corporate claim to constitutional rights can present a major obstacle for citizens who want to effectively regulate and control corporations. So what can we do about it?

Essentially, we need a coordinated legal movement that can challenge the pro-corporate interpretation of the law that has been steadily spreading for the last three decades. The goal of such a movement would be to offer an interpretation of the law that says that corporations are not entitled to Bill of Rights protections—and that the rights of citizens to govern themselves should be more important than the rights of corporations to maximize profits.

Before we discuss some potential strategies that We The People could adopt, we think it is important first to understand how, over the last three decades, a well-orchestrated corporate legal movement has successfully worked to establish an increasingly corporate-friendly jurisprudence. This will give us a sense of what we are up against, as well as help us to determine an appropriate response.

Important strands of the contemporary pro-business legal movement can be traced to the infamous "Powell Memorandum," a memo written by Supreme Court Justice Lewis F. Powell Jr. in August 1971, just two months before he was named to the bench, where he would become a fervent defender of corporate rights (as his decisions in cases such as *Bellotti* and *Pacific Gas & Electric,* discusses above, demonstrate*)*. The memo came in response to what Powell deemed "an attack on the American Enterprise System" from a variety of revolutionaries "who would destroy the entire system, both political and economic." Powell exhorted the forces of business enterprise to organize and then outlined a coherent (and ultimately catalytic) approach to restoring the preeminence of business enterprise to American values.[47]

In a section entitled "Neglected Opportunity in the Courts," Powell wrote that "the judiciary may be the most important instrument for social, economic and political change." After predictably bemoaning the judicial activism of "liberal" groups like the ACLU, Powell put the onus on the Chamber of Commerce: "This is a vast opportunity for the Chamber, if it is willing to undertake the role of spokesman for American business, and if, in turn, business is willing to provide the funds."

Fast-forward to 2002, when the National Chamber Litigation Center (NCLC), which proudly traces its origin to the Powell Memorandum celebrated its twenty-fifth "silver anniversary": "25 Years of Service to the Business Community" blares a statement on the center's website, bragging that the center "has participated in more than 700 cases in a wide range of business-related issues at every level of the judicial system and before many regulatory agencies."[48]

"NCLC's ambitious advocacy program has grown to include all aspects of employment relations, environmental regulation and enforcement, government contracts, as well as other cutting-edge legal issues in the areas of class action reform, product liability, toxic torts, and punitive damages," the release explains.[49]

According to its website, the center's ambitious and aggressive legal approaches include initiating legislation that "individual businesses might be reluctant to file or that no single business could fight alone and going head-to-head against federal and state government agencies on behalf of the business community"; submitting amicus curiae (friend-of-the-court) briefs to persuade the courts to rule in favor of business ("NCLC presents unique and compelling legal arguments and policy perspectives that can often surpass the help that the lawyers for the involved parties are able to provide. . . . Even the Chief Deputy Clerk of the U.S. Supreme Court has praised the quality of amicus briefs filed by NCLC on behalf of the Chamber"); and running a "moot court program" to help "a company's own litigation preparation by conducting complete 'trial runs' prior to oral argument. Initially designed to assist inexperienced counsel, these invaluable practice sessions are even used by veteran practitioners."[50]

The NCLC has been especially active on the issue of corporate constitutional rights. In the *Nike* case, for example, the center hired Kenneth Starr to draft an amicus brief defending Nike's right to free speech and urging the Court to issue a clear (and very narrow) definition of what counts as commercial speech. The center also issued briefs in support of corporate free speech in *Lorillard Tobacco Company v. Reilly* (where the Court struck down a Massachusetts law prohibiting tobacco advertising within 1,000 feet of a playground or school) and *Vaughey v. Montana Chamber of Commerce* (where a Montana initiative that restricted corporate political participation in state initiatives was declared unconstitutional).

Another of the most active groups in the "business civil liberties" movement is the Washington Legal Foundation (WLF). As the organization proudly notes on its website, "For many years, WLF has been a vigilant guardian of the civil rights of the business community. Those rights include the First Amendment right to speak truthfully on commercial matters, the Fifth Amendment protection against uncompensated government confiscation of private property, the right to engage in business without unnecessary government regulation, and the right to maintain the privacy of trade secrets and internal corporate affairs in the absence of an overriding public interest in disclosure."[51]

"I like to think of us as a small business version of the American Civil Liberties Union," WLF chairman Dan Popeo explains. "Only our stress is on economic civil liberties."[52]

Although WLF has a small staff of fifteen to thirty-four (depending on the budget and workload), its governing body is a "legal policy advisory board" of fifty-five lawyers, judges, and legal academics from the most prestigious schools in the country. In addition, forty-eight firms donated professional services to the WLF in 1993, among them such prestigious (or infamous) names as Arnold & Porter, Covington & Burling, and Vinson & Elkins (Enron's law firm). Corporate funders and foundations include ScheringPlough, Bristol-Myers Squibb, ExxonMobil, Kimberley-Clark, Textron, 3M, Chase Manhattan, Caterpillar, ADM, Citicorp, Philip Morris, Eli Lilly, Warner-Lambert, Nabisco, Cigna, Sprint, and many others. In 2002, WLF had a budget of $3.7 million.[53]

Since its founding in 1977, the WLF has produced more than 1,360 publications, litigated more than 800 court cases, and participated in more than 600 administrative and regulatory procedures.[54] The WLF coordinates a steady stream of legal backgrounders, written by prestigious judges, academics, and lawyers, to encourage the press and others to understand current legal debates from the perspective of corporate and property rights. The organization also regularly places opinion pieces in the nation's leading news outlets and regularly buys op-ads in the *New York Times*.

Over the past decade, the WLF has filed amicus briefs and distributed legal backgrounders advocating the expansion and protection of commercial rights in a variety of ways:

- Opposing FDA trans-fat labeling requirements.[55]
- Opposing EPA enforcement actions against pesticides.[56]
- Filing several lawsuits challenging the FDA's ban on promoting drugs for unapproved uses.[57]
- Standing up for Nike's right to commercial speech in the *Kasky* case.[58]
- Supporting breast implant manufacturers' and asbestos makers' rights to advertise while they are involved in a lawsuit, a practice that plaintiffs' attorneys describe as an attempt to taint prospective jury members.[59]
- Arguing that proposed restrictions on "point of sale" advertising, packaging, warning labels, and disclosures sought by the federal government against tobacco violate the industry's First Amendment rights.[60]
- Arguing that the Bipartisan Campaign Reform Act of 2002 encroaches on the fundamental First Amendment rights of free speech and association.[61]
- Opposing legislation, regulations, and lawsuits that seek to compel the FDA to label foods that contain genetically modified food ingredients.[62]
- Opposing global restrictions on advertising, particularly those that follow standards set in European countries, which are much more restrictive than those in the United States.[63]
- Opposing FCC regulations on horizontal ownership by cable operators and vertical relationships with their program suppliers.[64]

- Opposing a California law that restricts misleading claims about environmentally friendly products.[65]
- Opposing city ordinances banning tobacco and alcohol advertising.[66]
- Opposing congressional attempts to eliminate tax deductions for advertising expenses associated with liquor and tobacco.[67]
- Opposing state and federal attempts to tax tobacco and use the proceeds to fund antitobacco TV ads.[68]
- Opposing the regulation of product placement in movies.[69]
- Opposing court orders in Ohio and elsewhere that required executives convicted of violating environmental laws to join the Sierra Club as part of their sentence.[70]
- Supporting the right of malt liquor makers to use the name *Crazy Horse* after the Bureau of Alcohol, Tobacco, and Firearms (BATF) restricted its use.[71]
- Opposing attempts to ban the use of cartoon figures such as "Joe Camel" to market dangerous products.[72]
- Supporting direct-to-consumer advertising of prescription drugs.[73]
- Supporting the right of telephone carriers to use their customers' business records without first obtaining the customers' prior affirmative consent.[74]
- Opposing Massachusetts's attempt to regulate cigarette advertisements on billboards within 1,000 feet of schools, playgrounds, and churches. ("We protect the free speech of Nazis and white supremacists, but we restrict what people can say about their lawful products," WLF's Richard Samp commented; "somehow, that just doesn't seem right.")[75]
- Supporting a petition by Pfizer to the FDA by calling upon the FDA to respect the drug industry's right to "respond on an equal footing with its critics" by not subjecting such responses to its drug labeling and advertising requirements.[76]
- Filing a complaint with the Securities and Exchange Commission (SEC) to investigate stock losses caused by class action litigation practices allegedly designed to drive down the price of the stock and unfairly force the target company to settle a case.[77]

Additionally, using the Fifth Amendment to file suit against uncompensated taking of private property, the WLF has mounted serious legal challenges to the use of legal trust funds (money collected from pooled short-term interest paid on trust accounts that lawyers set up to temporarily hold certain client funds) to fund pro bono services for indigent clients. "We are finally in a position we've fought more than a decade to reach—a position where we can deal a death blow to the single most important source of income for radical legal groups across the country," wrote WLF chairman Dan Popeo in a fund-raising letter. Among the "radical" groups that Popeo is referring to are "groups dedicated to the homeless, to minorities, to gay and lesbian causes, and any other group that has drawn money from hard-working Americans like you and me to support its radical cause!"[78] Although the Supreme Court ruled 5–4 that the funds were constitutional in March 2003,[79] Richard Samp, WLF's chief counsel, said his clients were considering mounting a First Amendment challenge to the funds.[80]

WLF also issued a legal backgrounder warning citizens of Passaic County, New Jersey, that by adopting a resolution granting citizens unprecedented authority to search industrial plants and report the hazards they discover they are potentially creating legal and "civil liberties ramifications" for local business, governments, and themselves.[81]

Like the National Chamber Litigation Center, the Washington Legal Foundation has found that persistence pays.

In addition to the NCLC and the WLF, ideological conservatives have built perhaps the most influential legal network in this country, the more broadly conservative/libertarian Federalist Society for Law and Public Policy Studies. Though not focused on protecting business enterprise with quite the same fervor as the WLF, the Federalist Society's core principles of selective government interference tend to be quite consistent with the corporate agenda. Glancing through the society's forums and publications, one can find arguments to abolish the Securities and Exchange Commission, to limit the directives of the Environmental Protection Agency and the Occupational Safety and Health Administration, and to scale back the public sector in general.

Founded in 1982 by a handful of conservative law students, the Federalist Society now boasts more than 20,000 professional members with chapters in sixty cities and 5,000 students with 145 campus chapters. The society sponsors an annual National Lawyers Convention, a Speakers Bureau for organizing lectures and debates, and fifteen Practice Groups.[82]

A 2001 report by the Institute for Democracy Studies entitled "The Federalist Society and the Challenge to a Democratic Jurisprudence" details the influence that the Federalist Society and other conservative activist legal groups have had in dominating America's legal system.

> The push for significant restrictions on Congress's authority to legislate goes far beyond public skepticism about the efficacy of government programs, a renewed desire for regulatory efficiency, and necessary streamlining. Strategic constitutional challenges are being mounted across the state-level and federal judiciary in areas that were previously viewed as settled law and enjoyed widespread consensus. Meanwhile, an extensive network of large foundations, attorneys in prominent private and public interest law firms, activist groups, and political interests are expanding their institutional capacity while demonstrating growing sophistication in organizing toward their strategic goals.
>
> At the heart of this process is the Federalist Society, an often underestimated but increasingly powerful and influential organization of conservatives and right-wing libertarians in the bar. . . . The Federalist Society is more than a group of lawyers with reactionary ideas. Although the Society never argues a motion or files a case, it is quietly gaining influence in key areas of the American judicial system.[83]

According to the *New York Times*, about a quarter of the candidates interviewed by the Bush administration for judgeships were recommended by the Federalist Society. "The organization counts among its 25,000 members some of the most influential officials in the Bush administration," wrote the *Times*. "Many federal judges are ardent supporters."[84]

Though NCLC, WLF, and the Federalist Society are three of the biggest, journalist David Helvarg has documented at least twenty-two "free-enterprise" legal foundations created since the early 1970s to expand the business community's claims to constitutional rights and push the legal system's acceptance of certain business-friendly (and antiregulation) doctrines.[85]

Corporations also influence the judiciary through "educational" trips to plush vacation spots where corporate-funded foundations and centers offer seminars on corporate-friendly doctrines. As the Community Rights Council explains:

> Every year, more and more federal judges fly to resort locations to attend privately funded seminars. All of a judge's expenses are paid for, including tuition, transportation, food, lodging, and various leisure activities. These trips, which cost thousands of dollars per judge, are privately bankrolled by corporations and foundations. Meanwhile the same funders are simultaneously financing federal court litigation touching upon the same topics covered in the seminars. . . . Indeed, in 1998, more than ten percent of the nation's judges jetted off to a luxury resort to attend a private seminar. The education judges receive at these trips is one-sided, with the pro-market, anti-regulatory seminars . . . dominating the market of private judicial education.[86]

Between 1992 and 1998, 237 federal judges reported attending 539 seminars sponsored by the "Big Three" seminar sponsors, George Mason University's Law and Economics Center (LEC), the Foundation for Research on Economics and the Environment (FREE), and the Liberty Fund. LEC seminars have been held at such luxury vacation spots as Amelia Island, Florida; Hilton Head, South Carolina; and Marco Island, Florida, and have featured such programs as "an intensive course of study in price theory taught from a property rights perspective with an emphasis on the economics effects of alternative legal regulations." FREE seminars held in Bozeman, Montana (with plenty of "time for cycling, fishing, golfing, hiking, and horseback riding") include lectures with titles such as "The Environment—A CEO's perspective."[87]

Pro-business legal groups are also becoming increasingly involved in financing judicial elections in the thirty-eight states that elect judges either directly or through "retention" elections.

Instead of working to convince and persuade judges of their interpretation of the law, pro-business groups are now working to make sure the people selected to interpret the law are already on their side.

In 2000, campaign spending on judicial races hit $45.6 million, a 61 percent increase over its 1998 peak and twice as much as in 1994. According to *Mother Jones* magazine, in the late 1990s, "The U.S. Chamber of Commerce joined with the Business Roundtable to set up a complex network of front groups that anonymously filtered corporate money into often divisive local television ad campaigns. . . . The Chamber claimed victory in 21 of 24 judicial elections it worked on in eight states, as well as 11 attorneys general races . . . since 1998, major corporations . . . have spent more than $100 million through front groups to remake courts that have long been a refuge for consumers and employees."[88]

In Mississippi, for example, where the Chamber of Commerce ranks the courts the worst in the nation on fairness to business interests, the chamber has "pumped millions of dollars into judicial races there in order to defeat judges it views as unfriendly."[89] In Ohio, meanwhile, the Chamber of Commerce used a front group called Citizens for a Strong Ohio to raise $1 million to support judicial candidates in 2002.[90] In January of 2004, Tom Donohue, president of the Chamber, announced that his group would "put its clout and dollars into a number of state judicial and attorney general races this year. We're going to pick the ones where we think the American business community is getting an unfair shake because of the behavior of either the governor or the state attorney general or the justices of the state Supreme Court."[91]

Unfortunately, there are no comparable legal societies that are organized to disseminate and support the opposing view—that the rights of citizens to govern themselves are more important than the rights of corporations to make money, that our collective well-being should trump narrow property rights, and that citizen democracy depends on the ability of citizens to govern themselves.

Although there are some small progressive law societies, their focus is not on stemming the "business civil liberties" movement. One such society is the American Constitutional Society. Founded in 2001 to counteract the dominance of the conservative Federalist Society, the group as of 2004 had chapters in at least ten cities and eighty campuses and is continuing to grow.[92] Challenging corporate power and corporate rights, however, is not one of the American Constitutional Society's key areas of practice. Instead, the group's initial priorities fall into more bread-and-butter liberal issues like civil rights and gun control. There is also the American Civil Liberties Union (ACLU), which may be the closest thing to a powerful "progressive" legal organization, but unfortunately the ACLU has not yet made the distinction between corporate rights and our rights. In the *Nike v. Kasky* case, the ACLU of Northern California filed an amicus brief on behalf of Nike. Another notable group is the Public Citizen Litigation Group, which specializes in federal health and safety regulation, consumer litigation, open government, union democracy, separation of powers, and the First Amendment. However, its resources are limited in comparison to corporate-funded legal groups. Members of the National Lawyer's Guild (NLG) have also worked on challenging corporate rights. NLG has a Committee on Corporations, the Constitution & Human Rights. However, the NLG is relatively small, with chapters in only four cities.

To a certain extent, a legal society founded to challenge corporate rights could adopt many of the same techniques as the Washington Legal Foundation, which has been extremely effective in coordinating a "business civil rights" movement through a series of amicus briefs, legal backgrounders, and op-eds. However, we need to recognize that corporations will always be able to outspend their challengers; as a sovereign people, we cannot expect our Constitution to survive so many corporate assaults by merely delegating its defense to paid legal experts.

We believe that the most effective approach would be to essentially cut the rug out from under these corporate challenges to citizen sovereignty. Since many of the challenges are based on the premise that the Bill of Rights protections apply to corporations, perhaps instead of arguing specific interpretations of various amendments (such as what counts as commercial speech) we should be approaching the question from a more fundamental level. Perhaps we need to ask whether Bill of Rights protections should even apply to corporations in the first place. Because if they don't, then the whole premise of many of the arguments of the corporate rights legal movement is undercut.

So what basis would we have for saying corporations have no protections under the Bill of Rights? As we discussed in the beginning of this chapter, what rights corporations should have is largely an outgrowth of how we view the corporation. If we treat the corporation as a mere creature of the state, then it seems natural to limit the rights of corporations. But if corporations are to be treated as independent and natural persons, then it would logically follow that they should enjoy the rights of individuals.

The problem dates back to the late nineteenth century, when the popular and legal conception of corporations shifted from artificial entities to natural entities. Whereas the artificial entity theory supported the view that corporations enjoyed no rights and privileges except those directly granted in their charters, under the natural entity theory, corporations were able to fit themselves into a system of law based on the rights, privileges, and responsibilities of individuals. As legal historian Morton J. Horwitz explains, "Since corporations could no longer be treated as special creatures of the state, they were entitled to the same privileges as all other individuals and groups. . . . [T]he state thus lost any special claims arising out of the original theory of corporate creation to regulate corporations."[93]

Since corporations are not individuals, however, this had troubling consequences. As legal scholar Christopher Stone has explained, "There already existed a body of law addressed to 'persons' and the corporation was eased into this body of law in the simplest way possible: by ignoring, one by one, the earlier qualms about whether the corporation ('that invisible intangible, and artificial being' as chief Justice Marshall had called it) could be a person, too. As a result, many possible approaches to controlling corporations that would have taken special account of their special organizational natures were not developed as they might have been."[94]

In practice, then, the legal doctrine of "corporate person-hood" has affected our conception of corporations and the way that we accommodate them in our law and society. Shoehorning corporations into a system of law organized around individual persons, as Stone noted, meant that we did not develop a system of law that could appropriately deal with the institutional qualities of the corporation, apart from the relationship between owners and managers. Meanwhile, the idea of "corporate personhood" has helped to justify the corporation as a part of society, a sort of "corporate citizen." If we think of corporations as persons or citizens, we have a tendency to think that they are just like us, and that they should enjoy the same rights as we do.

Once upon a time, of course, corporations were seen as faceless institutions, with "no body to kick, no soul to damn," as one famous saying went. But as professor Roland Marchand has explained in *Creating the Corporate Soul: The Rise of Public Relations and Corporate Imagery in American Big Business,*[95] corporations have worked hard to shed their soulless image and become like people in the eyes of real human beings. Consider, for a minute, to what extent corporations go to endow themselves with human qualities through their advertising. Corporations claim to be "like a good neighbor." They want to be seen as caring. As public relations expert Chris Komisarjevsky has put it, "It's absolutely fundamental that a corporation today has as much a human and personal characteristic as anything else. . . . If you walked down the street with a microphone and a camera and you stopped [people] on the street . . . they will describe [corporations] in very human terms."[96] Corporations also tend to associate themselves with real people, whether through spokespeople or even through their logos. Consider such corporate "persons" as Orville Redenbacher, Aunt Jemima, Uncle Ben, Colonel Sanders, the Maytag repairman, the Pillsbury Dough-boy, and the Michelin Man, among countless others. These are all tools that corporations have used to try to integrate themselves into society as "persons."

But corporations are not persons. Corporations can live forever. Corporations can exist and operate in multiple locations at the same time. Corporations can own other corporations and be owned by people. Corporations can fuse two bodies into one. Corporations grow to full adulthood the second they are created. Corporations cannot be put in jail for their crimes. Corporations don't need air, water, or food. Corporations are incapable of feeling guilt, shame, love, or any other emotion.

By eliding these crucial differences between corporations and persons and sustaining a doctrine of corporate personhood, we have allowed these forms of business to enjoy many of the rights of being a person but few of the responsibilities.

But if corporations were persons, then what kind of person would a corporation be? According to Dr. Robert Hare, a world-renowned expert on psychopaths, corporations fit most of the clinical definitions of psychopaths. As lawyer Joel Bakan explains:

> When we asked Dr. Hare to apply his diagnostic checklist of psychopathic traits (italicized below) to the corporation's institutional character, he found there was a close match. The corporation is *irresponsible*, Dr. Hare said, because "in an attempt to satisfy the corporate goal, everybody else is put at risk." Corporations try to "*manipulate* everything, including public opinion, and they are *grandiose*, always insisting "that we're number one, we're the best." A *lack of empathy* and *asocial tendencies* are also key characteristics of the corporation, says Hare—"their behavior indicates that they don't really concern themselves with their victims"; and corporations often *refuse to accept responsibility for their own actions* and are *unable to feel remorse*: "if [corporations] get caught [breaking the law], they pay big fines and they . . . continue doing what they did before anyway. . . . Finally, according to Dr. Hare, corporations relate to others *superficially*—"their whole goal is to present themselves to the public in a way that is appealing to the public [but] in fact may not be representative of what th[e] organization is really like."[97]

As a society, we tend to deal with psychopaths by putting them in situations where they can't harm anybody else and by

CHALLENGING THE CORPORATE CLAIM | 77

trying to rehabilitate them. We do not give them all kinds of rights and privileges and let them run rampant.

In recent years, a growing number of activist groups, including the Program on Corporations Law and Democracy (POCLAD), the Women's International League for Peace and Freedom (WILPF), ReclaimDemocracy.org, and the Community Environmental Legal Defense Fund (CELDF),[98] have seized upon this idea of "corporate personhood" as a way of explaining the illegitimate legal advantages that corporations have enjoyed. The basic argument is that the Bill of Rights was intended for real people. Corporations are not real people. Therefore they don't deserve Bill of Rights protections. Case closed.

"Corporate personhood is an effective issue for engaging people," explains Jeff Milchen, an organizer and the executive director of grassroots group ReclaimDemocracy.org. "Why do corporations have more rights than you? It's one issue that can cut across the political spectrum very well."[99]

Many working on the issue of corporate personhood advocate a constitutional amendment that would say specifically that corporations are not persons. We believe that any amendment should circumvent debate over the question of corporate personhood and more directly state that Bill of Rights protections do not apply to corporations, which should be considered mere creatures of the state.

At this point, however, there is little practical reason to believe such an amendment would pass any time soon. Of 18,000 proposed amendments to the U.S. Constitution that have been introduced in Congress since 1789, only 33 have emerged with the required two-thirds majority of both the House of Representatives and the Senate. And of those 33, only 27 have been ratified into law by three-quarters of the states.[100] Therefore, although such an amendment might be effective if enacted, at this point in time it would be overwhelmingly difficult. And although it might be a useful pedagogical method of framing the issue of corporate constitutional rights, a constitutional amendment should not distract us from doing the many things that might actually make a difference in the immediate future.

TYING CONSTITUTIONAL QUESTIONS
TO REAL BATTLES

One approach to bringing about a more democracy-friendly system of jurisprudence is to begin reframing many of our struggles against corporations as questions of citizen rights versus the rights of corporations. Consider the example of Turlock, the California town that is being challenged by Wal-Mart over its decision to ban most new or expanding discount stores that exceed 100,000 square feet and devote at least 5 percent of the space to groceries and other nontaxable items. Whose rights are more important? The right of the citizens of Turlock to decide, democratically, what kind of community they would like to live in? Or the rights of Wal-Mart, a corporation, to build a store bigger than 100,000 square feet in a community that clearly does not want such a large retail store?

Though the citizens of Turlock plan to defend themselves against Wal-Mart's legal bullying, they have not yet challenged the fundamental basis of Wal-Mart's claim: that the corporation is entitled to constitutional protections that render Turlock's law unfairly discriminatory. And likely, given the current state of jurisprudence, such an approach would not get them very far. At the same time, however, battlegrounds such as this can offer opportunities for citizens to advance legal strategies that challenge corporate claims to Bill of Rights protections and perhaps even begin to frame direct challenges.

In western Pennsylvania, for example, a number of small towns, responding to public health hazards posed by sludge dumpers, have begun to extend their struggle in this direction, marking a new battleground where citizens are asserting that their rights of self-governance are more important than the rights of corporations to make money.

Consider the tale of Porter Township, which initially tried to deal with city sludge dumpers from nearby Pittsburgh by enacting unusually high fines targeted at these companies. When these companies brought a lawsuit challenging the town's right to regulate sludge, the town's board of supervisors, acting under the guidance of the Community Environmental Legal Defense

Fund (CELDF), passed a law in December 2002 that said that corporations don't have such rights in Porter Township. "A corporation is a legal fiction created by the express permission of the people," the ordinance reads. "Democracy means government by the people. Only citizens of Porter Township should be able to participate in the democratic process in Porter Township and enjoy a republican form of government therein."[101] Licking Township, another small Pennsylvania town, joined Porter in February 2003 in outlawing corporate constitutional rights. Meanwhile, also help from CELDF, approximately ten small Pennsylvania towns have banned corporate hog farming from their borders, also inviting Fourteenth Amendment discrimination challenges.

As more grassroots community struggles like these end up in court, there will be more and more opporunities for citizens to challenge the corporate claims to constitutional rights. Cases where such claims are at stake, such as the *Nike v. Kasky* case, also offer opportunities to raise a hue and cry over the corporate claim to constitutional rights.[102]

A recent case that offered a good example of the potential for organizing a large number of people around these issues is the corporate challenge to the Federal Trade Commission's Do-Not-Call registry. Though the antitelemarketing registry was incredibly popular, with the users of at least 50 million telephone numbers signing up for it within weeks, telemarketing trade groups protested, claiming First Amendment protections for their corporate clients' commercial speech. Federal district judge Edward W. Nottingham of Denver validated the telemarketers' claim in October 2003, but the Tenth Circuit Court of Appeals reversed Nottingham's decision and upheld the law in February 2004.[103] However, telemarketing groups have vowed to challenge the decision by seeking review by the Supreme Court, posing the possibility that corporate claims to the First Amendment could undermine a law that was so popular that Congress acted in record time to support it after Nottingham's decision.

As corporations continue to claim constitutional protections in attempts to overturn popular laws like the Do-Not-Call registry, We The People can respond by exposing the fallacies and destructive dangers of corporate claims to constitutional rights, and the fact that conferring such rights imperils the ability of citizens to effectively protect themselves from many of the excesses of corporate power.

———

One of the primary themes of this book is that citizens can most effectively control corporations by restoring democracy. However, to be able to place meaningful limitations on corporations through citizen government, we must have a system of jurisprudence that respects the rights of citizens to set their own rules and recognizes that corporations are fundamentally servants of the people, state-created business organizations that exist to promote the general welfare.

In the broadest sense, then, the struggle we face is one to reestablish our rights of self-governance. If corporations can effectively invalidate laws we have enacted to protect ourselves by claiming to have the same rights as citizens, then our rights to protect ourselves will be severely circumscribed.

Over the last three decades, corporations have worked assiduously to foster a system of jurisprudence that places a higher value on the rights of businesses to maximize profit than on the rights of citizens to govern themselves. Our challenge lies not only in reversing this dangerous development, but also in establishing an alternative, more democratic view of the law.

As we have noted, doing this will require that we pay much greater attention to the law. In part that will require us to build a broader popular understanding of the law. To do this, we can start by building a network of like-minded activists, academics, lawyers, and lawmakers concerned with the recent growth of corporate legal rights and come up with strategies to help reassert the legal rights and interested in developing strategies to reverse this process and restore citizen sovereignty.

3 | Fixing the Gears of Corporate Governance

*"My job as a businessman is to be a profit center
and to maximize return to the shareholder."*

—former Enron CEO Jeffrey Skilling (from his days
at the Harvard Business School)

On May 28, 2003, ExxonMobil shareholders gathered together for a contentious meeting in Dallas, Texas, where the
world's largest oil company (and second largest company of any
type) is headquartered.

Robert Monks, a noted shareholder activist and an Exxon-
Mobil shareholder in attendance, described the meeting as a
"milestone which we should not pass without examination."
Sitting there, he observed "the needless restrictions on shareholder communication, the minatory security apparatus, the
anal fixation on the clock, the enlistment of apparently 'bought'
testimony on particular resolutions, the deliberate slighting of
those who exercise their right to appear."[1]

Walking out, Monks thought, "Chapters of Russian history flashed through my mind. Maybe it was the talk of Emperors (during my allotted four minutes, I had called Exxon's CEO an emperor); after all, a hundred years ago, the masses had petitioned the Tsar for reform. But the enduring image is not so much Tsarist Russia as the Stalinist show trials of the 1930s. I felt diminished for having participated in this charade."[2]

For others, meanwhile, the concern was ExxonMobil's continued refusal to acknowledge global warming as a potential environmental problem. In the leadup to the meeting, Greenpeace activists dressed as tigers had invaded the company's headquarters and served notice on ExxonMobil's management for crimes against the global environment.

At the annual meeting, the company's directors announced the results of two resolutions filed by Campaign ExxonMobil, a shareholder consortium of faith-based and environmental groups working to get the company to address the problem of global warming.[3] The first would have required the company to prepare a report "describing any operating, financial and reputational risks to the company associated with climate change and explaining how the company will mitigate those risks." That proposal won 22.2 percent of the shareholder vote (one share, one vote). A second proposal asking the company to produce a report on how it will respond to "rising regulatory, competitive and public pressure to significantly develop renewable energy sources" won 21.3 percent.[4]

Shareholders also voted on ten other shareholder proposals on a range of issues, from requiring the company to rewrite its equal employment opportunity policy to explicitly prohibiting discrimination based on sexual orientation to requiring that the board review its policies related to human rights. The board of directors recommended against all twelve shareholder resolutions, and all suffered substantial defeats.[5]

Shareholders at the meeting were also faced with the task of selecting a board of directors that would ostensibly oversee management on their behalf. With only twelve candidates competing for twelve spots on the board of directors, the winning twelve-member board received 96.7 percent of the shareholder votes cast. Like shareholders at most corporations, ExxonMobil share-holders were faced with a Soviet-style election with one and only one choice.

And though it was a contentious meeting, the outcome was never really in doubt. The company's management, led by CEO and board chairman Lee Raymond, was always in control, and got everything it wanted. As Monks described it, the meeting "showed the power of contemporary corporate management to nullify even the slender rights of shareholder/owners to moni-tor that which is theirs."[6]

The problem that Monks points to—the lack of shareholder control—is not a new problem. For many years, corporate man-agement has enjoyed near total control over company opera-tions, leaving owners largely powerless. Changes in corporate law over decades have put ever more power into the hands of management, and shareholders have been too diffuse and poorly organized to exert any meaningful influence.

But whereas shareholders were at least allowed to attend the ExxonMobil meeting, the company's employees, customers, and other stakeholders were not, unless they also happened to be shareholders. For example, the meeting was not open to the low-income community members who live near and breathe the emis-sions from the company's refineries. Nor was it open to consumers whose money allows the corporation to grow and prosper. Like al-most all major companies, ExxonMobil has no formal mecha-nisms for seeking input from anybody except shareholders, and even the shareholders have only a minimal ability to offer input.

Still, every shareholder and every manager and director of ExxonMobil also lives on Planet Earth. Why would they con-tinue to support ExxonMobil's refusal to admit that global warming is a real problem, given that the overwhelming scien-tific evidence shows that the planet is getting warmer and the burning of fossil fuels probably has something to do with that?[7]

The answer appears disturbingly simple. For an oil company, questioning the disastrous impacts of the continuous produc-tion and use of fossil fuels is not a profitable thing to do. And ExxonMobil, as a corporation, is focused first and foremost on one thing: making a profit. As ExxonMobil's directors argued in response to the proposal to require the company to explain how it "will respond to rising regulatory, competitive and public pressure to significantly develop renewable energy sources," the company's shareholders should vote against the proposal because renewable sources of energy are too expensive, and therefore not profitable.[8]

ExxonMobil would also rather not call attention to the disastrous ecological consequences of the continued use of the product it sells; the company's managers had at least learned that much from its famous Valdez oil spill. ExxonMobil's continued financial success depends on the continued consumption of petroleum. And for the managers of the company—theoretically acting in the financial interests of the shareholders—it makes sense to continue to deny that global warming is a problem, especially while alternative sources of energy are more expensive and difficult for the company to control.

Of course, ExxonMobil's managers may be mistaken in their conviction that denying the potential consequences of global warming is a wise financial decision. The shareholders supporting the resolution argued that it is actually in the best interest of the company to start dealing with global warming now. But even the resolution requiring the company to do so (which the Securities and Exchange Commission ruled the company didn't have to address again in 2004)[9] was still framed around the premise that ExxonMobil should be making a profit first and foremost. It does not require ExxonMobil, as the world's largest oil company, to acknowledge any inherent responsibility to also be a good steward of the planet.

THE TYRANNY OF THE BOTTOM LINE

Though it comes across starkly in the ExxonMobil example, this kind of blind imperative to maximize profit occurs over and over again at most companies. Managers, driven by the laws and incentives that guide corporate behavior, have repeatedly gone so far as to put people's lives in danger if there is money to be made in the process.

This is the story behind many numerous corporate decisions that have caused serious damage, physical injury, and even death. It is the story behind the Ford Pinto, where a simple fuel-tank redesign that would have saved thousands of lives was intentionally not undertaken because it would have cost the company $10 per car, and given Ford's internal value judgment that the cost per death (factoring in lawsuits) would be $200,000, the design change was determined not to be cost-effective.[10] It is the story behind General Motors deciding that fixing a defect in its gasoline tanks at a cost of $8.59 per car was more expensive than the $2.40 per car it would have to pay to settle lawsuits for the estimated 500 fatalities a year the faulty gas tanks would cause.[11] It is the story behind the cost-benefit analysis that preceeds decisions whether or not to use pollution-control technologies as well as other antisocial behaviors that corporations rationally engage in simply because to do otherwise would cost more.

In this chapter, we ask: Is there anything that can be done about this problem within the corporation itself? Can the gears of large, publicly traded corporations be made to operate so that the corporations do not wreak such destruction on society?

Having looked at a variety of approaches, we are ultimately skeptical that the corporation can be fundamentally reformed from the inside. The simple fact that we run up against, over and over, is that for-profit business corporations are organized to make money, a defining purpose that often clashes with the broader public interest.

As we explore in this chapter and throughout the book, the consequences of the corporation's single-minded pursuit of profit, when not properly regulated and checked, are incredibly destructive for society. In pursuit of profit, corporations regularly pollute the environment, treat workers as disposable parts, and gouge and rip off consumers.

The question then becomes: Is this a problem that can be dealt with by reengineering the corporation from within? Or is it a problem that we can only address through vigorous external restraints on corporate behavior, largely through citizen-driven regulation?

Ultimately, we are concerned that efforts to reform the dynamics of corporate governance ignore the fundamental nature of the corporation and what drives it to accumulate power. Our underlying concern is that corporations already enjoy too much power in society, while citizens possess too little. To truly control corporations, we need to address this imbalance by restoring citizen democracy and reducing corporate encroachment upon the public sphere.

Still, there are many important things we can accomplish within the corporate governance structure to mitigate the harmful consequences of profit maximization. Ultimately, making corporations less focused on maximizing profits will make it easier for citizens to control them externally. Therefore, we believe that the subject of corporate governance is worthy of sustained attention. At the very least, understanding the way that corporations operate can help us to better fashion regulations to control them.

Since corporations are arguably the most powerful institutions in the world, we believe that we have no choice but to examine this set of questions and see whether the principles of democracy can be made to apply to corporations.

THE SHAREHOLDERS

Shareholders are the owners of the company. They are the estimated 84 million Americans[12] (as well as millions of foreign investors) who own stock in U.S. corporations, either directly or through mutual funds or pension funds. Other corporations are also shareholders, as are a variety of other institutions, including churches, universities, and other nonprofits.

Though shareholders are the owners of the company, they do not actually play any meaningful ownership role. In general, shareholders are largely passive investors.

Because putting your money into the stock market is considered one of the best ways to make your money grow (the average value of stocks has historically grown at about 8 percent a year, far more than bonds or CDs or other major forms of investment), these 84 million Americans invest in stocks. Accordingly, they choose their stocks by considering whether the company looks like a good investment (i.e., whether it looks like the value of the company's stock will rise based on projected growth). If it appears that a company has a poor financial future, investors will sell their stock.

Increasingly, more and more investors own stock through mutual funds and pension funds, which essentially means that somebody else is doing the buying and selling on their behalf. But the goal is the same: to maximize return on investment and make the most money possible. And the profit pressure is even more acute, since fund managers make their living by picking winners.

In their ownership capacity, shareholders have two primary responsibilities. One is that they select a board of directors to run the corporation on their behalf. The other is that they can introduce and vote on shareholder resolutions, which advise the company to adopt certain policies, like expensing stock options or producing a report on the consequences of global warming. Unfortunately, their power in both capacities is exceedingly limited. At most corporations, shareholders only get one slate of directors to choose from, a slate of directors that is nominated by either the current board of directors or management, or both. Meanwhile, shareholder resolutions very rarely win a majority of shareholder votes (one vote per share). And when they do, the vote is almost always not binding on management. The one thing that shareholders can do, however, is to buy and sell their ownership shares. And though each individual decision makes little difference, the cumulative effect of buying and selling millions of shares can alter the stock price and send a message to the corporation.

It's important to note, however, that many shareholders care about more than just making money. Many also have another relationship with the company in which they own stock. For example, it is common that workers own stock in the company where they work. Many corporate stockholders may also be regular customers. Finally, many shareholders may more generally be concerned with the destructive behaviors of corporations, as the $151 billion invested in two hundred socially responsible mutual funds demonstrates.[13] However, shareholders' ability to register these concerns within the corporation is still extremely limited.

THE DIRECTORS

The role of the directors is to oversee the management to ensure that the company is being run in the best interests of the shareholders. A Delaware law states, "The laws governing the organization and governance of public as well as privately held companies in the United States universally establish that the business and affairs of the corporation are to be managed by or under the direction of its board of directors."[14]

Though directors are technically elected by the shareholders, such elections tend to be little more than the rubber-stamping of a board of directors selected by the current directors, management, or both. At three-quarters of U.S. corporations, the CEO is also the chairman of the board.

Directors have a duty to act in the best interest of the corporation and its owners, which has generally been taken to mean their financial interest. This fiduciary duty essentially has two components: the duty of care and the duty of loyalty. Under these duties, directors are expected to behave reasonably, prudently, and in good faith in serving what they believe to be the best interest of the corporation, always putting the interests of the corporation ahead of their own interests. Though shareholders can sue when they believe directors have violated their fiduciary duty to shareholders, the bar for filing a suit is actually quite high. That is because courts rely on something called the "business judgment rule," which generally prevents courts from second-guessing the decisions of directors, and thus gives directors a good deal of freedom in deciding what to do. As Robert Monks and Nell Minow have explained it, "The business judgment rule begins with the reasonable assumption that directors should not be judged in hindsight, so we should not ask that all of their decisions be the right ones."[15] In practice, however, "the courts will go to the greatest possible lengths to defer to directors' business judgment unless there is a clear showing of fraud or bad faith."[16] Therefore, Monks and Minow argue that the existence of a "fiduciary standard is perhaps the most powerful myth underlying the corporate system."[17]

On average, directors earn $20,000 per meeting and $141,000 a year per board.[18] And since directors generally owe their lucrative nominations for the board to management (as opposed to the shareholders), there is a tendency among directors to acquiesce to the intentions of management. However, even though corporate law does offer them a certain degree of latitude in running the company, directors who are blatantly irresponsible (fiscally or otherwise) could face civil lawsuits.

THE MANAGERS

On a day-to-day basis, it is the managers who run the corporation, giving the orders and making the key decisions. Though technically they are responsible to the board of directors, since management plays an important role in selecting the board of directors and since the CEO is often the chairman of the board, the lines between managers and directors can sometimes get blurry. This creates problems of accountability.

What motivates managers? In general, money and power. As we have witnessed in recent years, when given the opportunity to enrich themselves at the expense of their shareholders, many executives will take that opportunity. Therefore, one of the underlying questions of corporate governance has always been: How can corporations be set up so that managers will run the company in the best interest of the owners, especially since owners have so little power in the corporate governance structure and so little information regarding day-to-day activities?

Perhaps the most common way to align the interests of managers and shareholders has been to make the managers into shareholders themselves. Indeed, at almost all large companies, top managers are major stockholders. This way, both managers and shareholders have the same interest in mind: keep the stock price up. But this can create another problem. Companies like

Enron, WorldCom, HealthSouth, and others went belly-up because executives, with boatloads of stock in their possession (much of which was doled out in the form of options), were motivated to "cook the books," to pump up the stock price. Then they cashed out by selling their stock before the house of cards they built crumbled.

However, even without a major investment in company stock, executives would still be focused on the stock price, since the stock price is the primary measure of a company's health and therefore management's success. A declining stock price is bad news for a corporation on a number of levels, and any manager who wants to keep his or her job knows this. So, although shareholders don't have much direct control over the company, managers do what they can to keep shareholders happy in the abstract by keeping quarterly earnings reports strong, knowing full well that if more investors are selling than are buying, the stock price will sag, and the first people to take the blame will be the top executives.

This principle is reinforced by corporate law, which essentially codifies the principle that corporations are to be run in the best interest of shareholders.

THE PARADOX OF CORPORATE GOVERNANCE

All this sets up a confusing dynamic. On the one hand, owners are completely disenfranchised. The corporation is run without their input, and managers are largely unaccountable to anybody. Yet, at the same time, corporations are run primarily for the financial benefit of shareholders—often with disastrous consequences and at great cost to workers, consumers, the environment, other stakeholders, and, paradoxically, sometimes even to shareholders themselves. Though it sounds contradictory, that is how corporations operate. Accordingly, attempts to use corporate governance to mitigate the harmful tendencies of large corporations essentially fall into two approaches.

In one approach, socially conscious investors use the powers of ownership that are given to them (shareholder resolutions, the ability to buy and sell) to pressure corporations to alter their behavior. Although this can yield some modest results, the truth is that the corporate governance structure makes it extremely difficult for shareholders to leverage much pressure on management. Meanwhile, because stock ownership is distributed unequally (just 1 percent of investors control about half the shares) and votes are granted based on the number of shares owned (as opposed to the real democracy of one person, one vote), and because most investors are primarily concerned with the company's finances, even when shareholders do get a say, that say will only reflect the opinions and concerns of primarily wealthy shareholders and large institutional investors primarily concerned with making money—hardly a representative sample of the public affected by the activities of the corporation.

The second set of approaches involves trying to change the laws and incentives that drive the corporation's unrelenting focus on maximizing shareholder profit in the first place. Potential reforms under this approach include making directors and managers responsible for protecting the public good (instead of just shareholder value), changing investment incentives, increasing the influence of a wider group of stakeholders, and requiring corporations to measure and make public a broad range of performance yardsticks (instead of just their finances). Though these reforms have varying potential benefits, none appear particularly capable of significantly altering the corporation's primary purpose.

COULD AND SHOULD SHAREHOLDERS HAVE MORE CONTROL OF CORPORATIONS?

As we have discussed, one of the problems of corporate governance is that corporations are run without any effective oversight from their owners. Therefore, managers are directly accountable, in effect, to no one.

The separation of ownership and control is a phenomenon that has been recognized as problematic throughout most of the twentieth century. Two related trends helped to distance owners from corporations in the late nineteenth century. The first was the rise of limited liability, as discussed in Chapter 1. In many (though not all) early corporations, investors could be held liable for outstanding debts of the company they owned. This made investing a serious affair and pushed investors to keep a close watch on corporate operations, since their own fortunes were at stake. But by the mid-nineteenth century, increasing attempts to draw more outside investment to corporations helped make limited liability the norm. Investors were now responsible only for their original investment. As a result, they became more invested in the stock market as a whole but less concerned about the day-to-day activities of any of the particular companies in which they invested.[19] As Monks and Minow note, "limiting the liability of investors in corporate enterprises had a potentially pernicious effect in decreasing the personal responsibility on which the integrity of democratic institutions depends."[20]

Meanwhile, as corporations began to grow in size and scope, more people were getting into the stock market. Both the size of companies and the increasing dispersion of stock ownership made it more difficult for investors to collectively monitor the companies they owned. Whereas in the 1830s, a typical day at the Exchange saw only about a few hundred trades, a typical day in the 1850s saw a few hundred thousand shares trade hands, and by 1886, the Exchange had its first million-share day.[21] With more and more investors getting into the stock market, each individual investor had less and less of an ownership stake.

As ownership grew more dispersed and companies grew bigger and more complicated, the old model of owners overseeing operations became less and less feasible. Instead, a new managerial class took over responsibility for the day-to-day operations and a quiet revolution transformed the way that corporations operated. Companies increasingly became more efficient, multidivisional firms operated on managerial principles.[22]

Shareholders also became much less influential. In 1932, Adolf Berle and Gardiner Means published their famous book, *The Modern Corporation and Private Property*, which for the first time focused public attention on the widespread inability of shareholders to control the corporations that they owned. Berle and Means determined that of the largest two hundred companies, in only forty-six did any one shareholder group control enough of the shares (generally 15 to 20 percent) to maintain "working control" of the company. That meant that in 77 percent of the top two hundred companies, managers were essentially running the show with no effective shareholder control.[23]

More than seventy years later, the disconnect between ownership and management is even more acute. Today roughly 50 percent of all households have some stake in the stock market, either as direct shareowners or through mutual funds or pension funds. As of 2002, that included 52.7 million households and 84.3 million individual investors.[24] Millions of retirees, workers, and family men and women have invested some of their money into equities in the hopes that the money will grow in value and allow them to improve the quality of life for themselves and their families. They are everyday people, watching their 401(k)s and IRAs, hoping they can send their children to a good college or retire in comfort if only they make the right investment choices.

But by and large, these investors do not think very much about their role as owners of corporations. Most do not scour the fine print of their company's annual reports or even know much, if anything, about the board of directors. And why should they? After all, they are such a diffuse and poorly organized group that it would be nearly impossible for them to meaningfully participate in corporate decision-making processes anyway. They move money in and out of company stocks in tiny blips, and their individual decisions (unless these involve a particularly large chunk of stock) are not at all significant by themselves. Most own diversified portfolios and are rarely invested enough in any single corporation to care much about it. As attorney Michael E. Murphy has noted, "The paradox of widespread ownership and limited access to power [is] a central feature of corporate enterprise in the United States. . . . [This] dispersion of ownership . . . divides and fragments shareholder action in corporate governance."[25]

Monks and Minow suggest that this lack of accountability to shareholders actually undermines the legitimacy of the corporation itself: "Management accountability to shareholders is more than an economically beneficial arrangement; it is the basis on which we, as a matter of public policy, give legitimacy to the impact that private entities have on our lives. We could no more create a private entity without accountability than we would a public one."[26]

However, although individual ownership of stock is becoming ever more diffuse, there is a second ownership trend that has the potential to counter the problem of diffusion: the increased growth of institutional investors (such as mutual funds and pension funds), which pool ownership into the hands of one fiduciary, who can command significant leverage.

Between 1990 and 1999, the total equities held by households increased 443 percent, from $1.81 trillion to $8.01 trillion. But the total equities held by mutual funds increased three times as fast, growing from $233 billion to $3.36 trillion (up 1,442 percent).[27] In 1990, there were only 228 stock mutual funds with 5.8 million accounts. By 1999, there were 3,952 mutual funds with 149 million accounts.[28]

Increasingly, other institutional investors besides mutual funds are also holding significant stakes in the stock market: $2.50 trillion was in private pension funds in 1999 (up from $595 billion in 1990, up 420 percent), and $2.04 trillion rested in state and local retirement funds (up from $271 billion in 1990, up 754 percent).[29] Another sizeable chunk of stocks is owned by insurance companies, which in 1999 owned $1.17 trillion worth of stock (up from $162 billion in 1990, up 720 percent). Bank trusts and estates, meanwhile, owned $336 billion in 1999 (up from $190 billion in 1990, up 177 percent).[30]

This growth of institutional ownership is a double-edged sword. On the one hand, it further distances individual investors from the companies they own. Indeed, most investors probably have little idea of what corporations they own through their mutual and pension funds. It is often impossible for them to know, since these funds change holdings all the time without letting investors know. Meanwhile, many fund managers are constantly getting in and out of different stocks to maximize their returns and beat the market average (in order to get a pay bonus). If they don't like the way a company is being run, they will likely sell their shares rather than try to change the company.

Additionally, when investors own stocks through mutual funds or pension funds, they do not get to vote their annual proxy ballots at the companies in which they own stock. The managers of the funds vote their proxies. Though a new proxy disclosure rule passed by the SEC in 2003 now requires funds to tell investors how they voted their proxies at companies they own, it has not yet noticeably affected the way that fund managers vote the proxies of their individual investors. The majority of fund managers continue to support the policies of management, which presents a not insignificant obstacle to meaningful shareholder activism.

On the other hand, as institutional investors grow bigger and control more and more shares, they can begin to meaningfully exercise some of the responsibilities and powers of ownership. Though the majority of institutional investors (particularly mutual funds) tend to be passive owners and reinforce the policies of management, a growing number of large state pension funds, union pension funds, and socially responsible mutual funds are taking an increasingly active role. At the end of 2002, the California Public Employees Retirement Fund (CalPERS) had $128.7 billion in assets, making it the third largest pension fund in the world; the California State Teachers Retirement Fund had $88.1 billion in assets. Meanwhile, the New York State Common Retirement Fund had $95.9 billion in assets (sixth largest in the world), and the New York State Teachers Retirement Fund had $66.4 billion in assets. The New York City Retirement Fund had $65.9 billion in assets.[31] The managers of all these funds have demonstrated a commitment to playing an active role in the companies they own.

For example, in a 2002 report entitled "The Power of the Purse," California treasurer Phil Angelides, the state's chief investment officer and a trustee of more than $270 billion in state pension and taxpayer funds, exhorted other institutional investors, particularly other state pension funds, to be more active and directed in their investments.

> Investors need to send a clear message: company conduct counts. . . . Indeed, company executives who relocate offshore to avoid taxes or bend environmental laws or exploit their workforce would not think twice about enriching themselves while shortchanging their shareholders. The California State Treasurer's Office already is setting an example by prohibiting business dealings with expatriate U.S. corporations that relocate offshore—in name only—to dodge taxes and escape legal protections for shareholders. . . . Investors can and must play a pivotal role in renewing faith in our financial system. Without their full commitment, there can be no systemic reform and lasting change.

Increasingly, state pension funds are also taking the social consequences of their investments more seriously and trying to influence the corporations in their portfolios to make positive changes. In November 2003, for example, the comptrollers of New York State and New York City and the treasurers of California, Oregon, Maine, Connecticut, Vermont, and New Mexico, along with pension fund chairs for two unions (the Communications Workers of America (CWA) and the Service Employees International Union (SEIU)), launched an "Investor Network on Climate Risk." The goal is to use the approximately $1 trillion in combined assets that these funds represent to pressure companies into addressing the risks of global warming, as well as to call on regulators to require better disclosure of the risks.[32]

"As fiduciaries, we must take it upon ourselves to identify the emerging environmental challenges facing the companies in which we are shareholders, to demand more information, and to spur needed actions to respond to those challenges," says Angelides.[33]

Meanwhile, two hundred socially responsible investment funds accounted for $151 billion worth of assets (about 1 percent of all assets in the stock market).[34] Union pension funds have also become increasingly active. In the wake of the corporate accounting fraud scandals, unions have increasingly made shareholder resolutions a priority. In 2003, they submitted almost 400 shareholder proposals, most of which dealt with issues of corporate governance and executive pay.

However, significant obstacles remain before even large, institutional investors exerting meaningful control. Under current rules, getting 49.9 percent of the shareholder vote is meaningless, except as a way of drawing attention to an issue. And even if approved, shareholder proposals are almost always nonbinding. Although 170 shareholder resolutions received a majority vote in 2003, only 36 companies have made the changes so far. Yet this is better than the "only a handful of companies" that would respond positively in previous years to shareholder resolutions that won a majority of votes.[35]

As we noted earlier, most corporate board elections are a sham. Instead of having any meaningful say in who sits on the board of directors, shareholders are typically presented with one and only one slate of directors to choose from at the annual shareholder meeting. This board, which is supposed to represent the interests of shareholders, is almost always nominated by the current board, by management, or by both. At roughly three-quarters of U.S. corporations, the CEO of the company also serves as chairman of the board, further blurring the lines between the board of directors and management.[36] "Since the CEO determines what information directors receive, it's no exaggeration to say that, in most instances, directors understand the company through the CEO's eyes," Harvard Business School researcher Jay W. Lorsch concludes in a study of corporate boards. "In addition, the CEO controls the agenda, the meeting process, and, though less important on many boards, he or she still plays a key role in the selection of new outside directors."[37]

The result is a kind of managerial capitalism in which shareholders are largely impotent and the board of directors is primarily a tool of management. This was the case with Enron, WorldCom, Tyco, Adelphia, and other companies where executives used the company as a trough to gorge themselves.

The storyline at many of the scandal-ridden companies was eerily similar: directors with close ties to management failed to question even the most suspicious dealings, essentially rubber-stamping everything management put before them. Executives at these companies received outrageous compensation packages, were given generous "loans" worth hundreds of millions of dollars that they never had any intention of repaying, and engaged in all kinds of accounting chicanery that boosted the company stock temporarily and helped them get rich through the timely exercising of stock options.

In the case of WorldCom, for example, court-appointed monitor Richard C. Breeden blamed the company's bankruptcy on the unchecked power of former CEO Bernard Ebbers. "As CEO, Ebbers was allowed nearly imperial reign over the affairs of the company, without the board of directors exercising any apparent restraint on his actions, even though he did not appear to possess the experience or training to be remotely qualified for his position," Breeden wrote.[38]

Though ultimately the market did catch on and the grossly overvalued stock prices of these companies plummeted, it was often too late. The executives had already become rich on stock sales, leaving unsuspecting workers and investors holding the bag. The *Financial Times* found that the top 208 executives and directors at the twenty-five largest companies that went bankrupt between January 2001 and July 2002 made off with a combined $3.3 billion in reported salary between 1999 and 2001 (about $15.9 million over the three-year-period per executive) as their companies collapsed, 100,000 workers lost their jobs, and investors lost hundreds of billions of dollars.[39] Meanwhile, at the twenty-five biggest companies whose stock price fell at least 75 percent from its high as the market bubble collapsed, 466 directors and executives at these companies cashed out on a whopping $23 billion in stock (almost $50 million per executive) before the crash.[40]

Of course, under the current rules, directors have little incentive to speak up and rock the boat. Since they are generally nominated by management, challenging management could result in losing a rather cushy and prestigious position.[41] Since there is little threat that shareholders will boot them (since there are virtually no meaningful board elections), directors are not inclined to pay much attention to shareholder complaints. And as of this writing, not a single director from a scandal-ridden company has been charged by a federal prosecutor in connection with any of the recent corporate scandals.[42]

Concerns about boards of directors being corrupt ciphers unable to stand up to management became mainstream in the wake of the corporate scandals of 2002. For example, the Conference Board, a good barometer of mainstream business thinking, concluded, after some hand-wringing, that the CEO and the chairman of the board should, in fact, be different people and that the chairman of the board should be an independent director:

> The primary concern in many of these [scandals] is that strong CEOs appear to have exerted a dominant influence on their boards, often stifling the efforts of directors to play the central oversight role needed to ensure a healthy system of corporate governance. In such circumstances, boards have often either lacked the structure and information to perform their roles properly, or they have simply abdicated their responsibilities to provide the oversight required of them.[43]

Separating the chairman and CEO roles was also one of the seventy-eight corporate governance reforms recommended by Breeden in a report designed to help MCI/WorldCom emerge from bankruptcy with a model corporate governance system. Breeden also recommended that directors not serve more than ten years and that the company nominate new directors each year. Additionally, he suggested a three-member governance committee to oversee board nominations, among many other worthwhile improvements.[44]

Meanwhile, both the New York Stock Exchange and the Nasdaq changed their listing standards to require that listed companies have a majority of independent directors, among other corporate governance reforms.[45] The Sarbanes-Oxley Act required the audit committee to be independent (though it said nothing about the rest of board).

Obviously, it is important to have directors who are independent of management. But the concept of board independence remains narrow, since it generally refers only to directors who have no direct financial ties to the company. Indeed, many so-called "independent directors" on corporate boards are CEOs from other corporations (CEOs make up the largest occupational group represented on corporate boards[46]) or longtime corporate directors who have served on many boards. Though they may technically be independent (in that they don't have any direct relationship with the company), there is often very little independence of perspective among directors on how a corporation should operate and for whose benefit.

Realizing that the dominance of managers in selecting corporate directors poses a problem of accountability, in 2004 the SEC proposed a new rule that would allow minority shareholders, under certain special circumstances, to have access to corporate proxy statements (currently controlled by management) for the purposes of nominating candidates to the board of directors.

The rule set up a two-step process for gaining access to the proxy statements. First, shareholders representing 1 percent of company stock can call for a shareholder vote on whether they can nominate directors. Then, if a majority of shareholders agree, the next year the shareholder group can nominate up to three directors, depending on the size of the board. Alternately, if at least 35 percent of shareholders withhold votes for one or more directors, investors are also allowed to nominate directors.

The mainstream business community reacted harshly to these efforts to open up the nominating process, arguing that the proposal would give what business executives like to label "special-interest groups" (such as labor and environmentalists) too much power. The Chamber of Commerce even threatened to sue the SEC over the proposal, arguing that the federal agency could not force corporations to open up the director nomination process to minority shareholders because the authority to do so was in the domain of state corporate law.

As the business community notes, minority shareholders such as socially responsible funds and union, state, and other pension funds would have the ability to nominate directors under the new proxy access rule. But we would argue that this would be a positive development that could make boards more diverse and more representative of the different constituencies that they should be representing. (As we write this, the rule is still under consideration, but the business community is working hard to defeat it.)

If enacted, such reform would be particularly effective at companies where cumulative voting is practiced. Cumulative voting, the practice of allowing voters to select as many candidates as there are seats and then giving the seats to the top-ranking vote getters, increases the chances of minority-supported directors to get on the board because it changes board elections from a simple majority rules system to a ranking system. Unfortunately, cumulative voting has fallen out of favor in corporate board elections over the last several decades. In the 1940s, roughly 40 percent of the 2,900 largest companies had cumulative voting. In 1992, only 14 percent of *Fortune* 500 companies had cumulative voting. Among Delaware companies (60 percent of *Fortune* 500 companies are incorporated in Delaware), only 11 percent had cumulative voting.[47]

Giving shareholders more control over the selection of board members would make board members more accountable to shareholders and would likely make it harder for executives to run away with the store, as they did at Enron and WorldCom. But it is unclear how significant the ability of shareholders to nominate directors would be in terms of making corporations accountable to the broader public. After all, without changing the incentives and mandates driving the corporation, directors will still have one underlying duty—to maximize profit—regardless of who selects them to the board of directors. And more shareholder control might even make the situation worse by putting even more pressure on directors and managers to maximize profit.

Still, some investors do care about making companies more socially responsible. After all, as we have noted, socially responsible funds boast as much as $151 billion worth of investments. And, as we noted, many of the biggest pension funds are also becoming increasingly aggressive in pushing for certain corporate reforms.

But how far can this go? For example, are shareholders as a whole willing to subvert some of their own economic self-interest to support more socially responsible ends? We are not so sure.

THE POSSIBILITIES AND LIMITS
OF SHAREHOLDER ACTION

Under current conditions, there are two main ways that socially conscious shareholders can potentially have an impact on corporations. The first is through shareholder resolutions calling on companies to change. The second is through not investing in companies whose products they don't support.

In response to the corporate scandals of 2002, shareholders at major companies became more active than they had ever been before. According to the Investor Responsibility Research Center, shareholder resolutions at major companies hit 1,082 in 2003, up from 800 the year before. Even more significantly, the number of resolutions that won the support of the majority of shares nearly doubled, jumping from 98 in 2002 to 166 in 2003.[48] (The plateau of resolutions remained steady in 2004, with shareholders filing more than 1,100 proposals.)[49]

Shareholders introduced resolutions related to a wide range of social and environmental issues—everything from human rights to discrimination policy to use of sweatshops to climate change to fair trade coffee. But the most common, and most successful, dealt with questions of corporate governance and CEO pay.

Outrageous CEO pay is widely acknowledged to be a symptom of much that has gone wrong in corporate America in recent years. Warren Buffett has suggested that the willingness to address it should be considered "the acid test of corporate reform."[50]

During the 1990s, CEO pay grew by a whopping 571 percent. For the same period, average worker pay grew by just 37 percent, barely outpacing inflation (which rose 32 percent during the 1990s). Had the minimum wage increased at the same rate as CEO pay, it would have reached $25.50 an hour by the end of the decade. Instead, it stood at just $5.15 an hour.[51] The ratio of average CEO pay to average worker pay reached 531:1 in 2000. To put this number in perspective, by late afternoon on January 1, the average CEO had already earned as much money as the average worker would earn the whole year. Though the average CEO pay has fallen in the last few years as some of the more outrageous options-drenched pay packages have been cut back, the median CEO package continues to rise.[52] And with the decline of stock options, corporations have been moving to different forms of "stealth compensation," (e.g., corporate jets, lavish homes, etc.), which are often harder to track. On both a global and historical level, U.S. executive compensation stands out as a gross aberration. In 2003, the ratio of CEO pay to worker pay was 282:1. Most other industrialized countries have a typical ratio of closer to 25:1. In 1964, the U.S. ratio was also approximately 25:1; in 1982 it was 42:1.[53]

As executive salaries grew dramatically in the 1990s, shareholders sat by idly, seemingly uninterested in how much top executives were making; as long as company stock was going up, they, too, could get rich. But with the collapse of the stock market, many shareholders lost their tolerance for excessive CEO salaries. As *Business Week* noted in May 2003, "Across Corporate America, proxy resolutions aimed at curbing CEO pay are winning unprecedented victories. Most are sponsored by union and public pension funds, which are capitalizing on investor ire over fat pay packages at poorly performing companies."[54]

In total, more than forty shareholder resolutions on the issue of executive pay received majority support in 2003, up from just three in 2002. Additionally, thirty resolutions calling for the expensing of stock options received majority support.[55]

In June 2003, the SEC approved a proposal submitted by the New York Stock Exchange that would require shareholders to approve most equity compensation plans for executives, including stock option programs. The proposal was a modest step. It did not, for example, apply to incoming executives, and it stopped far short of giving shareholders the right to vote on the total compensation package or on the plan each year.[56]

In England, a new law passed in 2003 requires all companies to put their annual executive compensation plans up to a vote each year. And in May 2003, 51 percent of GlaxoSmithKline

shareholders rejected a $36 million (£22 million) golden para-
chute package for CEO Jean-Pierre Garnier, marking the first
time that shareholders had ever rejected an executive pay package.[57] Though the vote was nonbinding, GlaxoSmithKline ac-
quiesced to shareholder demands and also got rid of two board
members responsible for setting compensation policies.[58]

Certainly, reducing excessive executive salaries is a desirable
goal. Not only are such pay packages unfair, but they also represent a disturbing transfer of wealth from stockholders and employees to executives. If corporations are to serve the public
good, they should be a source of shared prosperity, not private
plunder. Meanwhile, such pay disparities further skew the increasingly polarized distribution of wealth in this country,
which is now at levels equivalent to the period just preceding
the Great Depression.[59]

However, we should be clear: though the rise in resolutions
concerning executive pay was largely the result of a popular
backlash against what had become an epidemic of oversized pay
packages, one of the reasons the resolutions were so successful is
that they also were in the self-interest of shareholders. Put simply, shareholders would rather see the money go back into the
company (or go to them in the form of dividends) than go to
overcompensated executives.

But can shareholder activism also work to make companies
change in ways that may not offer as clear a financial benefit for
shareholders?

The answer seems to be: maybe, a little bit.

Though shareholder activists have been filing resolutions at
major corporations for about three decades, not a single major
proposal to make a company more socially responsible has won
a majority vote.

This, however, does not mean that it won't happen in the future or that shareholder resolutions are not an effective tactic as
part of a larger campaign to change corporate policies. Indeed,
winning 15 or 20 percent of shares can send a very strong signal
to a corporation that a not insignificant percentage of investors
are concerned enough about the company's operations to vote
against management.

For example, as part of a campaign to get Staples Inc. to increase the percentage of recycled content in the paper it sells, the socially responsible investing firm Calvert Group filed a shareholder resolution at the company. At the same time, Trillium Asset Management, another socially responsible investor, engaged in talks with Staples's management. Coupled with a sustained protest campaign organized by environmental groups, the shareholders' activism proved effective in getting Staples to increase the percentage of recycled content in the paper they sell to 30 percent.

Domini Social Investments, one of the leading shareholder activist funds, filed seventy resolutions at more than thirty companies between 1994 and 2003. Though none received a majority, Domini does cite a couple of instances where shareholder resolutions opened up a dialogue with management and played an important role in a broader corporate campaign. For example, Domini representatives say that the fund's shareholder dialogues helped to get Proctor & Gamble, the largest coffee buyer in the United States, to begin buying and selling fair trade coffee. Domini also participated in a successful campaign to get McDonald's and Disney to produce their first public reports on global labor compliance.[60]

The growth of shareholder activism is clearly a positive trend that has already produced some notable changes in corporate behavior and is likely to continue to do so. However, a couple of important cautions about the potential of shareholder activism as an effective means for making corporations socially responsible are in order here.

First, as we have noted, the shareholder resolutions that have enjoyed the most support involve changes to corporate governance or executive compensation. Resolutions involving a social or environmental cause face much stiffer odds. Though it is true that many investors do want corporations to be more socially responsible in the abstract, investors often do not seem to want companies to do so at the expense of their personal retirement savings. Still, some trends do indicate that shareholder activism will continue to grow as a means of pressuring corporations to address specific issues. For one, the number of assets engaged in some form of socially responsible investing (defined by the Social Investment Forum as investing that uses one or more of the three core socially responsible investing strategies: screening, shareholder advocacy, and community investing) grew from $1.19 trillion in 1997 to $2.16 trillion in 2003.[61] For another, the average percentage of votes that shareholder resolutions introduced by these funds received rose from 8.7 percent in 2001 to 11.4 percent in 2003 (the number of shareholder resolutions sponsored by socially responsible investors increased from 269 in 2001 to 310 in 2003).[62] However, even with the impressive growth in socially responsible investing, we are still a long way from the point where a majority of investors are in a position to direct the companies they own to be more socially responsible.

One reason is that shareholder resolutions are almost always nonbinding, so even a majority vote can be ignored. And since boards of directors are largely unaccountable to shareholders (for reasons we have already discussed), it is very difficult for even an organized group of shareholders to force a company to make the desired changes when management refuses to do so.

In addition, those institutional investors that do engage in shareholder activism are bound by a responsibility to the individual investors whose savings are invested in the funds. For example, while California treasurer Phil Angelides argues that the assets in California's public pension funds should be used to make corporate America more responsible, he is also responsible for the retirement security of tens of thousands of state employees. Therefore, he has to be sure that any efforts to reform corporate America do not come at the expense of the retirement security of California state employees.

In fact, by law, the fiduciary of pension funds must act "solely in the interests of the participants and beneficiaries and for the exclusive purpose of providing benefits to [them] and defraying [administrative expenses]." As law professor Daniel J. H. Greenwood notes, "Since fiduciaries are required to act in the best interest of [participants] there is little left for them to do but assess how to maximize those benefits."[63]

Though socially responsible investment funds do engage in shareholder activism, they also sell themselves primarily on their rate of return, arguing that while corporate social responsibility might be the right thing to do, it is also a good investment strategy that will outperform the rest of the market in the long run.

Hence, shareholder resolutions are frequently framed as proposals that will actually be good for the corporate bottom line. As many socially responsible investors note, there is a convincing argument to be made that companies that engage in socially responsible behaviors can be better investments in the long run because they build lasting relationships with customers and workers and enjoy a good reputation that is ultimately good for business.

Companies that switch to cleaner technologies, for example, often find that, over time, the new technologies are actually more efficient and more cost-effective and can save the company money by allowing it to avoid many of the costs associated with government regulation. Yet, in the short term, the benefits are not so clear, given that they often involve large initial capital outlays. And since investors are increasingly focused on short-term profit (as we will discuss later in this chapter), companies are often discouraged from making such improvements.

Meanwhile, there are other socially responsible policies that are hard to justify financially in either the short or the long term. Moving jobs overseas or cutting jobs outright, for example, is almost always going to generate a cost savings and a profit boost.

Analysts and shareholders regularly criticize managers who fail to cut costs to keep up with the competition. Consider Costco, which pays its employees significantly more than competitor Wal-Mart and gives them better benefits.[64] Yet, even after turning a 25 percent profit in the first quarter of 2004, Costco's stock fell 4 percent.[65] "One of the criticisms from Wall Street has been they're too nice to their employees," said one portfolio manager who owns Costco stock.[66]

Thus, arguing that the most socially responsible companies are also the best investments is an inherently limited framework. At some point, the two objectives will clash. If profit remains the primary goal, there is only so far companies can conceivably go in the direction of corporate social responsibility before it becomes too much of a drag on the bottom line.

Even if shareholders did want to sacrifice financial returns for social ends, it is not clear that they would be able to do so. The entire system of investing is based on the premise that shareholders want only one thing: to maximize profits. The laws of fiduciary duty reinforce this point; corporations have a duty to look out for the financial well-being of shareholders, as do pension fund trustees. Meanwhile, very few companies even offer investors the opportunity to be part of a socially responsible enterprise.

SOCIAL SCREENING

Another way that investors try to pressure corporations into socially responsible behavior is by avoiding companies whose products and practices they consider undesirable, an investing practice known as social screening. Some form of screening is practiced by virtually all of the $2.16 trillion worth of assets that engage in some form of socially responsible investing, with tobacco ($124 billion) and alcohol ($93.4 billion) being the most popular mutual fund screens.[67]

Additionally, other funds whose managers are concerned with the consequences of their investments, such as labor pension funds and state pension funds, also engage in social screening to varying degrees.

According to the Social Investment Forum, roughly one in nine dollars under professional management in the United States today is involved in some form of social screening, broadly construed.[68]

Social screening is intended to reward companies with good social, labor, and environmental practices. However, there is no evidence that the market as a whole puts any premium on socially responsible practices. All other things being equal, companies that sell tobacco, alcohol, and weapons do not appear to be any worse off than companies that sell other kinds of products. The reason for this is simple: the vast majority of investors either don't know where their money is invested or don't care as long as they are earning a profit. Even the most popular screen— tobacco—is avoided by less than 1 percent of the money invested in the market.

Social screening is also difficult because there are hardly any publicly traded corporations that are thoroughly socially responsible. Certain companies may be better than others in various categories, but anybody who is investing in the stock market is going to have to own stock in corporations that do something that is reprehensible to somebody. The fundamental problem, as we will explore shortly, is that the large publicly traded corporation has certain structural flaws that make destructive antisocial behavior the norm.

Social screening suffers from the same problem as shareholder activism. All mutual funds, even socially responsible ones, are first and foremost organized to make money for their investors. And even socially responsible funds sell themselves primarily according to their rate of return. Hence there is only so much they can do. If investors were more concerned about making the world a better place, they would be putting much more money into things like community investment, where their capital can help communities that are underserved by traditional financial services. And though community investing is a growing field, investors still put only about $1 into community investing for every $1,000 they put in the stock market.[69]

In short, social screening is not a particularly effective technique for getting corporations to change their behavior. Though we support the many investors who do not want to grow rich from investments in tobacco companies, weapons manufacturers, and companies that use sweatshop labor or do any of the many other things that socially responsible funds screen for, we do not believe that screening by itself is a meaningful challenge to those corporations that engage in destructive behavior.

THE LIMITS OF SHAREHOLDER POWER

Here, we come to the end of what shareholders can do to make companies they own more socially responsible. The problem that we run up against, again and again, is that shareholders are primarily investors, and from their aggregate point of view, the corporation should exist primarily to increase their wealth, a principle that is reinforced in the prevailing interpretation of corporate law. Shareholder interest is therefore not a proxy for the public interest. Of course, the enlightened self-interest of investors, if properly channeled, can yield some desirable results: fewer Enrons and WorldComs, more reasonable executive salaries, and some modest social responsibility initiatives. Occasionally, shareholders who care about more than just the bottom line can pressure corporations to consider more dramatic changes. But, as we have seen, shareholder action can only take us so far.

Additionally, we think it is worth asking whether shareholder resolutions are the best way to effect industrywide corporate accountability policies, even for questions like corporate governance and CEO pay, in which shareholders have a direct interest. Consider the issue of executive pay. In order to effectively reduce executive pay at even a single company, shareholders generally have to wage a concerted effort to win majority support. Magnify that across even the hundred largest corporations, and that's an overwhelming amount of effort. But what if that same amount of effort went into getting Congress to pass a law placing limits on executive compensation? Rep. Martin Sabo (D-Minn.), for example, has regularly introduced a proposal called the "Income Equity Act" that would eliminate all tax deductions for compensation above twenty-five times that received by the lowest-paid worker at the company (executive compensation is typically written off as a business expense by most corporations). Though the proposal has never picked up much momentum in Congress, it would certainly be a more comprehensive approach to limiting outrageous compensation than trying to execute pay caps at corporations one by one through shareholder resolutions.

Of course, shareholder resolutions that get industry leaders to change their policies can start a process that can ultimately end up with the particular reform being codified into law. Often, once leading corporations have changed their policies on specific issues, others will follow and Congress will sometimes even enact commensurate regulations (since industry leaders who have adopted a policy are not likely to oppose related laws anymore). In the campaign to change certain environmental policies within the paper industry, for example, activists decided to target companies like Boise Cascade and Staples because both of these companies are industry leaders whose policies can set a standard for the entire industry.[70]

THE PROBLEM OF SHAREHOLDER PRIMACY

In the prior section, we discussed ways that shareholders could be part of the solution. Although there are certainly things that shareholders can do to make the corporations they own behave better, their ability to do so is circumscribed by the fact that their profit-maximizing interests are also a part of the problem.

All state corporate laws say, in some form or other, that directors are to run corporations for the benefit of the corporation and its shareholders.[71] This responsibility has generally been interpreted by courts as a duty to maximize shareholder profit. And if directors ignore this responsibility, shareholders can bring a derivative lawsuit against them for violating their duty to the corporation (though the money goes back to the company, not to the shareholders, so the incentive for doing so is limited).

As professor Greenwood has observed, "Virtually all the major groups of corporate law scholars today agree on the centrality of the shareholder to corporate law . . . that virtually the sole task of corporate law is to ensure that managers act as agents for the shareholder owners."[72] Or, as management consultant Allan Kennedy has written, "Since the mid 1980s, I have witnessed a new phenomenon related to the purpose of business. One by one, company after company has come to embrace a new driving purpose for its activities: shareholder value."[73]

This doctrine of "shareholder primacy" was most famously elaborated in the 1919 Michigan Supreme Court case of *Dodge v. Ford Motor Co.* The case was brought by the Dodge brothers, minority owners in Ford Motor Company who challenged majority owner Henry Ford's decision not to issue a special dividend but to instead put the money back into the business to help out workers. "My ambition," Ford told the court, "is to employ still more men, to spread the benefits of this industrial system to the greatest possible number, to help them build up their lives and their homes. To do this we are putting the greatest share of our profits back in the business."[74]

But the Michigan Supreme Court ruled that Ford's reinvestment plan, based on social instead of financial goals, violated his duty to shareholders. "A business corporation is organized and carried on primarily for the profit of stockholders," the court ruled. "The powers of the directors are to be used for that end."[75]

"To this day," writes law professor Lawrence Mitchell, "*Dodge v. Ford* remains the leading case on corporate purpose."[76]

The consequence of this focus on maximizing shareholder value is that a corporation's relationships to its other stakeholders are less important. If shipping jobs overseas is cheaper, so much for the company's loyalty to its workers. If violating an emissions law (or, just as common, lobbying to weaken the law) is cheaper than complying, and government enforcement is lax and penalties are relatively insignificant (as is usually the case), so much for clean air. If misleading and deceptive advertising will sell more products, so much for honesty.

Robert Hinkley, who worked for more than two decades as a corporate lawyer, has argued that this legal construct of "shareholder primacy" is at the root of considerable social and ecological harm:

> Corporate law thus casts ethical and social concerns as irrelevant, or as stumbling blocks to the corporation's fundamental mandate. That's the effect the law has inside the corporation. Outside the corporation the effect is more devastating. It is the law that leads corporations to actively disregard harm to all interests other than those of shareholders. When toxic chemicals are spilled, forests destroyed, employees left in poverty, or communities devastated through plant shutdowns, corporations view these as unimportant side effects outside their area of concern. But when the company's stock price dips, that's a disaster.
>
> In the end, the natural result is that corporate bottom line goes up, and the state of the public good goes down. This is called privatizing the gain and externalizing the cost.[77]

Or, as future Enron CEO Jeffrey Skilling wrote when still a student at Harvard Business School, if his company were producing a product that might cause harm—or even death—to customers, "I'd keep making and selling the product. My job as a businessman is to be a profit center and to maximize return to the shareholders. It's the government's job to step in if a product is dangerous."[78]

Though many corporate managers may be fine upstanding citizens in their private lives, the profit-driven ethos of the corporation, based in the prevailing interpretation of state corporate law, forces them to do many things that might otherwise make them cringe—lay off thousands of employees, dump pollutants into a stream, release a product that has not been adequately tested—in order to maximize shareholder value.

In *Tyranny of the Bottom Line*, accounting professor Ralph Estes explains how even well-intentioned executives operate under pressure to "deliver the numbers," that is, make decisions that cause harm to company employees, the communities the company operates in, and the environment. "The manager is held hostage by the scorekeeping system," Estes writes. "And the manager's decisions determine the corporation's behavior and its effects on us. The corporation now is too often an amoral agent of iniquity, doing harm in the name of profit."[79]

Although the focus on shareholder profit is based in the prevailing interpretation of state corporate law, it has been profoundly amplified in recent years by the changing nature of stock investment in America. In short, the last two decades have witnessed an explosion in the number of investors and investments, coupled with rising expectations and demands on what a reasonable return of investment should be.[80] This has put increasing pressure on corporate managers to meet those demands and "deliver the numbers."

As we have already explained, most of the growth in stock ownership has been through mutual funds, retirement accounts, and pension plans.[81] The rise in mutual funds is particularly significant because it has put an increased focus on the rate of return. All mutual funds, even socially responsible funds, sell themselves based on their rate of return. And, as we have noted, most investors in mutual funds likely have little idea what companies they own indirectly through their funds. Because funds sell themselves based on their rate of return, this puts incredible pressure on individual fund managers to beat the averages and can encourage ruthless buying and selling to gain the best-performing fund. As Mitchell notes, "Since bonuses [for money managers] can easily exceed 50 percent of salary, the incentive to perform is very strong indeed. . . . Compensation depends on how you do in the short run and that gives money managers and the funds they manage every incentive to pressure corporations to increase their short-term performance."[82]

Meanwhile, the growth of discount online trading systems and generally declining transaction costs has made frequent stock trading easier (consider the day-trading phenomenon), and the globalization of equities markets has brought even more investors into the fold.

So how has all this manifested itself? The clearest trend is a dramatic rise in the rate at which shares are changing hands. In 1990, the turnover was 46 percent, which meant that the average investor held on to stock a little more than two years ($1/.46 = 2.17$ years). Turnover increased to 78 percent in 1999. In 2000, it hit 88 percent, and in 2002 it hit 105 percent, meaning that for the first time the average holding period for a share was less than one year. As of this writing, the percent turnover in 2004 was 116 percent, a new record. That's almost ten times what it was in 1960, when the percent turnover was just 12 percent.[83]

The increasingly rapid rate of turnover is the clearest indication that investors are putting more pressure than ever on corporations to demonstrate a rising stock price over a short period of time, either by demonstrating real profits or by spinning a convincing story about how exploding profits are just around the corner. Investors, both directly and through mutual funds, have demonstrated that they are not willing to hold on to a stock for years anymore. They want a good return on their investments now, and if they don't get it they are going to sell and put their money elsewhere. This has translated into an increasingly acute focus on quarterly earnings per share on Wall

Street. As financial journalist Alex Berenson describes it in *The Number*, his take on the corporate scandals:

> More than any other number, earnings per share determines whether a company's shares will rise or fall, whether its chief executive will be rewarded or fired, whether it will build a new headquarters or endure a round of layoffs. On Wall Street, a place of little subtlety, earnings per share is known simply as "the number." . . . Earnings per share is the number for which all other numbers are sacrificed.[84]

Because there are so many individual and institutional money managers perpetually buying and selling, managers of publicly held corporations must seek continual growth and expansion to impress investors, analysts, bankers, and credit rating agencies. If they fail to show good numbers, their stock price will fall and the company will suffer. A low price makes the company a target for a takeover. It also means that managers are likely to lose their jobs.

With increased pressure on corporations to meet or beat quarterly Wall Street expectations, corporate leaders are focusing more and more on short-term profits at the expense of almost everything else, be it relationships with workers or customers, investments in long-term research, or (as we learned in the wake of the recent accounting scandals) any resemblance to truthful financial accounting. Certainly, it is true that corporations have always been focused on the bottom line. But the increased pressure from Wall Street in recent years has exacerbated this dynamic even further, putting more focus than ever on share price.

DOES SHAREHOLDER PRIMACY EVEN MAKE SENSE?

Before we explore some potential ways to mitigate the problem of shareholder primacy, we think it would be useful to start out by asking whether it actually makes sense for shareholders to enjoy such a privileged role in the corporation, and whether it is logical that shareholders should be the one constituency in whose interest the corporation is supposed to be run.

In Chapter 1, we explored how early American corporations were quasi-public institutions with a clear public duty. Some of the earliest corporations were themselves townships and commonwealths. Corporations were needed to accomplish tasks that required big investments, like building bridges and canals. But although early corporations obviously depended on investors, they also had a mandate to serve the public interest. And corporations that failed to serve this mission could be in danger of losing their charters, which certainly would be bad for investors. Since companies were smaller and investors were often directly responsible for the company's actions, shareholders played a much greater role in management than they do today.

Over the years, as we have noted, the nature of investing changed dramatically. As corporations grew in size and political sophistication, the threat of charter revocation for violating the public good vanished, and limited liability became the rule, investment became passive and disconnected. While a stock offering remained a good way to raise capital, individual investors were much less important to the company.

Today, most investors contribute very little, if anything, to the corporation. Most stockholders today own shares that they did not originally purchase from the company in exchange for investment capital. Rather, they purchased them from another investor, who purchased them from another investor, until, somewhere down the line, somebody made a direct investment in the company and got a stock certificate in exchange.

The simple fact is that the stock market of today is not actually a significant source of investment capital for corporations. In 1999, for example, the value of new common stock issued was $106 billion. The value of all shares traded was $20.4 trillion. So about half of 1 percent was actually invested directly in a corporation. And when you add in stock buybacks, shareholders actually made a negative contribution to direct investment.[85] As *Business Ethics* editor Marjorie Kelly explains in *The Divine Right of Capital*, a critique of shareholder primacy, "though we speak of stock market activities as investing, there is only the smallest bit of direct investment in companies going on. What is at work is speculation, the trading of shares from one speculator to another."[86]

So, if today's shareholders contribute virtually nothing to the corporate enterprise, why do their interests factor so dominantly in the calculus of corporate decision making? After all, why are passive shareholders (many of whom don't even vote their proxies) more important than the employees who make the corporation function, the communities where the corporation operates, the consumers who buy the corporation's products, the pensioners who used to work at the company, and the environment that supports all living systems? All of these enable the corporation to operate and are affected by its operations. Why does maximizing profit for shareholders matter most? Why is it only shareholders who have a vote in corporate elections? Why is it only shareholders who are supposed to be represented by the board of directors? And why is it only shareholders who can hold the board of directors legally accountable?

Marjorie Kelly argues that there is no reason for it, other than antiquated mythology. She equates the rights of shareholders to extract capital from their corporations with the divine right of kings to extract wealth from their subjects. She argues that both the divine right of capital and the divine right of kings come from the same myth. "At root," Kelly writes, "what really governs corporations is an idea that is the intellectual descendant of the great chain of being: the notion that only those who possess wealth matter. . . . We accept that corporations are pieces of private property owned by shareholders, just as our ancestors believed that nations were private territories owned by kings."[87]

Kelly argues that although we overthrew the idea of the divine right of kings through a series of revolutions establishing our political democracy long ago, we have failed to establish a commensurate economic democracy. When it comes to capital, then, we are still in a feudal mindset.

To get out of this mindset, we should start by asking: What is the primary purpose of the corporation? Is it to make money for shareholders? Or is it to provide goods and services, to provide steady jobs, and to be an engine of public prosperity? We believe that business could strive to do all of these. And we think most people would agree with us. After all, when polled, 95 percent of respondents said they believe that corporations should do more than just make profits, and, in fact, "should sometimes sacrifice some profit for the sake of making things better for their workers and communities."[88]

But if we want corporations to operate with a broader public purpose, they cannot be ruthlessly focused on maximizing profits for shareholders. Put simply, sometimes serving a broader public purpose is going to come at the expense of maximizing profits for shareholders.

ADDRESSING SHAREHOLDER PRIMACY

So, what is to be done? Is there any way to fix the incentives and rules that drive corporate America so that corporations operate with a focus on their responsibility to society first and a focus on their profits second? Or, at the very least, that they make sure that profits do not have harmful social and environmental costs?

As we see it, there are a few different approaches to addressing the problem of shareholder primacy, each of which has both promise and shortcomings. One is to change the laws that define the duties and responsibilities of the corporation, its directors, and its officers. Another is to institutionalize various stakeholders who represent noninvestor concerns in the corporate governance structure, possibly through broader stakeholder ownership. A third is to develop and promulgate new legal theories of corporate governance that take into account a more expansive purpose of the corporation. A fourth is to change the attitudes and expectations of investors so that there is less external pressure on corporations to maximize profit. The final approach we offer is to simply require corporations to disclose all their activities publicly instead of just disclosing their finances, essentially forcing them to evaluate their performance based on a number of nonfinancial indicators, and thus giving concerned shareholders a greater ability to measure a broader set of corporate behaviors.

All these reforms are worth exploring and would, if enacted, be mutually reinforcing. Certainly, it will be easier to control corporations if we can mitigate some of the internal forces that drive them to be so destructive. But we should be aware that rewiring the corporation to make it more accountable is ultimately a poor substitute for establishing meaningful citizen control over corporations through democratically created laws. Nevertheless, a rewiring can obviously be quite helpful in achieving that ultimate goal by making companies more aligned with the public welfare in the first place.

EXPANDING THE DUTIES
AND RESPONSIBILITIES OF DIRECTORS

Perhaps the most straightforward way to make corporations pay attention to more than just shareholder profits is to force them to do so by changing the laws defining the duties and responsibilities of directors and officers.

Such an approach is nicely encapsulated in a proposal called the Code for Corporate Responsibility. The Code is intended to hit the shareholder primacy nail straight on the head. Robert Hinkley, the author of the Code, argues that since shareholder primacy is based in the corporate law of each state, the fix is simple: amend the law that says directors and officers are responsible for maximizing shareholder profit and add a simple twenty-eight-word phrase: *"but not at the expense of the environment, human rights, the public health or safety, the communities in which the corporation operates, or the dignity of its employees."*

"As long as directors, managers and employees are guided only by the doctrine of shareholder primacy, their companies will continue to do damage to the environment, human rights, the public health and safety, the dignity of employees and the welfare of their communities," explains Hinkley. "As long as companies continue to grow in size, such damage will become more extensive right along with it."[89]

But by redefining the duties of directors and officers, Hinkley argues, the corporation can be made to be responsible and accountable to a broader set of interests.

> The Code will . . . give employees and communities more leverage to deal with corporations. At a minimum, the Code will guarantee a living wage, the right to collectively bargain and the right to work in a safe environment. In fact, the Code may change many employers' attitudes towards unions. Such employers may actually encourage union participation so they can enter into collective bargaining agreements that are assured of complying with the Code.
>
> Finally, no longer will a major employer in a community be able to threaten to leave town unless the community accedes to the company's demands. Companies that create economic hardship will be responsible for compensating the community for the damage they cause. This may cause companies to negotiate with towns prior to making a plant closure decision and factor into that decision the cost of such compensation. This may or may not result in fewer closures, but it will put a stop to closures where the local community is left to pick up the pieces on its own.[90]

Hinkley suggests that, ideally, the Code would be enforceable by private citizens, through a private right of action. Directors and officers would have strict liability, meaning they would be responsible for any harm, regardless of whether or not they were negligent. Hinkley also recommends giving businesses a fifteen-year transition period before the law would go into effect: enough time to make necessary changes and phase out potentially harmful practices. He argues that the new standard would not hamper entrepreneurial initiative because it would not apply to corporations below a certain size and, perhaps more importantly, it would not eliminate the profit motive. It would merely modify it.

A draft version of the Code was introduced as a bill in the California State Senate in early 2004, but it failed to get out of committee.[91] Legislators cited concerns about the Code's vagueness. The Code was also introduced in the Minnesota legislature but was tabled when questions arose about the bill's language.[92]

Could the Code be made more specific? Perhaps, instead of holding directors and officers responsible for violating general principles, the Code could create a process for establishing specific, quantifiable duties, as most regulatory and criminal law does. Certainly, all states have a plethora of specific laws relating to such things as the environment and employee rights. Perhaps holding directors and officers responsible for violations makes sense, either civilly or criminally, or both. After all, one of the problems of the current system of corporate governance is that it is difficult to hold any one individual responsible because there is always somebody else to blame: employees report to managers, managers report to directors, directors report to shareholders, and shareholders have limited liability and are too diffuse and distanced from the corporation to ever be held responsible. Meanwhile, at each level, there is a natural filtering out of bad news.

But if directors and officers were held responsible for specific corporate wrongdoings regardless of their role in directly creating such problems, surely they would make it their business to know what was going on and make sure that systems were put in place to ensure legal compliance.[93] As Hinkley suggests, "The threat of civil litigation and possible criminal sanctions will serve as a powerful deterrent to violating the Code. It will cause directors to change the way they run their companies, much the way the securities laws that were passed in the 1930s caused them to change the way they offered securities to the public and distributed information to investors on an ongoing basis. They will become much more cautious."[94]

Even the American Bar Association (ABA) has supported more responsibility for directors and offered some specific suggestions. In its Task Force report on corporate responsibility, the ABA suggests the following "specific oversight matters": "assessing major risks facing the company; and ensuring that reasonable processes are in place to maintain the integrity of the company and the corresponding accountability of senior management, including processes relating to integrity of financial reporting, compliance with law and corporate codes of legal and ethical conduct, and processes designed to prevent improper related party transactions."[95] But rather than allowing such codes to be part of the corporation's public relations arma-ture, the benefit of the Code is that it would actually make such duties binding and enforceable.

One caveat relating to the Code is the problem of forum shopping we dealt with in Chapter 1—that when it comes to in-corporation, corporations have their choice of fifty states. Hence, it is likely that any state that alone passes the Code will find that at the end of the fifteen-year implementation period, almost all the major corporations chartered there will have rein-corporated elsewhere. Although it is conceivable that all fifty states could pass the Code within fifteen years (or at least enough to send a clear signal that this is the way things are going), it would be quite difficult. Another option would be to include the Code as part of a federal chartering regime, an idea we explored in Chapter 1.

Ultimately, the Code for Corporate Responsibility offers a very powerful idea: that directors and officers should be held re-sponsible for protecting the public interest, not just maximizing shareholder profit. Placing this responsibility on directors and officers would definitely change the way that corporations oper-ate. But, as is always the case, the devil is in the details, and the details (and more importantly, the politics) of holding directors and officers responsible for protecting such a legally ambiguous concept as the public good are tricky. However, as activists and policymakers continue to advance this idea, the specific provi-sions of the Code will continue to be workshopped and refined, calling attention to the failures of our current system of corpo-rate law in the process.

PUTTING MORE STAKEHOLDER REPRESENTATIVES ON THE BOARD OF DIRECTORS

Another approach to changing the corporate decision-making process is to change who is responsible for making key decisions inside the corporation. Currently, the board of directors is sup-posed to represent the interests of shareholder-owners (though, as we have discussed, it is overwhelmingly unresponsive, even to its shareholders). However, if the board of directors also rep-resented other stakeholders, such as employees, consumers, and community members, then these various groups would theoretically have a say in how the corporation operates.

An imperfect example of how this might work is the German supervisory board, which is supposed to represent the interests of employees and owners and also sometimes includes bankers, local community leaders, suppliers, and customers. The supervisory board oversees the board of directors, which represents the interests of just shareholders. The supervisory board is supposed to be responsible for the long-term well-being of the firm and is based on the principle that employees have an important role to play in corporate governance.[96]

In practice, the composition of the German supervisory boards is often not substantially different from that of the management board. According to one study, 43 percent of supervisory boards include a former member of the management board and 61 percent of supervisory boards include an investor/shareholder.[97] When asked, supervisory board members almost uniformly say that they are responsible to shareholders. As one observer has noted, there is a "widespread impression that there is often too close a connection between the two boards, which can negatively affect the intensity of control exerted by the supervisory board."[98]

However, there seems to be no reason why we could not take this concept of the supervisory board and build upon it, making sure that communities, consumers, and other stakeholders have a say on such a board. Certainly, the more voices that have a say in what the corporation does, the more the corporation's actions will more closely reflect what a broad range of stakeholders would like to see the corporation do. Another approach to getting more stakeholders on the board would be to distribute ownership more widely among stakeholders instead of allowing it to be concentrated in the hands of shareholders who often have no other connection to the company.[99]

One major caveat to this stakeholder solution is that if a wide range of stakeholders did gain power or influence on the corporate board, they could likely have conflicting views on how the corporation should be run. Workers, for example, would want higher wages. But higher wages could mean higher prices for consumers. And lower prices advocated by consumers might have to come at the expense of lower environmental standards, and so on and so forth. This potential for disagreement led economist Adolf Berle and others to conclude that duties to multiple stakeholders could be so complex and conflicting that they would ultimately encourage managers to stop paying attention to the board and become autonomous.[100] As Seattle University law professor Kellye Testy has suggested, "stakeholder theory risks creating a free-for-all among stakeholders in the quest for control of the corporate enterprise, a free-for-all in which the already powerful are likely to continue to prevail. . . . Chief among those critiques is that the ambiguity in defining who is and who is not a 'stakeholder' will actually increase the power and discretion of management, because they will be beholden to no one in particular."[101]

THINKING OUTSIDE THE BOX
OF SHAREHOLDER PRIMACY

Another approach to the problem of shareholder primacy is to develop and promulgate new theories of corporate law to displace the prevailing doctrine of shareholder primacy. One such theory that holds some promise is the team production model of corporate governance.[102] Developed by economist Margaret M. Blair and law professor Lynn A. Stout, the team production model is based on the idea that all stakeholders—managers, employees, suppliers, the community, and the shareholders—are part of a team that makes the corporation what it is. Under this model, the board of directors becomes a "mediating hierarch" whose role is to be an independent arbiter between the claims of different stakeholders and to make sure that all constituencies are properly valued and rewarded for their contributions to the corporation. As Blair has written:

> The team production approach suggests that corporate performance must be measured in multiple dimensions, and that no single measure of corporate performance can tell the whole story of how well the corporation is doing. Share price

is important, because, even though it is noisy and subject to manipulation, it should at least reflect what one subset of financial investors on any given day think the value of their claim on the corporation is. But it also matters whether the corporation is meeting the expectations of other participants, not to mention whether it is fairly and accurately presenting its financial position to investors.[103]

Blair and Stout argue that the legal basis for shareholder primacy has been overblown. They argue that corporate law, as interpreted by the Delaware courts, has generally given directors and managers a good deal of freedom in how they want to run their companies under a loose interpretation of the business judgment rule.

"Judges have sanctioned directors' decisions to use corporate funds for charitable purposes; to reject business strategies that would increase profits at the expense of the local community; to avoid risky undertakings that would benefit shareholders at creditors' expense; to fend off a hostile take-over at a premium price in order to protect the interests of employees or the community," note Blair and Stout. "As these examples illustrate, modern corporate law does not adhere to the norm of shareholder primacy. To the contrary, *case law interpreting the business judgment rule often explicitly authorizes directors to sacrifice shareholders' interests to protect other constituencies.*"[104] [emphasis in original]

Blair and Stout also argue that there is nothing inevitable about shareholder primacy. Rather, they contend that it became dominant in the 1980s, when, in response to a stagnant economy in the 1960s and 1970s, companies began downsizing and restructuring. "This restructuring process has produced 'leaner and meaner' corporations that are more attentive than ever to shareholders' desires, and returns from share ownership have correspondingly increased."[105]

The caveat with the team production approach is the same caveat that applies to other stakeholder approaches: how to effectively mediate between different claims on the corporation. In the team production model, the board of directors is supposed to be the "mediating hierarch," an "institutional mechanism intended to facilitate trust among the team members."[106] But how is the board to decide fairly between the competing demands of different stakeholders, especially when stockholders are the only group allowed to select the board?

Certainly, the team production model offers an intriguing approach to the corporate governance question; it is a framework that allows and encourages directors to be more broadly accountable. But given the pressures of the stock market and the powers (albeit quite limited) of shareholders, it is not clear how we could get from shareholder primacy to a team production approach without either changing the ownership composition or also establishing an external prod (such as holding directors responsible for violating the rights of various constituencies, as Hinkley has suggested).

CHANGING THE INVESTMENT INCENTIVES

As we noted earlier, one of the key forces pressuring corporations to focus so intently on profit, particularly short-term profit, is the hyperkinetic nature of the stock market. More than ever, Wall Street investors are obsessively focused on quarterly earnings reports. They are ready to sell a stock based on the slightest negative financial news and buy another based on the slightest positive financial news. As the time horizon for holding stock has dropped precipitously over the last few decades, the pressure on corporate managers to constantly be increasing profits has grown, and with great consequences for the way that corporations are run. Managers are increasingly focused on meeting the latest quarterly earnings goals, knowing that if they don't, they are at risk of losing their jobs. As we noted earlier, many of the strategies underlying corporate social responsibility are long-term strategies. Yet, most investors aren't patient enough to wait for the long term. As a result, managers must constantly sacrifice long-term goals for short-term profit if they want to keep their jobs.

One approach to this problem would be to change the capital gains taxation rates to encourage long-term stock holding. This would take some of the incentive for short-term earnings away, which would free companies up to do things that, although not immediately profitable, are good long-term business strategies. This could include taking the time to build solid relationships with workers, customers, and suppliers, investing more in research and development, or pioneering more ecologically sustainable business practices.

Larry Mitchell suggests that this could be done by placing very high capital gains taxes on short-term speculative investments and much lower capital gains taxes on long-term investments. For example, if you hold stock for six days, 90 percent of your gains might be taxed; but if you hold stock for ten years, 15 percent of your gains might be taxed. What this kind of taxation scale would do is force investors to be a lot more careful about where they invest, keep their investments in one place longer, and make sure they believe that the company they are investing in has a good long-term plan. Stock turnover would decrease, and corporate managers would feel less pressure to pump up short-term earnings at the expense of long-term stability, which is beneficial for everybody involved in the corporation, particularly employees.[107]

The limitation of this approach is that, regardless of the time horizon, investors are still going to be interested in maximizing their return and companies will still be under pressure to demonstrate that they can be profitable if they want to attract investment. Whether over the short term or long term, maximizing profits would still likely come at the expense of other social goals, barring other changes.

Perhaps more significantly, since roughly half of all equity is held in tax-exempt accounts,[108] a change in the capital gains tax would have no effect on these shareholders.

Another approach to changing the incentives for investors would be to make investors more liable for the consequences of their investments through either a partial or even perhaps a full removal of limited liability. As we discussed earlier in this chapter, one of the developments that cleared the way for diffuse widespread ownership was limited liability for investors, which meant that investors would only be responsible for their initial investment. Yet, if investors were again responsible for the debts and lawsuits facing the corporation, they would be more careful about where they invest their money and be more aggressive about overseeing the activities of these companies.[109] However, we recognize that this is not likely to come about any time soon.

EXPANDING DISCLOSURE

Another approach to making corporations more publicly accountable is to require them to disclose much more information about their activities (especially violations, felonies, and other information concerning the damage they do to the public interest) in their annual report, which currently is focused primarily on the company's finances. Such an approach is reminiscent of the early days of U.S. corporations, when the public enjoyed full access to all corporate records.

Ralph Estes envisions an annual corporate report in which corporations would be required to account for all their activities, not just their finances. "By simply looking in the corporate report," Estes explains in *Tyranny of the Bottom Line*, "you could see how many people had died from workplace injuries last year, what that brown stuff is pouring out of the company's smokestacks, how the company has settled with customers over product problems, and how much top executives were making while they were 'downsizing' your job."[110]

In this context, the primary benefit of expanded disclosure is that it can change the yardsticks by which investors are able to measure corporate behavior. As Estes has suggested, "change the performance evaluation system and you change behavior. . . . If the corporation, through its scorekeeping system, truly moves to evaluate managers not on a single dimension but on the balance they achieve among several dimensions, then managers will respond by seeking a balance."[111]

Though disclosing information doesn't outright force any company to change what it is doing, it offers the powerful possibility of creating other indices with which to measure corporate performance besides just earnings per share. Expanded disclosure would empower employees, investors, and consumers to make better decisions about the corporations they support.

Enlightened consumers would stop buying services and products from certain corporations. Enlightened employees might choose to work elsewhere. Enlightened communities might refuse to let corporations site a plant or build a store. And enlightened investors might put their money elsewhere. The realization of what is actually going on at many of these corporations could trigger an increase in public demand for more fundamental change. Meanwhile, forcing companies to publicly report much more of what they do (with significant penalties for false reporting) would at least make them more aware of the consequences of their activities and policies.

One approach to requiring more disclosure would be to take advantage of the existing SEC financial disclosure system and expand the guidelines for what public companies are required to disclose on their annual 10-K form (which is currently focused on the company's finances) to include more complete information about the company's environmental, social, workers' rights, human rights, and criminal record.

In his younger and more idealistic days (1971), former SEC chairman Harvey Pitt wrote that SEC disclosure laws could be used to advance corporate social responsibility by calling for more complete disclosure of non-financial information. "The Commission has within its power the wherewithal to make corporations socially responsible and afford substantially higher degree of investor and public protection," wrote Pitt.[112] Today, a group of lawyers and activists known as the Corporate Sunshine Working Group[113] have encouraged the SEC to mandate more thorough disclosure standards under the argument that such information really does matter to investors, because hidden environmental and social liabilities can come back to bite investors.

As we come to the end of this chapter, we are left with two possible approaches to changing corporate governance to make corporations more socially responsible.

In one framework, the problem is that shareholders don't have enough control over the corporations they own, that renegade managers recklessly run corporations without any oversight from the shareholder owners, and if shareholders were capable of and willing to assert their ownership powers, corporations would act less recklessly. Additionally, many shareholders are also corporate employees, customers, and community members. As such, they should have a self-interest in steering corporations toward more socially responsible behaviors.

In another framework, it's clear that the prevailing operating principle of "shareholder primacy" (maximize returns for shareholders at all costs) is the root of most, if not all, destructive corporate behavior. Therefore, the most effective approaches should focus on broadening the purpose of the corporation to go beyond just maximizing shareholder gain and instead make corporations accountable to all their stakeholders: employees, customers, communities, and others. If we want corporations to serve the public good, they must be accountable to the greater public.

Though these two approaches may seem contradictory (are shareholders the solution, or are they the problem?), we believe that individual shareholders can be part of the solution even as we challenge the doctrine of shareholder primacy.

As we have noted, shareholders that want their companies to be more socially responsible can exercise their ownership rights by selecting directors and proposing and voting on shareholder resolutions. And though the rights of shareholders to do both of these things are severely limited under current corporate governance rules, both outlets could provide enough leverage within the corporation to at least make officials take note of the shareholders' concerns.

But to say that corporate owners should have more rights in selecting directors and voting on resolutions is not to say that the corporation need be run for the financial profit of shareholders to the exclusion of all else. Indeed, many shareholders are also workers, consumers, and other stakeholders whose interests cannot be so narrowly defined.

In this chapter, we have identified several approaches to mitigating the problem of shareholder primacy. For example, we could begin by placing different stakeholder representatives (worker, consumer, community, etc.) on the board of directors.

We could also change corporate laws to force directors and managers to consider the societal consequences of their actions. Additionally, we could mitigate the demands that investors place on corporate managers to maximize short-term profits by establishing tax policies that incentivize longer-term holdings.

Though it is not clear which, if any, of these approaches will be the most effective, what does seem clear is that shareholder primacy is a major design flaw in the corporation and, left unmitigated, means that virtually all large publicly traded corporations present an inherent danger to society because as profit-making machines they know no limits and boundaries: they will continue to grow and expand until they have destroyed everything in their paths.

Therefore, as we attempt to fashion market rules, crack down on corporate crime, and limit the poisonous influence of corporations in politics (the subject of the next three chapters, respectively), we must always keep in mind the problems inherent in the corporate governance structure. We must understand that large, publicly traded corporations are not benign institutions, but inherently destructive ones. As Robert Monks has put it, "the corporation is an externalizing machine, in the same way that a shark is a killing machine. . . . There isn't any question of malevolence or of will; the enterprise has within it, and the shark has within it, those characteristics that enable it to do that for which it was designed . . . [the corporation] is potentially very, very damaging to society."[114] Understanding the destructive dynamics inherent in the corporation can help us understand how to better place proper limits and regulations on corporate behavior and use certain levers within the corporation to force decision makers to confront the impacts that their corporations have on the rest of us.

Ultimately, what we are attempting to wrestle with in this book is that corporations have too much power in society and that citizens have lost many of the mechanisms by which they can effectively control corporations and limit their power. Although working within the system of corporate governance to make the corporation a less destructive institution can accomplish certain things, such an approach does not ultimately get at the question of who has the power, which we believe has to be the central question. Therefore, although corporate governance reform can make some inroads in taming the harmful behaviors of large corporations, these inroads are only truly valuable in the long run if they can help pave the way to meaningful citizen sovereignty.

4 | Freeing Markets from Corporate Control

"It is possible, because of its indirect social or moral effect, to prefer a system of small producers, each dependent for his success upon his own skill and character, to one in which the great mass of those engaged must accept the direction of the few."

—Judge Learned Hand, from his 1945 decision in
United States v. Aluminum Co. of America

As rolling blackouts swept through California in 2000 and 2001 and prices for electricity skyrocketed, many people were confused. How was it that in this modern era, in the most developed nation in the world, something as basic as electricity service could suffer such serious disruptions and such wild price fluctuations?

The reason, as it turned out, was somewhat simple. California had deregulated its energy market, meaning that state regulators had surrendered their ability to control energy prices and service. As a result, the state found itself at the mercy of the market, or rather at the mercy of power companies who realized that, with no external controls, they were now free to game the system as they liked to fatten their own bottom lines. California had surrendered its ability to intervene when it deregulated its energy markets. There was nothing state residents could do but sit back and suffer.[1]

Skyrocketing electricity prices forced the state of California into enormous debt and created unnecessary hardships for residents and small businesses. Calls went out for federal regulators to impose strict caps on the wholesale electricity prices. If prices were capped, it was argued, power suppliers would have no incentive to manipulate prices, since they'd have nothing to gain. And sure enough, when the Federal Energy Regulatory Commission finally imposed strict price caps on June 19, 2001, the worst of California's crisis ended.

The ensuing investigations echoed what many had suspected all along. According to reports, companies like Enron, Reliant, Duke, Dynegy, AES, and numerous others had withheld power that drove up demand, and then sold electricity at inflated prices during these manufactured emergencies. They shared crucial information about outages among themselves. They sold phantom "ancillary services" for emergency situations. They engaged in enough questionable activity to fill a 3,000-page report prepared by the state of California, which accused seventy energy companies and municipal utilities of using ten primary schemes to drive up prices. But the report noted: "This evidence, while substantial and compelling, is just the tip of the iceberg. As this investigation has shown, there is a snake under almost every rock one turns."[2]

A few weeks after California released its report, even the market fundamentalists at the Federal Energy Regulatory Commission (FERC)—whose chair, Pat Wood III, was appointed by President Bush at the behest of Enron's Ken Lay[3]—were forced to come to the same conclusion. In their own report on the California energy crisis, FERC found "significant market manipulation" and misconduct by more than thirty energy companies and recommended that the companies be forced to pay a $3.3 billion refund to the state of California.[4]

The California electricity crisis demonstrated that when left to their own devices, corporations will often do whatever it takes to increase their profits, regardless of the consequences. And sometimes these consequences can be quite serious.

In this chapter, we ask what role the government should play in regulating the economy, structuring markets, and providing essential services.

Ask most corporate leaders, and they will say, "not much." Over the last several decades, large corporations, with the backing of key politicians, think tanks, and economists, have successfully pushed an ideological agenda of deregulation, very limited antitrust enforcement, and privatization. The underlying intellectual framework they have used is that markets work best when government doesn't interfere because markets are perfectly self-regulating and corporations can be most efficient and innovative when they don't have to answer to centralized government bureaucrats. The astonishing thing about the wide acceptance of this view is that it fails to take into account the role that central planners play when a few behemoth corporations dominate the economy.

In this chapter, we will look back at recent events that have exposed this agenda for what it is: a thinly veiled corporate power grab. Though the idea of the "free" market might sound nice, it is largely an abstraction dreamed up by economists who spend far too much time playing with mathematical models and far too little time in the real world. Experience, however, shows that markets require rules and limits to work effectively and efficiently. Realizing this, the question becomes who will set those rules: the citizens, acting for their government, or the companies themselves, on behalf of their own economic interests?

This chapter has three parts. In the first part we look at the consequences of deregulation, focusing on electricity, telecommunications, and banking (three key sectors that were deregulated under industry pressure in recent years). These examples are important because they demonstrate what happens when government removes structural barriers and controls designed to keep corporations from abusing the public interest. These examples make the case for why industry-specific regulation is crucial, and how we can go about restoring it.

Next, we examine the need for vigorous antitrust policies that span most industrial sectors, recognizing that economies work best when there are many competing firms in any given market sector and no single firm is able to wield too much control. A vigorous antitrust policy that keeps corporations reasonably sized is important not just because it ensures a competitive market; it is also essential to keep large corporations from overwhelming the political process and obstructing our ability to control corporations through the regulatory process.

Finally, we briefly examine the need to place certain limits on the reach of markets and look at the dangers of corporate efforts to privatize certain parts of the public sphere. When corporations begin to control the delivery of essential services like water, education, and health care, we can find ourselves in a troubling situation where making money becomes more important than providing reliable and affordable service, and where corporations—largely accountable only to their shareholders—are granted control over captive markets with dependent customers.

THE FAILURES OF DEREGULATION

Deregulation became a central part of the corporate agenda during the late 1980s and 1990s, particularly for industries such as electricity, telecommunications, and banking, which had been regulated tightly since the New Deal era because of their general importance to the economy and the fact that they have certain unique features that require industry-specific regulations.

In order to "free" these industries from government regulation, corporations and their think-tank proxies argued that government was an inefficient arbiter and that a competitive free market could do a better job regulating the economy, parroting the familiar anti–big government tropes of the 1980s. They promised that if structural barriers that had been enacted to prevent conflicts of interest were removed, great efficiencies of scale would suddenly appear, and that there was no need to worry about conflicts of interest anymore because the competitive market would somehow keep corporations from abusing customers.

One of the leading proponents of deregulation was the pro-business Heritage Foundation. In a 1997 briefing paper entitled "Energizing America: A Blueprint for Deregulating the Electricity Market,"[5] for example, Heritage fellow Adam Thierer argued that regulation of electricity monopolies had caused a "lack of price competition and consumer choices, limited innovations, and a lackluster environmental record," whereas "deregulation of the electricity marketplace" promised "rich rewards."[6]

This kind of passionate sermonizing about deregulation ignored the fact that these industries had been regulated for good reasons—not merely because government bureaucrats wanted to create jobs for themselves.

One of the main problems with deregulation was that key industries were deregulated without ensuring the high levels of competition that would be necessary to keep in check certain abuses that could result from conflicts of interest and concentrated market power that government regulations had previously worked to prevent. And perversely, deregulation actually led to less, not more competition, by paving the way for new mergers. As economists Walter Adams and James W. Brock have noted:

> Rather than subjecting newly deregulated fields to stringent antitrust oversight, however, a radical laissez-faire stance was often adopted in which it was assumed that no government resistance to anticompetitive mergers and predatory practices would miraculously enable competition to flourish. . . . The lessons of a century of antitrust experience—competition is vulnerable to subversion by private interests; preventing concentration by blocking mergers is preferable to the dilemma of determining how to break up such structural concentrations of economic power once they have been allowed to take root—would have to be learned all over again in a number of deregulated fields.[7]

In industry after industry, the promises of better prices and better services rarely materialized. Instead, deregulation introduced a degree of unpredictability and instability in previously stable industries. As economist Robert Kuttner has explained it, "deregulation has given us higher prices, less reliability, poorer service. It has invited monopoly. It has invited price manipulation, and it certainly hasn't improved the efficiency of the economy if you think the economy is efficient when resources are allocated efficiently."[8]

It is also worth noting that most of the major corporate scandals of 2002 took place at companies in industries that had recently been deregulated. Part of the reason was that deregulation created a kind of gold-rush mentality in these industries, which ultimately put pressure on companies to cook their books to meet expectations and cover for significant blunders. As was obvious with Enron, deregulation opened up opportunities for abusive behaviors where they didn't previously exist. After gaining an exemption from certain provisions in the Public Utilities Holding Company Act (PUHCA, a New Deal era utility law designed to protect energy consumers by limiting the ability of power companies to merge and to invest in anything outside their core business), Enron rushed into new areas like water and broadband and weather derivatives, where it had no previous experience and the risks were significant. Enron CFO Andy Fastow's complex accounting schemes were largely motivated by an attempt to cover for these missteps.

ELECTRICITY

Ever since the New Deal, electricity had been regulated tightly because it is essential to how we live our lives and how we run our economy. As a society we have a very strong interest in making sure that electricity is produced and provided in a way that ensures that it is readily available and reasonably priced. If we didn't, we would run the risk of allowing utility corporations to take advantage of our need for electricity and jack up the price, knowing that customers have few immediate alternatives.

Additionally, there are certain conditions unique to electricity markets, such as high fixed costs and high barriers to entry, that make competition difficult, perhaps impossible. As Tyson Slocum of Public Citizen's Critical Mass Energy and Environment Program explains:

> Unlike other industries in the American economy, it is very difficult to foster competition in the electricity industry. Electricity's high overhead costs limit the number of players, since it requires hundreds of millions to build or buy a power plant. And building one is not easy, as construction can take years. Constraints on siting power plants also inhibit competition because plants must be near power lines and meet minimum public health standards, since those using natural gas, oil or coal (as 70% of U.S. plants do) produce harmful emissions.
>
> These constraints on power plant construction not only limit competition, but also the flexibility of supply to respond to changes in demand. Unlike other products, electricity cannot be stored after it is produced; it must be immediately consumed. The capital constraints that restrict the entry of new generators into the market, therefore, limit the ability of supply to match demand.
>
> And electricity, more than other products in the U.S. economy, features extreme fluctuations in demand. . . . Unless orderly advance planning is conducted to match supply with demand, shortages occur that drive up the price of electricity. And when the few corporations who control the power plants are left unregulated, there is tremendous incentive to withhold supply to create artificial shortages to drive up prices and profits. [9]

For these reasons, states traditionally have intervened to ensure that all prices and practices are "just and reasonable." Public utility commissions in all states set rates through an open, public process that consumers can use to ensure that electricity rates are reasonable and service is reliable, especially when they are organized through citizen utility boards and other collective associations.[10]

Under this system, prices were based on utility costs and expenditures, provided these costs and expenditures were themselves reasonable. Regulators have traditionally allowed service providers to make a steady and fair profit, which is one of the reasons that utility stocks were once seen as such a stable investment. Additionally, to ensure fair access to everybody, states have discounted rates to ensure that poor families can afford to access these services, and they have required that such services cannot be terminated at a time when they cannot be restored within a few hours (such as when utility offices are closed).[11]

This arrangement historically worked quite well. Energy corporations were kept in check by state regulators, their power and ability to engage in destructive behavior largely circumscribed by strict regulations.

Congress began to deregulate the system in 1992, when it passed the Energy Policy Act. This law took away the states' authority over wholesale power generation, authorizing and encouraging independent power producers to enter regionally accessible markets to compete with existing monopolies. It required utilities to open up their transmission lines to these wholesale generators, as well as to energy traders like Enron.

But true deregulation depended on states passing legislation that restructured their utilities, breaking up the old-fashioned vertical monopolies in which the same company generated the power and provided retail service. By forcing the separation of wholesale power generators and retail distributors, the theory was that that wholesale providers would compete to sell energy at the lowest price to utilities. Utilities, in turn, would pass those savings along to retail consumers.

However, energy deregulation failed to bring about the key condition that was supposed to make it work: competition. Instead, there has been an increase in market sector consolidation. Prior to 1992, the ten largest electric utilities owned about 33 percent of the nation's generating capacity. By 2000, the top ten companies owned half of all capacity, while the top twenty companies owned 75 percent,[12] creating increased likelihood of the kind of collusion and price manipulation that took place in California.

Without sufficient competition, wholesale prices didn't fall once the markets were deregulated. They rose. California was only the most extreme example. Since 1994, wholesale prices in the deregulated New England states, for example, have risen from about $12 per month to almost $50 per month per megawatt hour, with wild price fluctuations up to $70 an hour. This forced Connecticut to raise electricity rates for residential consumers (the governor argued that the higher price would entice "competitors" to enter the market). Meanwhile, in the Pennsylvania-New Jersey-Maryland market, which was deregulated in 1998, wholesale prices have risen about 40 percent, from $22.52 to $31.58 per megawatt hour, with dramatic price fluctuations reaching as high as $76.[13] In New Jersey, four-year rate caps expired on August 1, 2003. Days later, natural gas utilities raised their rates between 7 and 12 percent.[14] In the Maryland area, rate caps were to end on July 1, 2004, and in May, energy supplier Pepco warned customers to expect to pay $150 more a year as a result of a predicted 26 percent increase in electricity prices and a 15 percent increase in utility bills.[15]

In Montana, six years of deregulation have transformed the state's power prices from among the lowest in the region to among the highest, with a 10 percent increase in electricity prices coming in a single year.[16]

As Slocum put it, "America has painfully learned what happens when deregulation is applied to an industry with inelastic supply and demand, high capital costs and prohibitively expensive transaction costs."[17]

Meanwhile, the reliability of service declined. Again, California serves as the obvious example. But the great Northeast blackout of August 2003 that left 50 million Americans and Canadians without power was another wake-up call. As Public Citizen explained:

Deregulation is the main factor behind the blackouts. First, America's transmission system was designed to accommodate local electricity markets, not the large, freewheeling trading of electricity and movement of power over long

distances under deregulation. Sending power over a much
wider area strains a transmission system designed to serve
local utilities. Second, deregulation means utilities are no
longer required to reinvest their profits back into the transmission system. That's why reinvestment in wires has fallen
by hundreds of millions of dollars since deregulation: energy
companies simply aren't willing to invest their money where
there's no chance of making runaway profits.[18]

In 1990, utilities spent $3.3 billion (in 2003 dollars) to upgrade
and maintain transmission lines. But in 2000, when substantially more power was moving through the grid, only $3 billion
went into maintaining and replacing transmission lines.[19]

Still, despite the failures of deregulation, big energy companies are continuing to push for further deregulation, including
the full repeal of the already weakened and gutted PUHCA. Instead of repealing PUHCA, a Congress interested in effective energy regulation would work to strengthen it and once again
restore very clear limits on what utility companies can and cannot do and, particularly, how big electric companies can grow
and how far they can expand from their original service mandates.[20] As far as rolling back electricity deregulation, restoring
PUHCA would be an effective step.

Of course, given Congress's continued support for deregulation, even fighting to save PUHCA will be an uphill struggle. In
2003, for example, various versions of a controversial omnibus
energy bill would have repealed PUHCA altogether.

Still, despite the brazen ambitions of utility companies and
their political allies, resistance to energy deregulation seems to
be growing across the country. Although as many as twenty-five
states initially planned to deregulate, at least ten have delayed
or backtracked on plans to do so now that the potential consequences are clearer.

Another alternative to deregulation that is gaining popularity is local control of utilities. After noticing that Sacramento
and Los Angeles were largely unaffected by California's electricity crisis because they generated and controlled their own power
through publicly owned utilities, the citizens of San Francisco

organized a referendum to take back control of their power system from Pacific Gas and Electric in 2001. Despite being outspent by $2 million, they lost by just 1 percent of the vote.[21]

Across the country, 2,100 municipalities own their own utilities; there are an additional 900 energy cooperatives. In 1999, the Department of Energy found that, on average, customers who owned their utilities paid 18 percent less than customers of investor-owned utilities.[22] As the New Rules Project explains, "Because customer-owned utilities are democratically and locally controlled, and service rather than profit oriented, we should encourage their formation. In today's topsy-turvy electricity world, states should encourage the formation not only of customer-owned distribution utilities, but public transmission utilities as well."[23] To put it simply: when the means to generate and distribute electricity are locally owned and locally controlled, people aren't going to rip themselves off to make a profit for shareholders

Local control also brings other benefits. As the big northeastern blackout of August 2003 demonstrated, large parts of the national power grid are potentially vulnerable when there is a failure in one location. And when a very minor set of triggers can shut down power for 50 million people, a strong case can be made that the security of our national energy system would be greatly improved with decentralized local control.[24] If energy production is localized and thus decentralized, it becomes much more difficult for anyone to deliberately cause widespread disruptions to service. Smaller local utilities also don't build the kinds of giant power plants that are prime potential targets for terrorist attacks. Additionally, local control can facilitate efforts to introduce more sustainable energy technologies, such as wind, solar, or hydrogen, as some communities have already done.

TELECOMMUNICATIONS

One of the arguments for deregulation was that the market does a better job of allocating resources than government regulators. Yet deregulation of the telecommunications industry produced just the opposite result: a stunning misallocation of investment capital, with billions of dollars wastefully thrown toward building excess capacity based on outlandish predictions that Internet traffic would grow by 1,000 percent a year, doubling every ninety days, a prediction originally attributed to World-Com.[25]

Almost half a trillion dollars poured into developing all kinds of high-tech fiberoptic networks, routers, wireless systems, and other technologies that were to be the wave of the future: roughly twice what the federal government spent on the interstate highway system over the last fifty years.[26] Networks were built up over the air, over the land, and under the sea. As one insider put it, "Business plans all looked alike. Massively parallel systems were being built up."[27] And once companies realized they had made massive investment errors, they turned to ways to cover these mistakes up, such as trading excess capacity with each other to make it look like they were actually doing business on these networks, a scam known as round-tripping.

By the end of the boom, telecom firms had accumulated a whopping $306.4 billion in debt, money that would have to be paid off somehow. As Lee Selwyn, the president of a telecommunications consulting firm, put it, "When you have a major sector of the economy sucking up resources, it means resources are being diverted from other places. That forces prices up, it forces professional salaries up, and when that falls apart, we all pay."[28] Among the initial victims were the 400,000 workers who lost their jobs in the telecom collapse[29] and the millions of investors who lost an estimated combined $2 trillion as stock prices tumbled off their highs by 95 percent.[30] In 2002, the *Wall Street Journal* reported that only 2.7 percent of the installed fiber was actually being used and that "much of the remaining fiber—called 'dark fiber' in industry parlance—may remain dormant forever."[31]

Meanwhile, on the consumer end of things, the promised benefits of telecommunications deregulation have yet to materialize. Consumers Union and the Consumer Federation of America found that six years after the Telecommunications Act became law, local telephone charges had increased by 17 percent. New bill items, like monthly service charges, universal service fees, and in-state service fees were driving prices higher as well. Cable rates had risen a whopping 36 percent (from $26.57 in 1996 to $40.11 in 2002), mostly because, despite deregulation, 95 percent of American households still had only one choice for a cable company.[32] The problem, according to the consumer groups, was that although the industry was deregulated based on the assumption that competition would reduce prices, there was not actually any real competition:

> The Telecommunications Act was based on a faulty premise. It called for the deregulation of the telecommunications industry before competition existed or competitive forces had developed. It was based on the naïve assumption that firms wanted to enter each other's market and compete. Relaxing the government oversight of cable and phone monopolies has allowed them to merge, consolidate their control of core markets, and begin to expand their monopoly power into adjacent markets. . . . The vast majority of Americans continue to have only one choice of cable company and phone company.[33]

Verizon, the result of postderegulation mergers between Bell Atlantic and NYNEX and GTE, now has 80 million customers. And SBC, also the result of three mergers since 1996 (Southwestern Bell, Pacific Telesis, and Ameritech), now provides service to 72 million customers. Two firms controlling more than half of the nation's local phone service is hardly a model of competition.[34]

As Mark Cooper of the Consumer Federation of America and Gene Kimmelman of Consumers Union wrote in April 2004 to the Senate Commerce Committee: "Obviously the failure of market forces and lax public oversight has allowed cable companies to solidify their power and allowed telephone companies to consolidate in a manner that extends their dominance. This makes it even more difficult to jump start competition now than was the case in 1996. There's no doubt it is long past time to fix the flaws that do not, and we predicted would not, work for consumers."[35]

Like energy, telecommunications service does not fit easily into a competitive market structure. There are high fixed costs and high barriers to entry, making true competition difficult and unlikely. In the absence of competitive pressures, the pertinent question remains: Do we want to be able to exert control over the telecommunications industry to ensure that we enjoy reliable and affordable service? Or do we want to relinquish that control, allowing corporations to do as they will based on vague promises that somehow market forces will keep them in line?

BANKING AND FINANCIAL SERVICES

Like electricity and telecommunications, banking is a service whose stability is key to a functioning economy. The ability of people to save and borrow money is crucial to economic development and general prosperity. When the banking system fails, it can threaten the entire economy, as we learned during the Great Depression.

In response to the financial collapse of the Great Depression (which was caused, in part, by conflicts of interest on Wall Street that helped create an artificial boom through heavily leveraged and thus unstable positions), Congress passed the Glass-Steagall Banking Act, which separated commercial banking from investment banking and provided federal guarantees of bank deposits. The simple premise was that commercial banking needed to be stable. Banks shouldn't be allowed to put depositors' money at risk by investing in highly speculative ventures.

Another problem that arose in the lead-up to the stock market crash of 1929 was that big banks were pushing bad investments to unsuspecting investors at the wishes of their corporate banking clients, a situation similar to the Wall Street analyst scandals of recent years. Glass-Steagall made this kind of collaboration illegal by prohibiting mergers between investment banking and stock brokerage firms.[36]

A relatively stable banking system lasted for about four decades, until rising inflationary costs in the 1970s pressured banks to compete on deposit rates instead of having them regulated by the Securities and Exchange Commission. After the banks began to compete on rates, they had to get more aggressive with their own investments, which resulted in a new wave of deregulation that allowed banks to invest depositors' taxpayer-guaranteed money into ever riskier ventures, a development that eventually led to the savings-and-loan crisis. Tiny savings-and-loan associations, suddenly free to invest as they pleased, began investing wildly and irresponsibly. A variety of schemers and scammers pilfered, plundered, and gambled away immense sums of money, leaving taxpayers with an eventual bill estimated at $500 billion after 1,600 banks failed.[37] The aftermath of the scandal also made banks more hesitant to grant credit, creating collateral damage for ordinary borrowers.[38]

Undaunted, the big commercial banks clamored for still fewer restraints on the banking sector. Specifically, they wanted to get rid of Glass-Steagall, and they promised that great efficiencies would result from the kinds of consolidation between the big banks and brokerage firms that the law specifically prohibited. By 1997, the act had been weakened enough to allow banks to acquire securities firms outright, and by 1999, thanks to a lobbying effort led by Citibank and others, Glass-Steagall was essentially history and investment banking, insurance, and financial underwriting were back under the same umbrella again. The final compromise on Gramm-Leach-Bliley (the legislation that ultimately repealed Glass-Steagall) was brokered by then Treasury secretary Robert Rubin, who joined the newly formed Citigroup as a vice president just four days later. At the time of the legislation, Citibank had already merged with Travelers/American Express, in violation of Glass-Steagall (but technically legal because of a two-year window for compliance). Such was the arrogance of the company.

With the law's repeal, Wall Street conglomerates like J.P. Morgan Chase & Co. and Citigroup were now free to both lend money to and underwrite securities for Enron from their banking side, while their brokers advised investors to buy Enron's stock. (Citigroup, for instance, earned at least $167 million by selling various services to Enron between 1997 and 2001.[39])

Such investment advice was hardly impartial. Both banks had issued Enron huge loans that were disguised as energy trades, which enabled Enron to misstate the loan as cash flow from business operations, misleading investors, analysts, tax collectors, and employees. These big banks were also pivotal players—perhaps the architects—of the offshore special purpose entities that were used to hide the company's debt and that ultimately brought the company down.[40] As Senator Carl Levin (D-Mich.) testified in a Senate panel hearing he led on the banks' role in the collapse of Enron, "Citigroup and Chase . . . not only assisted Enron, they developed the deceptive pre-pays as a financial product and sold it to other companies as so-called balance sheet-friendly financing, earning millions of fees for themselves in the process."[41]

These banks must have known that Enron was a terrible investment, a house of cards. After all, they helped to build it. Yet, because it was in the interests of these conglomerates to keep that house of cards propped up, they didn't issue a peep about Enron's shaky finances.

Of course, Enron wasn't the only bum stock that the big Wall Street firms were pushing for all the wrong reasons. With many investment banking and brokerage firms now under the same roof as a result of deregulation, investment advisers were routinely taking their cues from bosses who were more concerned with pleasing big corporate clients than with giving good advice to small investors. As a result, analysts recommended that their clients buy stocks in companies that they privately derided as "crap" and "junk" for the sole reason that these companies were investment banking clients at their firm. These massive conflicts of interest resulted in an epidemic of worthless "buy" ratings. According to Weiss Ratings, an independent analyst whose revenues do not come from the companies they analyze, the vast majority of Wall Street investment analysts (many tied to the same banks that underwrote the companies they were covering) advised investors to "buy" or "hold" shares in Enron and other failing companies even as they were filing for Chapter 11 bankruptcies. Forty-seven of the fifty large brokerage firms covering companies that went bankrupt in the first four months of 2002 continued to recommend that investors buy or hold shares in the companies even as they were filing for Chapter 11.[42]

In some cases, the analyst-underwriter conflicts went even deeper. For example, Citigroups's telecom analyst Jack Grubman (who ultimately resigned in disgrace and paid a $15 million fine) helped raise money for Qwest, Global Crossing, and WorldCom, helping them plot strategy and attending board meetings while he was touting their stock to unsuspecting investors. Meanwhile, as a favor for throwing business toward the banks, executives at these companies received "kickbacks" in the form of early Initial Public Offering (IPO) allocations.[43]

Such conflicts of interest surely helped fuel the dot-com boom. The financial conglomerates had every incentive to keep pushing stock prices higher, as they were pulling in massive underwriting and investment banking fees from companies whose success was based solely on the hot air of irrational exuberance. It was conflicts like these that led two *Business Week* reporters to conclude that "it's starting to look as though the very model of the financial conglomerate is fundamentally flawed."[44]

Though New York State Attorney General Eliot Spitzer led the investigation into these kinds of conflicts of interest at ten major Wall Street banks (Citigroup, Morgan Stanley, Credit Suisse First Boston, Goldman Sachs, J.P. Morgan Chase, Bear Stearns, Lehman Brothers, DeutschBank, UBS Paine Webber, and Piper Jaffray), the penalty Spitzer and the SEC eventually agreed upon with the banks hardly fit the crime. The $1.4 billion settlement that regulators and banks agreed to in April 2003 amounted to little more than a slap on the wrist for these financial giants, who between them could bring in that much revenue in a matter of days.[45] And experts predicted that most of the settlement would wind up either being tax-deductible or covered by insurance companies.[46] The settlement did little to address the structural conflicts of interest that resulted from deregulation, even though Spitzer himself had concluded, "'I don't think there is any question that bringing many elements of financial services together has created more complex relationships that need to be properly controlled. Many of the conflicts that we are trying to unravel . . . come from the notion that the concentration of financial services would be a good and healthy thing for the economy."'[47] As Tom Schlesinger, executive director of the Financial Markets Center, explained it, "The rationale for repealing Glass-Steagall was that it would create more diversified banks and therefore more stability. What I see in these mega-banks is not diversification but more concentration of risk, which puts the taxpayers on the hook."[48]

Another area of the financial sector that underwent deregulation was the trading of derivatives (complex financial instruments that allow investors to make huge and potentially very risky bets). Derivatives first gained popularity among a few clever Wall Street traders in the mid-1980s. By the early 1990s, future Enron board member Wendy Lee Gramm had eased the regulations on derivatives as she ended her tenure as chair of the Commodities Futures Trading Commission, and the usage of derivatives began to spread to hundreds of less sophisticated money managers at otherwise solid businesses. Though congressional hearings and at least one GAO report[49] raised significant concerns about the infectious spread of derivatives, virtually every attempt to regulate derivatives in response was blocked, mostly by efforts coordinated by the International Swaps and Derivatives Association (ISDA), the derivatives trade group and its top lobbyist, Mark Brickell, a vice president of J.P. Morgan. According to law professor Frank Partnoy, a former derivatives salesman, unregulated derivatives trading played a key role in the majority of financial scandals of the past decade, including Long Term Capital Management, Orange County, Barings Bank, and Enron. In order to avoid massive risk taking that could have drastic consequences for our economy, derivatives need to be regulated.[50]

Ultimately, the question underlying deregulation in the financial sector is the same question we have asked elsewhere. Do we want to place limits to ensure that the banking sector is stable and operates in the public interest? Or do we want to give companies more freedom to do as their bottom-line-focused decision making tells them, trusting that the market will somehow work things out on its own? Banking is yet another sector where promises of deregulation never quite materialized, and where, once the experiment had begun, we realized that some of the restrictions we had enacted in the first place served a useful purpose after all.

THE NEED FOR REGULATED COMPETITION

Not every industry requires special government regulations to the degree that electricity, telecommunications, and banking do. But almost all require some form of regulation to ensure that no one company or group of companies is allowed to get so big that the market they operate in is no longer sufficiently competitive.

Indeed, as almost all economists will agree, competitive markets are generally good things. Competition is a wonderful spur to self-improvement, and companies that operate in a competitive market are forced to pay attention to basic things like price and quality, because if they don't, the competition will, and those who are slow to innovate will find themselves left behind. However, competitive markets require actual competition, and this is where the reality of concentrated corporate power conflicts with the corporate mantra of "free" markets.

Though they won't admit it, what corporations actually seem to want is a kind of corporate socialism, where a handful of "too-big-to-fail" corporations dominate each sector, propped up by massive corporate welfare and other government favors that help them cement their dominant position. This is almost the exact opposite of how a properly competitive market should work, with government operating as an impartial umpire making sure that everything is fair and competitive and no single competitor is enjoying any special favors.

Though we will not go into detail about corporate welfare here,[51] we think it's important to make a quick point about how, despite what corporations might say rhetorically about not wanting government intervention in the marketplace, they actually depend on a mélange of subsidies, bailouts, giveaways, tax loopholes, debt revocations, loan guarantees, discounted insurance, and other benefits that make already big and influential corporations become even bigger and more influential, costing taxpayers an estimated $93 billion a year in the process.[52]

As Ralph Nader has written, "Corporate welfare programs siphon funds from appropriate public investments, subsidize companies ripping minerals from federal lands, enable pharmaceutical companies to gouge consumers, perpetuate anti-competitive oligopolistic markets, injure our national security, and weaken our democracy."[53]

Federal bailouts are especially troubling. Economists Adams and Brock describe bailouts as a "perverse kind of 'lemon socialism' whereby profits are privatized while costs are publicly borne."[54] Yet, such is the consequence of allowing individual corporations to grow so big that their failure could have troubling economic ripples. As Adams and Brock write, "It underscores the importance of keeping the economic organizations at a size such that society can tolerate their mistakes and failures—a size that prevents private tragedies from becoming social catastrophes and that thereby prevents the public from being held a hostage to bigness."[55]

All in all, today's economic situation is a far cry from the competitive markets envisioned by Adam Smith, the Enlightenment- era economist regularly invoked by defenders of corporate capitalism, even though Smith had a profound distaste for corporations, which he thought were anticompetitive and inherently irresponsible. As author David Korten notes, "When Adam Smith conceptualized the idea of a market economy in his classic *Wealth of Nations*, he had in mind economies that allocated human and material resources justly and sustainably to meet the self-defined needs of people and community."[56]

In Smith's ideal economy, no individual actor is big enough to impose market terms on others and there is enough competition to keep individual businesses in check. All producers bear the costs of their own enterprise themselves. There are no government subsidies, protections, or other special advantages to unfairly privilege certain actors. All actors are responsible for producing their own goods and for any harms that might result. This is patently not the situation today. Today, aggressive antitrust regulation and enforcement is desperately needed to guarantee the benefits of a competitive economy.

And though economic models may insist that unregulated competition is an effective way of keeping corporations in check, experience shows otherwise. For example, in one recent worldwide study of 25,000 companies in twenty-four countries, the authors found that merger activity in any industry follows a predictable twenty-five-year pattern, with industries almost always winding up with just a few players controlling as much as 90 percent of the market.[57] Perhaps the reason for this is that, as we discussed in Chapter 3, corporations are set up to maximize profit first and foremost, and, as economic historian Richard B. DuBoff has written, "The bigger the corporation in size of assets or the larger its market share, the higher its rate of profit. . . . Large firms in concentrated industries earn systematically higher profits than all other firms, about 30 percent more . . . on average."[58]

The reason that concentration brings higher profits is simple. With little competition, firms can get away with charging higher prices, boosting their bottom line. Ultimately, consumers suffer the consequences. Charles Mueller, editor of the *Antitrust Law and Economics Review*, has suggested that monopoly power is present in about one-third of the U.S. economy and that, where present, it inflates prices by an average of 30 percent. This translates into about 10 percent of the country's GDP, or more than $1.1 trillion a year (or about $3,700 per person).[59]

There are other costs to concentration as well. One is that because there is less competitive pressure when industries are concentrated, the largest firms spend less on R&D and tend to stifle innovation far more than they promote it, since they benefit from the status quo. One famous study of sixty-one major inventions found that only sixteen were the result of organized corporate research.[60] As Ralph Nader, Mark Green, and Joel Seligman explained in *Taming the Giant Corporation:*

> The best innovation usually emerges from solo inventors or small and medium-sized firms—not our giant corporations . . . If you already dominate an industry, where is the incentive to take a chance on a new and costly approach? We don't associate inventiveness with the centralized planners of socialist economies, though the planners have substantial R&D resources under their control. The reason is that

they, like big businessmen, are not eager to give the green light to new ways which threaten their investment in old ways.[61]

"Study after study of the sources of inventions. . . . shows it tends to be mavericks, independents or outsiders," note economists Adams and Brock. "They tend not to have much money to work with. But they are all pursuing different ideas. You don't know in advance what the right idea is. It makes sense to have multiple approaches. When you have a collaboration, that tends to narrow everyone's thinking down to fewer and fewer dimensions."[62]

Concentration also makes companies less susceptible to consumer demands. With fewer competitors, consumers have fewer options to turn to if they don't like something about a product. Meanwhile, as companies grow bigger and bigger, they can afford to spend more and more on advertising, which in turn allows them to increasingly dictate consumer demands in the first place instead of having to respond to them. In 2004, annual U.S. spending on advertising was projected to reach $266.4 billion.[63] This is up from $212 billion in 2000, and from $33.3 billion in 1976.

Perhaps most importantly, economic power inevitably leads to political power. When corporations grow to enormous sizes and exert formidable control over markets, it is only a matter of time before they will also use their clout to dictate public policy. As professors DuBoff and Edward S. Herman put it, "Concentration, by magnifying the power of dominant corporations, diminishes the possibility that citizen voices will be heard in the management of public business."[64] Put simply, when a handful of dominant corporations control the economic and political spheres that govern their behavior, there is little chance for meaningful representative democracy.

Corporations generally argue that mergers are justified because they create efficiencies of scale that lower prices. However, these claims tend to be self-serving and largely overstated. "The annals of business history are laden with examples of combinations that decreased efficiency. . . . In the early 1900s the stifling effect of bigness on efficiency was frequently commented upon," writes DuBoff, who also notes that in almost all cases, efficiencies of scale are capped at relatively small sizes.[65]

THE EXAMPLE OF MEDIA CONCENTRATION

Corporate control of the media is one sector where concentrated ownership is now widely acknowledged to be a problem.

Today, ten transnational conglomerates with revenues ranging from roughly $8 billion to $35 billion a year thoroughly dominate the media landscape. The list includes Disney (ABC), AOL Time Warner (CNN), News Corporation (Fox), Viacom (CBS), Vivendi Universal, Sony, Liberty, Bertelsman, AT&T-Comcast, and General Electric (NBC). As media critics Robert McChesney and John Nichols explain, "The first tier owns all the commercial television networks, all the major Hollywood studios, four of the five firms that sell 90 percent of the music in the United States, a majority of the cable TV systems, all or part of most of the successful cable TV channels, and much, much, more." In the second tier are another roughly twelve to fifteen firms that do about $3 to $8 billion of business each year. Firms like Hearst, the New York Times Company, the Washington Post Company, Cox, Knight-Ridder, Tribune Company, and Gannett have holdings in two or three media sectors. [66]

Because today's media are essentially dominated by a handful of large corporate chains, much of the news looks and sounds the same, regardless of what channel we may be watching or what newspaper we may be reading. "It is an extraordinary degree of economic concentration. Such concentration of media ownership is clearly negative by any standard that cherishes free speech and diversity in democratic culture," write McChesney and Nichols.[67]

Corporate conglomerates prefer news stories that are cheap to produce, easy to draw an audience for, and conducive to promotional tie-ins. Instead of exposés on massive corporate rip-offs that require in-depth reporting, we are given sensationalist local crime stories that require little more than listening to a police scanner. Instead of stories about political processes that can have a direct impact on our lives, we are treated to irrelevant de-tails about the lives of celebrities who just happen to be in a major feature film that the media conglomerate's production studios are releasing. Instead of meaningful coverage of impor-tant world and national news, we are given sound bites.

"The primary effects of tightened corporate control are seri-ous reduction in staff, combined with pressure to do vastly less expensive and less controversial lifestyle and feature stories," write McChesney and Nichols. "Where there is 'news,' it often takes the form of canned crime reports that foster unrealistic and unnecessary fears. This is the magic elixir for the bottom line."[68]

In June 2003, the Federal Communications Commission voted to loosen media ownership rules (paving the way for still further consolidation) by allowing one company to own both broadcast and print media in the same market and allowing one broadcast company to own stations that reach more than 45 percent of the national audience (up from 35 percent).[69] The response was an unprecedented outpouring of protest, including an estimated 3 million letters, e-mails, and petition signatures.[70] One year later, a Circuit Court threw out the FCC rules, asserting that the FCC had failed to justify why loosening ownership rules was in the public interest.[71]

Even industry leaders such as Ted Turner were critical of the FCC's proposal. "If a young media entrepreneur were trying to get started today under these proposed rules, he or she wouldn't be able to buy a UHF station, as I did," Turner wrote. "They're all bought up. But even if someone did manage to buy a TV sta-tion, that wouldn't be enough. To compete, you have to have good programming and good distribution. Today both are owned by conglomerates that keep the best for themselves and leave the worst for you—if they sell anything to you at all. It's hard to compete when your suppliers are owned by your com-petitors."[72]

"Large media corporations are far more profit-focused and risk-averse. They sometimes confuse short-term profits and long-term value," Turner added. "They kill local programming because it's expensive, and they push national programming because it's cheap—even if it runs counter to local interests and community values. For a corporation to launch a new idea, you have to get the backing of executives who are obsessed with quarterly earnings and afraid of being fired for an idea that fails."[73]

It is widely understood that further consolidation of the media in the hands of just a few corporate conglomerates will significantly damage the media's ability to hold those in power accountable, while handicapping journalists' ability to serve as guardians of the public interest. In an industry like the media, which provides a valuable public service (essentially determining what people know about the world), competition is especially important, because it allows for a variety of voices and opinions. As Justice Hugo Black once put it: "The First Amendment rests on the assumption that the widest possible dissemination of information from diverse and antagonistic sources is essential to the welfare of the public."[74]

The most effective way to ensure the diversity necessary for a vibrant democracy is to enact competition rules, such as limits on cross-media ownership and vertical integration that essentially mandate diversity by prohibiting media conglomerates. For example, radio conglomerate Clear Channel shouldn't also be allowed to operate or exclusively book more than one hundred concert venues across the United States, producing about 70 percent of live concerts in the country, as it does.[75]

As McChesney has suggested, "What is needed, then, is a new media antitrust statute, similar in tone to the seminal Clayton and Sherman Acts, that lays out the general values to be enforced by the Justice Department and the Federal Trade Commission. . . . The objective should be to break up such media conglomerates as Time Warner, News Corporation, and Disney, so that their book publishing, magazine publishing, TV show production, movie production, TV stations, TV networks, amusement parks, retail store chains, cable TV channels, cable TV systems, and so on all become independent firms. With reduced barriers to entry in these specific markets, new firms could join in."[76]

FIXING OUR BUSTED SYSTEM
OF TRUST BUSTING

Though the media situation provides an example that has gained much prominence of late, it is hardly the only industry where tight corporate concentration has had troubling consequences. In 1998, for example, just four supermarket chains controlled more than 70 percent of the market in ninety-four large cities.[77] Just four meatpacking companies—ConAgra, IBP, Cargill, and Farmland National—currently control 87 percent of the nation's cattle slaughter, up from only 36 percent in 1980. They also control 54 percent of the hog slaughter and 70 percent of the sheep slaughter.[78] As law professor Peter Carstensen recently told a Senate agriculture panel, "packers have both the capacity and the incentive to engage in strategic conduct whose primary function is either to exploit their buyer power or entrench that power against potential competition."[79] In many cases, the same company controls almost all steps of food production and distribution, creating a vertical integration that borders on anticompetitive.[80]

Much of the current concentration in many industries is the result of a massive wave of mergers in the last twenty or so years. Between 1985 and 1999, the number of mergers valued at $5 million or more rose from 1,719 to 9,599 (a 558 percent rise), with the total value of those mergers rising from $149.6 billion to $3.402 trillion (a 2,274 percent rise).[81] The number of mergers valued at $1 billion or more grew from about 20 per year in the early 1990s to 208 in 2000.[82] Some of the mergers were of dizzying size: Pfizer's $116.1 billion takeover of Warner-Lambert Co. in 1999; America-On-Line's $106 billion takeover of Time Warner in 2000; Exxon's $86.4 billion takeover of Mobil in 1998; Travelers Group's $72.6 billion takeover of Citicorp in 1998. Between 1998 and 1999, there were twenty-four mergers worth $25 billion or more.[83] Though big mergers have slowed down a little in the last few years, they have by no means disappeared. In January 2004, for example, J.P. Morgan Chase & Co. acquired Bank One for $58 billion in the third largest banking merger in American history, making it the second largest

U.S. bank in assets at $1.1 trillion, just behind Citigroup's $1.2 trillion.[84] And, as we write, RJ Reynolds (the No. 2 cigarette maker in the U.S.) is trying to buy Brown and Williamson (the No. 3 cigarette maker in the U.S.). If merged, they would have a combined market share of 32.3 percent. Add in industry leader Philip Morris (which controls 49.4 percent of the market), and the top three firms now control 82 percent of the U.S. cigarette market already.[85]

This merger mania also ignores the fact that most mergers fail—on the order of 60 to 80 percent—"either because the merged entities fail to deliver hoped for 'synergies' through cost reductions, or because they underperform stock market trends more generally."[86] Bigness introduces its own set of bureaucratic inefficiencies.

The reason that so many of these mergers have been allowed is that the Federal Trade Commission and the Department of Justice have shown little interest in challenging them in recent decades. In the mid-1970s, about 1,500 antitrust cases a year were being brought before federal courts. Now, only between 200 and 300 cases are filed a year.[87] As antitrust expert Charles Mueller wrote in the late 1990s, "The Reagan and Bush administrations . . . were ideologically hostile to antitrust and the present (Clinton) administration—being politically weak and eager for "business" support—is rapidly compiling a pro-monopoly (non-enforcement) record which rivals that of the McKinley administration."[88]

The policy of light antitrust enforcement continued under the second Bush administration, which shocked many by settling the Microsoft antitrust case brought under the previous administration without breaking up the technology giant, extracting only minor concessions.[89] Testifying at a Senate hearing on "Antitrust Laws" shortly after the settlement, then Justice Department antitrust chief Charles James said he saw no problem with Microsoft retaining the 95 percent share of computer operating systems and 90 percent share in web browsers. "If that is the result the market dictates, free from all unlawful restraints imposed by Microsoft, I think that is the result that we have to live with under antitrust laws."[90] As Brock notes, "The notion of economics today has been twisted and confined and limited to represent one narrow, extreme ideological point of view, the *laissez-faire* point of view. It is not just economics, it is one particular ideology, masquerading as economic science, that has come to dominate the debate."[91]

Such a policy stands in contrast to Justice Learned Hand's majority opinion in the famous 1945 case *United States v. Aluminum Co. of America*, which held that Alcoa's 90 percent control of the virgin-aluminum ingot market was an illegal monopoly. Judge Hand wrote that "it is possible, because of its indirect social or moral effect, to prefer a system of small producers, each dependent for his success upon his own skill and character, to one in which the great mass of those engaged must accept the direction of the few." He also wrote that the prohibition of monopoly was "based upon the belief that great industrial consolidations are inherent undesirable, regardless of their economic results."[92]

Antitrust regulation in America dates back to 1890, when widespread anger about the dominant position of trusts and monopolies gave rise to the Sherman Act, which prohibited "every contract, combination . . . or conspiracy, in restraint of trade." However, even at the time the Act was widely acknowledged to be insufficient, and the government lost six of the first seven cases brought under the act, including the 1895 Sugar Trust case, where the Supreme Court allowed a combination controlling 98 percent of sugar to stand because it was "manufacturing" and not "interstate commerce."[93]

In 1914, Congress tightened antitrust rules by passing the Clayton Act and the Federal Trade Commission Act. The Clayton Act prohibited mergers and acquisitions where the effect "may be substantially to lessen competition, or tend to create a monopoly." The Federal Trade Commission Act created the Federal Trade Commission to monitor potential antitrust violations. It also outlawed "unfair methods of competition," though it did not define "unfair."

Since the language of both laws is somewhat vague, much is incumbent on those interpreting the law. Various administrations have had very different interpretations of the laws.

We believe that smaller corporations are to be desired for a number of reasons detailed in this chapter, and until we can directly limit their size and range of actions through some kind of chartering process, the most effective way to limit the size of corporations and restore properly competitive markets would be to more aggressively enforce antitrust law.

A new antitrust policy needs to take the approach that market concentration must be avoided because of its polluting effects in both the economic and the political spheres. The new policy should recognize that economies of scale and efficiency are not an unmitigated good and that their benefits are often overstated. It should also implicitly understand that the larger corporations become, the more power they will be able to exert over both prices and politics. And when that power rests with a handful of large corporations, democracy necessarily suffers. As Louis Brandeis once famously put it, "We can have democracy in this country, or we can have great wealth concentrated in the hands of a few, but we can't have both."

Developing a new antitrust policy could begin by setting up a congressionally appointed commission to assess the consequences of concentrated corporate ownership in specific sectors, much like how Congress created the Temporary National Economic Committee (TNEC) in 1938 to hold hearings on the concentration of economic power. Though the TNEC got derailed by World War II, Senator Joseph O'Mahoney, who led the committee, concluded by suggesting, "It is idle to think that huge collective institutions which carry on our modern business can continue to operate without more definite responsibility toward all the people of the Nation than they now have."[94] O'Mahoney ultimately recommended a system of federal chartering, which we discussed in Chapter 1.

A series of congressional hearings today could focus on the effects of concentrated ownership in such areas as media, agriculture, defense, and banking. One possible reform , suggested by Adams and Brock, would be to "amend the Clayton Act to prohibit all corporate mergers involving assets greater than some predetermined amount. Whether horizontal, vertical, or conglomerate, mergers involving firms exceeding this size threshold would be prohibited unless the merging firms could demonstrate—say, before an expert tribunal—that the propose merger would not be likely to lessen competition in any line of commerce; that it would enhance operating efficiency and contribute substantially to the merged firms' competitiveness; and that it would promote technological progress in demonstrably specific ways not otherwise available."[95]

Antitrust enforcement could also make more aggressive use of structural divestments and dissolutions. Of the 423 monopolization cases won by the government between 1890 and 1996, for example, only 63 (15 percent) resulted in a break-up.[96]

Any new antitrust policy should also come with major funding increases for the antitrust divisions of the Department of Justice and the Federal Trade Commission. As it stands, the current budgets of antitrust agencies charged with policing a $10 trillion economy total less than $200 million.[97]

In an era of corporate globalization, the issue of antitrust regulation for certain sectors may have to be addressed on a global level. Law professor Joseph Wilson, for example, has suggested an International Merger Control Regime.[98] But however we choose to address this issue, we must refute the canard that traditional antitrust rules shouldn't apply in an era of global markets.

PRIVATIZATION AND THE LIMITS OF MARKETS

Though well-regulated markets can often channel competitive pressures to work on behalf of the public good, we believe that there are certain essential services (such as water, health care, public education, prisons, and security-related operations) where the private sector has no place. Such services, we believe, must be guaranteed by citizen governments accountable to the people and not be left to corporations whose primary interest is to serve their shareholders.

Yet, increasingly many of these services are being turned over to the private sector under the destructive logic of privatization. Based on a disingenuous premise similar to that behind deregulation (government is inefficient, private corporations free from government control can do a better job), privatization represents a dangerous transfer of power from citizens to corporations, placing all of us at the mercy of for-profit corporations for the provision of a growing number of essential services.

Although government provision of these services may fall victim to those inefficiencies traditionally associated with monopoly control of any service, at least government is not under pressure to turn a profit, and at least government is accountable directly to the people. Corporations, on the other hand, are under pressure to turn a profit on these services at all costs, and much less accountable when they fail to provide adequate service.

Though privatization in many sectors is only beginning to gain popularity these days, its track record thus far is troubling.

Public education is an instructive example. The idea of turning public schools over to the private sector goes back at least a half-century to an article written by Milton Friedman in 1955, which called for the privatization of public schools.[99] Privatization of public schools is becoming increasingly popular with a variety of groups, including libertarians interested in shrinking the government, religious groups that denounce the secular liberalism of public education, and for-profit educational corporations looking to boost their bottom line.

As Barbara Miner, the editor of Rethinking Schools, has written, "in the last decade, privatization took on a new meaning, as for-profit companies hoped to get involved in education at a higher and qualitatively different level. Their goal: to run schools or entire school districts—from the hiring of teachers to the development of curricula and the teaching of students. In the process, they plan to compete with publicly run schools and redefine the very definition of public education."[100]

The opening salvo in the full-scale assault on public education began in Milwaukee, Wisconsin, where the Bradley Foundation has funded a campaign that played up a perceived crisis in the Milwaukee Public School System and disguised what critics describe as a racist and classist ideological agenda behind a proposed voucher system that favored "parental choice." By 1989, Wisconsin Act 336 had created the Milwaukee Parental Choice Program, the first private school choice program in the nation to provide public funds for private school enrollment. Jeffrey Leverich of the Wisconsin Education Association Council has suggested that Wisconsin's program is a model that conservative leaders expect to replicate across the nation: "The Bradley Foundation, along with a handful of other conservative foundations, has been extremely effective in advancing the message that government programs do not work and that private enterprise should replace them."[101]

The biggest and most important for-profit grade school corporation is Edison Schools, Inc. Formed in 1992, just a decade later it was running 136 schools serving 75,000 students in twenty-two states and the District of Columbia. Since Edison is a corporation, its first responsibility is to its shareholders, not to its students. Edison's track record so far has largely been one of cutting corners to achieve numbers, often with failing results for taxpayers. In Wichita, Kansas, for example, contracts with four Edison schools cost $250,000 more than comparable district schools; at one school the principal and assistant principal were removed after it was found that school personnel were improperly helping students on standardized tests. In Dallas, Texas, Edison was forced to renegotiate a five-year contract after the school board figured out that the existing contract was for $20 million more than the actual cost of running the seven schools. And in San Francisco, California, parents and school board members revoked Edison's charter when Edison's schools produced the worst test scores among city schools. As Miner has put it: "Fundamentally, privatization is about money, not educational reform."[102] And though it may go without saying, if we allow our schools to be run by corporations whose first and foremost concern is to make money, we have to wonder what kind of education our children are going to get.

Privatization battles are also taking place over water. Many U.S. water systems are overdue for repairs, and estimates for how much these repairs will cost over the next three decades range from $150 billion to $1 trillion. And since roughly 80 percent of Americans get their water from public utilities, the big question is whether local governments are willing to pay for those repairs.[103] In an era of tax cuts and budget shortfalls, the prospect of water privatization has become more appealing to many communities who don't want to pay for the repairs themselves.

If anybody has any illusions about the promises of water privatization, he or she should look no further than Atlanta, Georgia, which in 1998 signed a twenty-year, $428 million contract with United Water (a subsidiary of French conglomerate Suez) to operate the city's water system. The result was disastrous. United's idea of cutting costs was firing 400 of the 700 system employees and reducing training for the existing employees, which predictably resulted in a giant backlog of work orders. Maintenance projects hovered at a 50 percent completion rate. Broken water lines took up to two months to fix. Fire hydrants were found to be inoperative. United Water billed the city an additional $37.6 million for service authorizations, maintenance costs, and capital repairs, even though, as it turned out, United Water was trying to count routine maintenance as "capital repairs." To cut through the fraud, the city had to spend $1 million on inspections just to verify the company's reports. Ultimately, Atlanta cut the contract short, having learned its lesson that some things are just better left to the public sector.[104]

Water privatization battles are happening in communities across the country as we write, from Indianapolis, Indiana, to Stockton, California, from New Orleans, Louisiana, to Newark, New Jersey.[105] At stake is citizen control over this essential resource. Though community struggles against water privatization are obviously crucial, it is also important to note that a 1997 change in the tax code (lobbied for by the National Association of Water Companies) has proven a boon to water privatization, and should be repealed. The change gave tax-exempt status to cities that contract with private companies for up to twenty years, instead of just up to five years, as it had been before. This made a big difference, because tax-exempt status allows cities to borrow money at a significantly lower rate. [106]

Additionally, the use of private military companies in the Iraq war and the postwar occupation of Iraq has raised serious questions about the privatization of one of the most fundamental functions of government: national defense. Private military contractors, which represented roughly 10 percent of all military personnel in the initial phase of the Iraq campaign and which were later found to be involved in the torture of prisoners at the infamous Abu Ghraib prison, are not subject to the same accountability as U.S. soldiers (contracted personnel, for example, are not subject to the Uniform Code of Military Justice). The primary mandate of these companies is to maximize corporate profits, not to serve the national interest. Observers say the contractors' conflicting loyalty has the potential to undermine the integrity of battlefield operations, putting soldiers at risk. It has also led to widespread charges of contract-related fraud and abuse.[107]

We believe that services such as water, public education, and national defense are too important to leave to for-profit corporations, who are primarily driven to make money for shareholders. Put simply, corporations should not have control over essential services and other functions best provided for by collective governments.

———

Deregulation, privatization, and a loosened antitrust policy represent a dangerous power grab by large corporations. As large corporations increasingly knock down government regulations designed to keep them in check, their economic power will grow accordingly, giving them greater power to set the terms of engagement for workers and consumers, whose power is accordingly diminished. Meanwhile, in industries that were once tightly regulated for specific reasons, such as electricity, telecommunications, and banking, deregulation has cleared the way for many abusive practices that previously would have been impossible, while the promised benefits have rarely appeared. Finally, the growing threat of privatization represents an attack on the very idea of public services, calling on us to firmly establish proper limits to what activities it is proper for corporations to get involved in.

Economic power is also inevitably tied up with political power. The larger corporations are allowed to become, the more they will come to dominate regulatory processes, crowding out citizen control over decisions that establish the rules for markets. Thus, in order to restore the ability of citizens to exercise their own self- governance and control corporations through regulation, it should be obvious that corporations need to be brought down to size and, where unique industry features make bigness necessary, very tightly regulated. Stopping the march toward deregulation and privatization and establishing an aggressive antitrust policy are important ways to assert that citizens should be in control of the economy and that corporations cannot simply operate as they please.

5 | Cracking Down on Corporate Crime

"Managers do not have an ethical duty to obey economic regulatory laws just because the laws exist. They must determine the importance of these laws. The penalties Congress names for disobedience are a measure of how much it wants firms to sacrifice in order to adhere to the rules."

—Frank H. Easterbrook and Daniel R. Fischel (two leaders in the Chicago school of law and economics)

The year 2002 was the year that corporate crime hit the big time. Headline after headline told the story of greed and deception at companies like Enron, Adelphia, Tyco, Global Crossing, WorldCom, Arthur Andersen, and countless others. Millions of investors lost billions of dollars in their retirement savings, claiming that they had been misled by lying executives, cheating accountants, and greedy and conflicted brokers. Hundreds of thousands of workers lost their jobs in the inevitable bankruptcies. Meanwhile, a handful of unscrupulous executives had become fabulously wealthy in the process, some walking away with hundreds of millions of dollars of other people's money.

Though business leaders and their representatives in Washington originally tried to pass it off as the case of a "few bad apples," the continious cascade of corporate corruption soon made it apparent that this was more than a passing phase. Something was rotten to the core in the way business was being conducted in America, and some things needed to change.

By the end of July 2002, the president had signed into law the Sarbanes-Oxley Act, a new accounting reform bill that had swept through Congress in record time once the accounting fraud at WorldCom made public demand for reform unstoppable. The new law was largely based on the premise that the corporate scandals were rooted in problems in the accounting industry. Clean up the accounting industry and eliminate some of the egregious conflicts of interest, it was argued, and the problem would be solved.

Yet, other issues also came up for discussion. Many agreed that there were widespread problems in the corporate governance system, that management had enjoyed too much control over boards of directors, and that as a result boards had failed to stand up to the excesses of management. Stock options, the steroids of corporate greed, came under scrutiny as well for providing perverse incentives for executives to "cook the books." Most everybody agreed that the state of business ethics was in poor shape, that business leaders had become too greedy and lost their moral compass.

Still, most analyses nibbled around the edges, focusing on narrow and specific causes. Very few asked questions about whether there were certain problems inherent in the guiding principles of corporate America that made such a corporate crime wave inevitable. Minimal attention was paid to the simple fact that federal regulators and prosecutors have not taken corporate crime seriously in decades, if ever, fostering a business culture in which punishment for illegal activity was not considered a threat.

Meanwhile, the accounting scandals of Enron, WorldCom, and other companies blurred the definition of corporate crime. Whereas we generally think of corporate crime as crime carried out by a corporation or individuals acting on behalf of a corporation, at many of the scandal-ridden companies it was not always clear whether the executives at these companies were working on behalf of the company or whether they were simply out for themselves. Though they certainly abused their power as corporate leaders, their crimes might be more aptly described as white-collar crime, or crime committed by individual executives for their own benefit. Indeed, the main victims of many of these crimes were the company's owners: the shareholders for whom the corporations are supposed to be run.

The distinctions between what we call corporate crime and white-collar crime are important, because their different natures require different responses. However, they often occur in tandem. And the fact that both corporate and individual business crimes are so prevalent and problematic reflects a larger problem that we will attempt to deal with in this chapter: namely, that society (and in particular, government lawmakers, regulators, and prosecutors) does not consider the epidemic of corporations and corporate executives breaking the law to be a particularly serious problem.

Additionally, the scandals focused attention on only one kind of corporate crime: financial crime. It is important to note that the victims of this crime were primarily powerful and wealthy investors who are not used to being victimized by corporate crime. Arguably, this is one of the main reasons that the crimes received such much attention in both the media and in Washington, as compared to crimes of pollution, workplace injuries, and other frequently unremarked-upon violations.

Consider Enron. Almost all of the attention focused on how the company had inflated its earnings through a deceptive and complicated series of off-the-books partnerships and special-purpose entities that had helped executives to become fabulously wealthy. Yet other crimes went largely ignored. For example, Enron executives had manipulated the price of electricity and natural gas in California by withholding supplies to create an artificial shortage and gouge utilities by charging prices for power that were ten times higher than in previous years.[1] Overseas, the company had allegedly bribed foreign officials[2] and contributed to massive ecological damage by constructing natural gas pipelines through a pristine region of the South American rainforest.[3] Human Rights Watch had alleged that the company was complicit in human rights abuses committed by security forces hired to guard the company's Dabhol, India, power plant.[4]

And while even the Conference Board considered widespread accounting fraud at so many companies as "evidence [of] a clear breach of the basic compact that underlies corporate capitalism,"[5] there was barely a peep about the other crimes that these companies had committed. At WorldCom, for example, a wide range of dubious consumer abuses went largely unreported amid the focus on accounting fraud.[6]

Of course, given even the lackluster response to the financial crimes that victimized mostly wealthy Americans, it comes as perhaps no surprise that other types of corporate crime have merited even less response from our elected officials and appointed regulators, as well as the media and other watchdogs. For example, according to the AFL-CIO, serious OSHA violations that pose a substantial probability of death or injury carry an average penalty of only $871.[7]

Indeed, one might be tempted to ask: If corporations are capable of so brazenly violating the rights of even the most privileged elements of society (their own owners), then how extensive is the damage that they do to the rest of us? Was all the attention paid to the epidemic of accounting fraud cases diverting us from an understanding of the larger universe of corporate crime, fraud, and abuse that occurs all the time?

Ultimately, the challenge we face is to mitigate and eventually eradicate all kinds of corporate criminal activity, be it financial, environmental, consumer, workplace safety, or anything else. But financial crime is as good a starting point as any for understanding the basic dynamics of corporate crime enforcement and punishment.

We believe that the proliferation of corporate crime represents one of the most dangerous consequences of unchecked corporate power. Though we have touched upon ways to cut off corporate crime at its root elsewhere – for example, in Chapter 3 we discuss the incentives that drive corporations to maximize shareholder value at the expense of everything else—in this chapter we will focus more directly on the problem of corporations and their executives breaking the law and explore ways to meet this problem head on: with proper enforcement and proper sanctions.

ASSESSING THE PROBLEM OF CORPORATE CRIME

So, how widespread is the problem of corporate crime? The answer, unfortunately, is that we don't know. Our government has never considered it worth its time to figure out the extent of the problem, and few others have taken the time to study it, though bits and pieces can be found here and there.

For instance, the Government Accountability Office (GAO), the investigative arm of Congress, estimates that healthcare fraud alone costs up to $100 billion each year.[8] Another estimate suggested that the annual cost of antitrust or trade violations is at least $250 billion.[9] The direct cost of occupational injury and illnesses is estimated at $1 billion per week, and based on conservative estimates, the annual cost of these injuries is between $183.2 billion and $274.8 billion in direct and indirect costs.[10]

In 1994, accounting professor Ralph Estes calculated that the public costs of private corporations (for both legal and illegal activities) were $2.6 trillion. Estes based his calculations on costs to workers (injuries, deaths, illnesses), costs to consumers (price fixing, unsafe products), costs to communities (primarily health-related costs), and costs to the nation (overcharging for contracts, regulatory violations).[11]

By comparison, the FBI's estimate of the nation's combined total loss from robbery and property crimes (burglary, larceny-theft, and motor vehicle theft) was $17.2 billion in 2002.[12]

Corporations also cause more violence and death than ordinary street criminals. The U.S. national murder rate reported by the FBI is about 16,000 each year.[13] This is far less than the sum total of deaths related to corporate negligence and malfeasance. Consider the following:

- The Consumer Product Safety Commission estimates that 23,000 Americans die annually in accidents or hazards associated with consumer products.[14]
- More than 5,500 workers were killed on the job because of traumatic injuries in 2002 (an average of 15 a day), and another 4.7 million suffered other serious injuries or illnesses, according to the Bureau of Labor Statistics.[15]
- The AFL-CIO reports that deaths from occupational diseases claim the lives of an estimated 50,000 to 60,000 workers each year.[16]

These numbers do not include the thousands of annual deaths caused by cancers and other deaths linked to corporate pollution (the Natural Resources Defense Council [NRDC] estimates that 64,000 premature deaths are caused a year by air pollution),[17] accidental deaths from defective products, tainted food, the marketing of addictive substances such as tobacco (which alone is estimated to kill more than 400,000 people each year), and other causes.[18]

The few major investigations of corporate crime that have ever been conducted paint an extraordinary picture of the extent and cost of corporate crime:

- In his pioneering 1949 study, *White Collar Crime*, Edwin Sutherland found that the seventy large corporations he surveyed had an average of approximately four convictions each over the course of their existence. Measured by the standards that many states apply to ordinary individuals, Sutherland pointed out that these companies would have been considered "habitual criminals." Sutherland was particularly harsh in his characterization of corporate war profiteering ("profits are more important to large corporations than patriotism"), fraud, and tax evasion, characterizing these and other corporate crimes as a form of organized crime.[19]

- In a 1977 study of just one form of illegal corporate activity, the bribery of foreign officials, Congress reported that "more than 400 corporations [including 117 members of the *Fortune* 500] have admitted making questionable or illegal payments. The companies reported paying out well in excess of $300 million in corporate funds to foreign government officials, politicians, and political parties." The industrial sectors most deeply involved were drugs and health care; oil and gas production and services; food products; aerospace, airlines, and air services; and chemicals.[20]

- In 1979 the Justice Department issued the first large-scale comprehensive investigation of corporations directly related to their violations of law. It found that "approximately two-thirds of large corporations violated the law, some of them many times" over just a two-year period (1975–76). The auto, pharmaceutical, and oil refining industries accounted for almost one-half of all violations, and four out of every ten of the most serious violations. Actions that directly harmed the economy were more likely to receive greater penalties, whereas those affecting consumer product quality were "responded to with the least severe sanctions."[21]

- A *Multinational Monitor* magazine survey of corporate crime in the 1990s found that the most serious acts of corporate criminality (measured by the size of resulting fines) involved many of the largest and most well established companies in the United States. Six of the companies that made the list of "Top 100 Corporate Criminals" were criminal recidivists (made the list twice). The categories of crime included environmental (38), antitrust (20), fraud (13), campaign finance (7), food and drug (6), financial (4), false statements (3), illegal exports (3), illegal boycott (1), worker death (1), bribery (1), obstruction of justice (1), public corruption (1), and tax evasion (1).[22]

WHY DO CORPORATIONS AND EXECUTIVES BREAK THE LAW?

If we are going to frame an effective response to corporate crime, we need to start by figuring out why corporations and their executives break the law. The answer, it seems, is twofold: (1) because they can get away with it; and 2) because if they can get away with it, it means they will make money breaking the law, and since maximizing profit is the driving corporate purpose, corporations will engage in any behaviors that are profitable.

Here, we will not discuss the incentives that drive corporations to break the law, because we have already done so in Chapter 3. To summarize briefly, however, the prevailing interpretation of corporate law gives corporations one primary duty: to maximize shareholder profit. To accomplish that goal, corporations are forced to cast aside other concerns, like human rights, the environment, and workers' rights. Under such an approach, even following the law becomes subject to a cost-benefit analysis. And if, factoring in the likelihood and consequences of getting caught, it turns out to be more profitable to break the law than to follow it, corporations will often go ahead and break the law. Frank H. Easterbrook and Daniel R. Fischel, two leaders in the Chicago school of law and economics, have even suggested that "managers do not have an ethical duty to obey economic regulatory laws just because the laws exist. They must determine the importance of these laws. The penalties Congress names for disobedience are a measure of how much it wants firms to sacrifice in order to adhere to the rules; the idea of optional sanctions is based on the supposition that managers not only may but also should violate the rules when it is profitable to do so."[23]

The problem is that breaking the law is often quite profitable because when it comes to corporate crime, enforcement is generally poor and punishments are often weak and worth risking. Corporate crime is generally not seen as a serious problem by our society, and there is a widespread perspective among corporate decision makers that they can get away with it—and worse, that much of the wrongdoing they engage in is actually legal.

Hence, the challenge in dealing with corporate crime is essentially making sure that crime doesn't pay. At a most basic level, corporations and corporate executives need to understand that they will be caught and punished if they violate the law. This, of course, is one of the most basic tenets of law enforcement. If there are not meaningful consequences for breaking the laws, then laws will be frequently broken.

But if it were as simple as that, we could end the chapter now. Certainly, there is an element of needing to devote more law enforcement resources to corporate crime and toughen the penalties, which we will discuss in this chapter. But corporate crime is tricky for a number of reasons, including the fact that corporate misbehaviors are often the result of decisions and actions by a number of different people within a corporation and the fact that traditional law enforcement deterrents like incarceration do not apply. Also, as business institutions, corporations are unable to feel the guilt and shame that might prevent ordinary human beings from breaking the law.

Our discussion of appropriate responses to corporate crime will proceed as follows. First, we will explore each of them in the corporation (employees, executives, directors, shareholders) and examine how we could hold these different actors responsible for corporate misbehaviors. Then we will look at dealing with the corporation itself and appropriate law enforcement responses. Finally, we will turn to a discussion of enforcement and, building on suggestions for holding corporations and corporate executives responsible, offer some ideas for making corporate crime more of a law enforcement priority to ensure that these actors are actually held responsible.

WHO SHOULD BE HELD RESPONSIBLE?

One of the problems in framing a proper response to corporate crime is figuring out who should be responsible and who should be punished and how. Obviously, different corporate crimes require different responses. In cases like Enron, WorldCom, and many of the other recent scandals, the fraud appears to have been directed by top executives for their own personal gain (though this can be difficult to prove). In these cases it probably makes the most sense to punish those executives. But in other cases, such as the many cases where companies manufacture dangerous products, it is much harder to hold anybody in particular responsible. After all, it is rare that anybody at a corporation will set out to make a dangerous product. Rather, such a product could be the result of a number of things: inadequate testing, cheap materials, or faulty designs. In these cases, it may make the most sense to deal with the corporation as a whole.

Keeping in mind the underlying corporate purpose of maximizing shareholder value and the pressures associated with that, let us now address the different actors in the corporation and explore who should be held responsible when, and what the appropriate sanctions should be.

EMPLOYEES

Though sometimes it is low-level employees at a corporation that are responsible for carrying out corporate crimes, we generally don't advocate holding them primarily responsible. Certainly, employees should be prosecuted for consciously breaking the law and also encouraged to blow the whistle and report crimes when they see them. But, as we will explore a little later in this chapter, whistleblower protections are generally inadequate in this country. Generally, in terms of deterring corporate crime, focusing on individual employees makes little sense, because individual employees can be replaced, and if the underlying incentives are not changed, there is a high likelihood that the same thing will happen again with other employees. If it is the employees who are punished, management will not receive the sting and there will be little deterrent effect where it is most needed.

EXECUTIVES

Top executives should be held the most responsible, since they ostensibly run the corporation. However, it is important to distinguish between executive crimes that benefit the corporation as a whole and executive crimes that benefit the executives themselves.

In cases like Enron, WorldCom, Adelphia, Tyco, and most of the other recent scandals, it was the executives who primarily benefited, making millions personally while their primary victims were the corporation and its owners and employees. These executives were almost entirely out for themselves. They used the corporate form as a way to get rich, essentially orchestrating a massive transfer of wealth from shareholders, employees, and anyone else who might be involved into their own pockets. At Adelphia, for example, prosecutors have charged that Adelphia executives illegally used tens of millions of dollars in company money to buy luxury condominiums and golf courses. At Tyco, former CEO Dennis Kozlowski and former CFO Mark Swartz allegedly stole $600 million from the company in unauthorized bonuses, loans, and stock (which Kozlowksi used to buy such items as a $17,100 traveling toilet box and a $15,000 dog umbrella stand). At Enron, chairman Ken Lay cashed in $123 million in stock options in 2000 and CEO Jeffrey Skilling took home $60 million, taking advantage of an Enron stock that was rising primarily on the basis of hot air.

In such cases, it obviously makes sense to go after individual executives who used their privileged positions as corporate executives to engage in colossal heists that dwarf even the biggest bank robberies in both scope and size.

Historically, however, the punishment has rarely fit the crime for executives who cook up these frauds.

Take the crooks that went to prison for the savings-and-loan scams in the 1980s, which cost American taxpayers hundreds of billions of dollars. The few executives that were actually convicted of a crime were sentenced to an average of 36.4 months. Charles Keating, the Lincoln Savings & Loan executive who personified the scandals, drove away from the federal courthouse in a chauffeured luxury car after serving just 51 months (four years) in prison. Michael Milken, the notorious junk bond king who pocketed hundreds of millions of dollars in the 1980s before pleading guilty to securities fraud in 1990, was sentenced to a mere two years and three months in prison and kept a great deal of the money he made.

In general, executives who commit fraud are sentenced to prison only 63 percent of the time, and for an average of just

16 months. On the other hand, burglars convicted for swiping about $300 or less serve an average sentence of 55.6 months (four and a half years) and are sentenced to prison 89 percent of the time.[24] In 2002, out of a federal inmate population of 156,238, only 1,021 were white-collar criminals of all stripes (both corporate and individual fraudsters). And half of these criminals were being held at minimum-security "Club Feds."[25]

Shortly after Enron, the Justice Department began staging a few "perp walks" and ordered the Federal Bureau of Prisons to follow a new policy that ensured that corporate and other white-collar criminals sentenced to less than two years would serve at least some time in prisons rather than "community corrections centers" or halfway houses.[26] More substantially, Sarbanes-Oxley extended the penalties for financial fraud crimes, including mail and wire fraud (which prosecutors typically use when it is difficult to make other charges stick).[27] The law also established a new category of corporate financial crime, punishable by up to twenty-five years in prison. In addition, it made it a crime (punishable by up to twenty years in prison) to shred or otherwise tamper with records to obstruct or impede a government investigation.[28] When President Bush signed the law, he pledged that "for corporate leaders found guilty of fraud and theft, there will be no more easy money, just hard time."[29]

Certainly, in the wake of the recent financial scandals, the treatment of executives is beginning to change and prosecutors are beginning to take the problem of executives abusing their power for personal gain more seriously, though there is much more work to be done, as we will discuss later in this chapter.

But what about the executives who are instead complicit in corporate crimes such as pollution, price fixing, workplace deaths, contaminated foods, and hazardous consumer products—crimes that are often more the result of companywide, profit-driven cost cutting than the overzealous greed of any particular executive?

Typically, executives are less likely to be held responsible in these cases. It is usually difficult to tie any single corporate executive to a specific crime because such criminal outcomes are typically the result of a combination of decisions made by many different people. As law professor Christopher Stone has written, "In an enormously complex organization, the responsibility for the acts that say, brought to market a defective car or tainted meat are apt to be widely spread among many men—and machines."[30]

Stone also notes that executives are generally concerned with big-picture things like financial planning, budgets, personnel, and long-term strategy, and more importantly, that "men at the top of the corporation are 'protected' from incriminating evidence not only through the abstractness of their own affairs, but on account of natural screening of 'bad news.'" Additionally, "the law itself often results in systematic insulation of top-level officers from information of possible wrongdoing."[31] In other words, executives often don't want to know *how* targets are being met, just that they are being met. It is up to lower-level employees to figure out how to meet those targets, and if they have to externalize costs to a dangerous degree, that is none of management's business.

As Marshall Clinard and Peter Yeager note in their classic report, *Corporate Crime,* "executives may issue a directive to exhort employees to obey the law, yet they may fail to determine the general level of compliance within the firm. Instead of closely watching the day-to-day activities of subordinates, top executives simply use such output measures as sales, market shares, or profit margins to evaluate foreign operations, all of which tend to put pressure on lower levels of management."[32]

To a great extent, the entire driving force of the corporation—to maximize profit at any cost—is behind most institutional corporate crime. Executives will cut budgets for workplace safety not because they want to hurt workers per se, but because they are under pressure to maximize profits, and a cut here and there is a good way to do that. Such is the tyranny of the bottom line that we discussed in Chapter 3.

Yet, to a certain extent, these executives are complicit in the crimes. Lacking an affirmative duty or responsibility for protecting the safety of workers or making sure that meat is not contaminated, managers are free to cast these concerns aside when figuring out the most profitable path for the corporation. But if the laws were changed to hold top executives responsible for ensuring that corporations did not break specific rules, executives would be more likely to take an affirmative stance to make sure that, for example, workers didn't die on the job because of inadequate safety compliance.

Canada recently enacted a new workplace manslaughter law that should work this way. The "Westray" law, passed as a response to a 1992 mining disaster where twenty-six miners died from a methane gas explosion, penalizes corporate officers and directors for workplace conditions that cause serious injury or death.[33] The law also holds corporations liable for crimes of negligence resulting in foreseeable harms to individuals or the public "where the acts and omissions of its representatives taken as a whole exhibit a marked departure from the standard normally expected in the circumstances, even if no single individual has acted with criminal negligence."[34] Expected to come into force sometime in 2004, the law also creates a legal duty to prevent bodily harm to any other person, which industry representatives say could be interpreted as imposing criminal liability for dangerous products.[35]

Another model statute is California's Corporate Criminal Liability Act, which provides criminal sanctions for corporate executives and managers who conceal certain life-threatening and or injury-causing dangers associated with a company's products or workplace setting.[36]

Similarly, in 2002, in response to the cascade of accounting scandals, the SEC enacted a new rule that required CEOs and CFOs to personally vouch for their corporation's financial statements. The logic was that if executives could be held personally responsible for the numbers, they would be more likely to make sure that those numbers were accurate.

On the whole, however, the law could do a better job of enforcing specific responsibilities on executives to prevent their corporations from engaging in certain criminal activities. There are many environmental, consumer, and workplace safety standards that have no criminal sanctions and, as we have seen, weak civil penalties. Establishing significant sanctions for these crimes will not be easy. The automobile industry, for instance, has worked hard to block legislation that would impose criminal sanctions on knowing and willful violations of auto safety laws.[37] If executives faced the possibility of being held criminally responsible, you can bet they'd be extra careful to make sure that their company obeyed the law.

Still, a few points of caution are in order. One is that if executives were held civilly liable for certain corporate crimes and had to pay fines, these fines probably would be covered by some kind of executive liability insurance, and the corporation (ultimately the shareholders), not the executives, would wind up paying. Second, if executives were held criminally liable, prosecution would be difficult because, as we noted, responsibility for any crime is likely to be so widespread and executives are often kept in the dark about potential wrongdoing. Though it is tempting to want to assign blame to somebody, in most cases it is difficult to do so because the criminal outcome often has more to do with the corporate bureaucracy than the actions of any one executive. Still, in certain cases where executives willfully ignore information, it is more likely they can be held responsible.

Third, when it comes to using criminal law to prosecute corporate managers for not providing employees with a safe workplace, recent trends suggest that there may be less of a need for new laws than for a willingness to prosecute. However, there are some signs that this might be shifting. For example, in 1997, the *Wall Street Journal* expressed concern about the "growing number of employers . . . being charged with manslaughter, reckless homicide and assault" and the fact that "prosecutors in 14 states in recent years have sought jail time for employers, sending at least 12 to jail in 1990s."[38]

DIRECTORS

Directors are responsible for overseeing the corporation. Therefore, one could argue that it is directors who should ultimately be held responsible for what goes on at the corporation.

The problem with holding the board of directors responsible, however, is that directors are even less involved in the day-to-day details of the corporation than the executives. At most companies, the board of directors acts like a sort of outside advisory board, a group of experts to be consulted on major decisions. But the directors leave running the corporation to the managers.

Still, directors do have the ultimate authority in the corporate structure; they are the ones who have the authority to tell top executives what to do and to hire and fire them, as well. The logic of holding them responsible is the same as holding top executives responsible. If nobody is ultimately responsible, then there is nobody who will make sure that the corporation complies with the law. Hence, laws like Canada's "Westray" law and California's Corporate Criminal Liability Act make sense for directors as well as managers. Somebody needs to bottom-line the corporation's activities and be responsible for making sure that the corporation obeys the law.

Holding directors more responsible for corporate wrongdoing would force them to become more involved in the corporations they ostensibly oversee. As with holding executives responsible, holding directors responsible centralizes responsibility for corporate wrongdoing, providing a flashpoint for accountability.

The problem, however, is that the corporation is a large, complex organization, a bureaucracy where responsibility is necessarily diffuse. This makes it difficult to legitimately hold directors—or top executives—directly responsible for what the corporation does. Ultimately, the problem is the corporate structure itself, and holding individual executives and directors personally responsible for the criminal outcomes of an inherently criminogenic structure doesn't really get at the root of the problem.

SHAREHOLDERS

One other group we should consider is the shareholders. After all, they are the owners of the corporation. Shouldn't they be responsible for the behavior of the company that they own?

Once upon a time, of course, they were. In the early days of U.S. companies, there were few limited liability companies. Instead, investors could be held financially responsible when things went wrong at the company they owned (though not criminally liable). Today, of course, limited liability is standard, and investors can only lose as much as they put in, though shareholders can often wind up paying for criminal violations indirectly. Meanwhile, investors are such a diffuse group at most companies that it would be hard to legitimately hold them responsible. Certainly, it would be hard to draw a link between a shareholder at General Motors and a defective fuel tank.

But, then again, as we've noted, the corporate focus on maximizing shareholder profits is one of the driving forces behind corporate wrongdoing. One of the reasons that corporations engage in illegal activity is that they are focused on maximizing shareholder profit. Why is it, then, that shareholders should benefit from the profit making, but not bear any responsibility when things go wrong?

Law professor Henry Glasbeek has argued that, although shareholders typically maintain that they are passive, even innocent, bystanders, they should be prosecuted to the extent that they are "receivers of criminally obtained goods, namely the proceeds of corporate conduct that violates legal standards." Glasbeek suggests that "controlling shareholders of violating corporations should be prosecuted whenever their corporation has violated a regulatory or criminal law rule."[39]

Although holding shareholders responsible for corporate criminal activities has the potential to make investing a more serious affair, the problem is that ownership today is both so diffuse and so separate from control, as we discussed in Chapter 3, that there is simply no reasonable way to hold shareholders responsible. Moreover, shareholders probably suffer the most anyway in cases of corporate wrongdoing, since fines typically come out of company profits, not the salaries of executives and directors, and scandal is bad for the stock price.

GOING AFTER THE CORPORATION ITSELF

Although all these groups could be considered responsible for various corporate lawbreaking activities to varying degrees, they are also part of a larger entity: the corporation. And, as we have seen, there are many forces and pressures embedded in the corporation itself that lead corporations and their executives to cast ethical and legal concerns aside in maximizing profit.

Corporations do, in fact, commit criminal acts through elaborate processes, not just individual decision making. So, although it makes sense to go after corrupt individuals when they are knowingly involved in lawbreaking activities and intentionally using the corporate form as a personal get-rich-quick scheme, in most cases corporate crime is the result of multiple decisions spread throughout the corporation. Hence, in cases where there is clearly not just one executive to pinpoint, it makes sense to hold the entire corporation accountable.

As Clinard and Yeager have suggested, "only if the corporation itself is liable will it have powerful enough incentives to establish appropriate preventive, disciplinary, and reward policies to minimize executive and employee involvement in criminal conduct. If the corporation is not criminally liable, executives are encouraged to violate or fail to comply with laws in ways that are beneficial to the corporation."[40]

In the long-standing debate over corporate criminal liability, critics have suggested that corporations cannot commit a crime because they have no ability to meet the standard of criminal intent—are not capable of thinking or intending to do anything. Only individuals can intend. Yet punishing individuals alone fails to address the underlying dynamics and structural incentives that lead individuals in a corporate setting to break the law.

Additionally, since the corporation almost always has more assets than individual executives, the opportunity to seek restitution for the harms inflicted will almost always be greater.

Corporations are regularly fined for violations (though, as we will discuss shortly, it is usually not nearly enough). Some are even prosecuted criminally. Arthur Andersen, for example, was successfully prosecuted for obstruction of justice in 2002. In 2004, federal prosecutors charged Reliant Energy Services Inc. (along with four former or current employees) with conspiracy, fraud, and manipulating the price of electricity in connection with the California energy crisis. In announcing the indictment, Attorney General John Ashcroft noted that "when evidence shows that a company's corporate culture breeds corruption and disrespect for the law, the Department of Justice will not hesitate to bring criminal charges against the company itself."[41]

However, such instances are far more the exception than the rule. Though a January 2003 Department of Justice memo noted that prosecutors should "apply the same factors in determining whether to charge a corporation as they do with respect to individuals," the memo also included a provision that allows for "deferred prosecution agreements," or pretrial agreements whereby prosecutors can decide not to prosecute a company in exchange for its cooperation in the investigation of individuals within the corporation.[42] According to the *Corporate Crime Reporter (CCR)*, pretrial diversions have traditionally been saved for minor cases, not major corporate crime cases. The *U.S. Attorney's Manual*, which gives guidance on federal prosecution policy, says that a major objective of pretrial diversions is to "save prosecutive and judicial resources for concentration on major cases." But the Justice Department's memo extends this immunity to big corporations.[43] "This is a favorable change for companies," Alan Vinegrad, a white-collar defense attorney with Covington & Burling, told *CCR*, adding that it is conceivable that the Justice Department can cut these kinds of deals with companies without filing any public notice that might bring public attention to the case.[44]

And then, even in the rare cases where governments do decide to go after corporations, there is the issue of proper punishment.

Consider perhaps the most massive corporate crime in history, a giant conspiracy in the 1940s by three companies (GM, Firestone, and Standard Oil of California) to buy up one hundred electric trolley systems in forty-five cities across the country (including New York, Philadelphia, Baltimore, St. Louis, Oakland, Salt Lake City, and Los Angeles) and replace them with gas- and diesel-powered buses, monopolizing the sale of buses and related products in the process. This destruction of urban electrical train systems literally paved the way for smog-producing, gas-guzzling cars and buses that have been degrading air quality for more than fifty years. It also paved the way for massive suburban sprawl and all of its negative consequences. Though GM,

Firestone, and Standard Oil were convicted of a criminal conspiracy, they were fined a measly $5,000 each. The executives involved were fined $1 each. Nobody went to jail.

Almost all corporate fines amount to little more than slaps on the wrist. In many cases, they amount to less than the profit gained from breaking the law in the first place. Hence, when corporate decision makers do the math and realize that the chances of getting caught are limited and that even if they get caught, the fine will be minor, the cold-blooded cost-benefit analysis of corporate decision making will tell them to risk violating the law.

At the most basic level, then, it would make sense to enact stiffer penalties on corporations. Assuming a basic cost-benefit analysis, corporations will be less likely to engage in activities that could get them in legal trouble if the fines are more substantial and the likelihood of getting caught is greater.

GOING BEYOND FINES

Although fines are important to deter corporations from breaking the law, sometimes they are not enough. Often corporations also require changes in internal policies and procedures to ensure future compliance with the law.

Such internal policy changes could include requiring the offending corporation to institute an effective compliance program, increasing public awareness by publicizing the corporation's misdeeds (e.g., in a full-page notice in the largest newspapers in both the state and the affected community), and increasing the public's ability to monitor the company by forcing companies to pay a certain percentage of the fines to independent watchdogs.

Law professor Christopher Stone also suggests that corporations be required to hire an independent, public director whose specific mandate is to represent the public interest rather than the interests of any internal stakeholder.[45] This public director would be empowered to recommend certain changes relevant to the crime and particular to the corporation's business. Such directors are different than traditional directors in the corporation, because they would be given the court-ordered authority to require additional reforms.

As Stone and others have suggested, the appointment of corporate monitors or public directors could also help root out specific sources of corruption within a company because individual employees with concerns about the way the company was being run would have a place to turn. By establishing internal reforms, including new forms of communication, public directors could also help government agencies draw up appropriate new regulations.[46] To be effective, however, public directors should be given sufficient time and resources, including staff with the necessary expertise, to determine the source of any particular problems within the company.

In a limited way, this approach to changing internal policies was used in the SEC's enforcement proceeding against WorldCom. Richard C. Breeden, a court-appointed corporate monitor, issued seventy-eight recommendations to address explicit abuses by top management that were instrumental in the company's collapse. The measures involved establishing a "maximum wage" for the new CEO (which can only be exceeded by a vote of the shareholders); placing limits on severance packages; banning the personal use of corporate jets and other property; increasing the frequency of director elections and allowing shareholders to nominate candidates directly with access to the company's proxy solicitation statement; increasing the independence of board members, board training, and board ability to act independently of management; strengthening internal legal compliance controls; and placing limits on outside board memberships by the CEO and members of the board.[47]

The U.S. Sentencing Commission's (USSC) 2002 proposed guidelines for organizations, meanwhile, order a corporation to "publicize the nature of the offense committed, the fact of conviction, the nature of the punishment imposed, and the steps that will be taken to prevent the recurrence of similar offenses." The guidelines also allow courts to order corporations to develop and submit a plan showing how they would prevent and detect future violations of law. Interpreted broadly, the guidelines would allow courts to force corporations to adopt changes in environmental, occupational safety, and other policies.[48] Some in the corporate community have decried the proposed guidelines for encouraging the "micro-management" of corporations, even though the guidelines restrain the courts from imposing compliance measures that are unrelated to the offense.[49]

In certain cases, we would even suggest that certain structural changes in the corporation are necessary to put an end to destructive and illegal corporate behavior. Certain conflicts of interest, anticompetitive behaviors, and illegal practices, we would argue, can only be addressed by forcing corporations to deconcentrate and divest themselves of specific subsidiaries.[50] Bigger is not always better, as we saw in Chapter 4. Just like we sometimes have to reset a broken bone for the body to properly heal, so it may sometimes be necessary to fundamentally restructure the corporation to address the primary causes of criminal behavior.

One such approach would be to force a parent corporation to divest itself of a particular business that is continuously or regularly in violation of the law, or of a particular division that is responsible for using certain life-threatening technologies or producing an inherently dangerous product.[51] These subsidiaries should be isolated and forced into receivership or rechartered as a nonprofit with a limited lifespan so that the technology or product at issue can be phased out over a determined period of time. We can use the revenues from this nonprofit to retrain workers for another job elsewhere, help subcontractors (e.g., tobacco farmers) transition to a new source of income, and attend to any associated environmental or public health costs.

For example, in Chapter 1, we touched upon former FDA commissioner David Kessler's suggestion that associated conglomerates be forced to divest themselves of tobacco corporations as a matter of public health policy. The same argument could be made for other industrial sectors that have seriously harmed public health and the environment, such as the chlorine industry.[52]

In addition, there may be instances where the profit-making incentives that drive corporations to break the law have the potential to cause enough damage to the national interest that public ownership is the best option. As the Justice Department concluded in 1979, "public ownership, or nationalization, is one alternative means of socially controlling certain large corporations, possibly the means of last resort. As a viable alternative in the context of corporate crime control, public ownership should be considered only for those large industries that have become oligopolies with little or no competition and socially irresponsible both to national interests and those of the consumer."[53]

We do not necessarily believe that a crime has to be proven in order for the people to exercise their collective authority to initiate a corporate rechartering process. There may be other goals that justify such action. National security arguments could also be invoked for operating certain industries in the public sector. This is particularly true with certain essential services like water and electricity that we have collectively decided that everyone has the right to access at a reasonable rate.[54]

REVOKING CHARTERS AND LICENSES

In especially extreme cases, where corruption seems endemic and reform seems quixotic, we should take seriously the possibility of revoking a corporation's state-granted charter.

As we discussed in Chapter 1, all corporations derive their right to exist from a state-granted charter; that is, their right to exist is ultimately a privilege that We, The People, have granted. Since governments exist to promote the general well-being of the governed, we would argue that corporations that consistently violate the law and damage the public good should have their charters revoked.

Charter revocation is a sanction that has been endorsed by an increasing number of politicians, including New York attorney general Eliot Spitzer, who declared during his 1998 campaign that "when a corporation is convicted of repeated felonies that harm or endanger the lives of human beings or destroy our environment, the corporation should be put to death, its corporate existence ended, and its assets taken and sold at public auction."[55] Although it is extremely rare that charters of large corporations are revoked, small corporations regularly lose their charters. In 2001–2002 alone, for example, the state of

California suspended the charters for 58,000 small corporations for failure to pay taxes or file proper statements.[56]

Revoking the charter of a large corporation naturally raises concerns about potential harm to innocent employees, suppliers, and customers. Yet such concerns could be addressed through a court-supervised transition process similar to what occurs after corporations declare bankruptcy. The federal government has forced certain union locals into such "receivership" as part of an ongoing effort to root out corruption. In a similar manner, should a court deem it appropriate to force large, recidivist corporations out of business, the corporation's assets could be distributed to certain stakeholders through a court-supervised process.

A less draconian approach—worth considering when a specific industrial facility, or corrupt division of a corporation, is identified as the source of lawbreaking or harm—is revoking the relevant operating licenses or permits.

A cursory review of news stories in the last decade indicates that licenses are regularly revoked to shut down businesses that are considered a community nuisance, including bars and night clubs, liquor stores, adult cinemas, racetracks, juvenile camps, restaurants, fish farms, taxi and shuttle services, hospitals, landfills, gravel pits, tire dumps, and other operations.

For large corporations the process can be similar, although their operating authorities are usually obtained from federal and state regulatory agencies.

In June 2003, for example, the Federal Energy Regulatory Commission (FERC) used this sanction for the first time when it voted to strip Enron and its related affiliates of their right to trade electricity and natural gas after finding the company manipulated electricity prices during California's energy crisis of 2000–2001.[57]

State officials have also shut down corporate operations that blatantly flout the law by revoking their licenses. In July 2003, for example, the Ohio Department of Agriculture ordered Buckeye Egg Farm to shut down, revoking twelve permits and denying eleven others that allowed the farm to operate. "The pollution and nuisance problems caused by this farm during the last decade were intolerable," department director Fred Dailey explained.[58]

Federal regulatory agencies, however, invariably balk at the suggestion of applying this sanction more broadly, especially when there is an absence of significant public pressure. The FCC, for instance, issued a terse denial of a petition to deny the renewal of licenses for sixty-three radio stations operated by Clear Channel, although the company had clearly violated the FCC's good character rules on thirty-six occasions over the previous three years. Among the violations were misleading the public about the rules for radio contests; broadcasting conversations without obtaining permission of the second party to the conversation; broadcasting obscene and indecent material during daylight hours when children are probably listening; and practicing animal cruelty in violation of state law for the purpose of promoting an on-air personality.[59]

As FCC commissioner Michael Copps has noted, "Most people do not even know that they can challenge the renewal of a local radio or television station if they believe that the station is not living up to its obligation due to a lack of local coverage, a lack of diversity, excessive indecency and violence, or for other concerns important to the community."[60] Yet over the past seventy years, fewer than half a dozen broadcasting licenses have ever been revoked.[61]

GOVERNMENT DEBARMENT AND SUSPENSION

For the many corporations for whom government contracts constitute a significant portion of their business, disqualifying lawbreaking companies from being eligible for government contracts can be an appropriate sanction.[62]

The federal government spends $265 billion a year on goods and services, making it the largest consumer in the world.[63] Yet, it is not a particularly discriminating consumer when it comes to doing business with companies that have a criminal record. According to the Project on Government Oversight (POGO), between 1990 and 2001, the top ten federal contractors between them had 280 instances of misconduct and alleged misconduct and paid more than $1.97 billion in fines, penalties, restitution, settlements, and cleanup costs. Lockheed Martin, for example, which won $19 billion in contracts in 1999, paid $232 million in fines for sixty-three violations between 1990 and 2001. Boeing, which received $14.2 billion in 1999, paid $358 million in fines for thirty-six violations. Four of the top ten government contractors had at least two criminal convictions. Yet only one of the top forty-three contractors (General Electric) was ever suspended or debarred from doing business with the government, and then for just five days.[64]

Under law, federal agencies are required to award contracts to "responsible sources."[65] This requirement is implemented through a Federal Acquisition Regulation (FAR), which requires that government purchases be made from "responsible" contractors.[66]

In December 2000, the Clinton administration issued a new FAR standard that stated that a satisfactory record of integrity and business ethics must include a record of compliance with specific environmental, labor, employment, antitrust, consumer protection, and tax laws. It also included a disclosure provision that required that prospective contractors certify in their bids or proposals any violations of these laws in the previous three years. The rule, however, was not mandatory.[67]

Once the Bush administration took over in January 2001, the rule was quickly revoked. Contractors are still required by the FAR to be "responsible sources," but without an explicit standard there is no specific guidance that government contracting officers must follow for applying the debarment sanction. In addition, contractors no longer have to certify their record of compliance with the law. As a result, companies with a record of lawbreaking continue to be eligible to receive contracts.[68]

In May 2004, for example, just months after being indicted for its role in the California energy crisis, Reliant received a new contract from the Pentagon to supply electricity to Army bases and facilities, including Walter Reed Hospital.[69]

There are occasional circumstances in which corporate misbehavior is so egregious that the government will refuse to contract with the company. For example, the General Services

Administration (GSA) banned Enron and Arthur Andersen from federal contracts in 2002 (though by that time neither company was in much shape to bid for government contracts). Still, the GSA did offer a useful rule of thumb in banning the companies: "Suspension from Government procurements is appropriate where adequate evidence shows that a company or person has committed misconduct related to business ethics and integrity, or other irregularities relevant to their present responsibility, and where a pending investigation or legal proceeding is examining those questionable activities."[70]

The GSA also barred MCI/WorldCom from government contracts in July 2003, but not before the company, fresh off the largest accounting fraud on record ($11 billion), had won a $45 million contract to rebuild the wireless network in Baghdad, Iraq (even though the company is not a wireless carrier and had no prior experience in building such a network). Oddly enough, that contract was awarded on the same day the SEC and WorldCom/MCI announced a proposed penalty of $500 million to settle the SEC's investigation into accounting fraud.[71] The suspension also came after the House of Representatives itself signed a new $17 million contract with WorldCom/ MCI to provide high-speed data services between Washington and members' district offices.[72]

By January 2004, MCI/WorldCom was back in the good graces of the government. The GSA lifted the sanctions just three days before the government's long-distance telephone contract with the company was set to expire.[73]

Despite reluctance to use it forcefully, the debarment sanction offers a good carrot-and-stick approach to get corporations to obey the law: law-abiding corporations are eligible for lucrative government contracts; lawbreaking corporations are not.[74] All levels of government should be encouraged to apply such a standard to corporations with which they might contract.[75] At the most basic level, we can ask: Why should taxpayer money be used to reward companies that consistently break the law and harm the public?

Of course, problems can sometimes arise when applying the debarment sanction to manufacturers who are the sole source of specific goods or services. In cases like these, ancillary remedies may be appropriate, such as compulsory licensing agreements that allow other manufacturers to provide the relevant goods or services. Alternatively, a sole-source contractor could be forced to provide such goods or services at cost for a designated period of time.

ENFORCING THE LAW

Now that we have explored different remedies and sanctions that would be effective in deterring and punishing corporations and their executives, we need to turn our attention to a separate but equally difficult problem: enforcing the law.

The problem that we run up against is that, despite its massive impact on society, corporate crime is not considered a law enforcement priority.

Although the corporate scandals of 2002 made the public hungry to see CEOs in handcuffs and put some public pressure on government prosecutors, even that outrage just focused on the very narrow slice of corporate crime—financial crime—that affects mostly wealthy investors. The truth is that corporate crime is a much larger problem than most people understand, and in general, both the will and the resources to deal with the problem are grossly inadequate.

There are a couple of reasons for this.

On the most basic level, "Those who are responsible for the system of criminal justice are afraid to antagonize businessmen; among other consequences, such antagonism may result in a reduction of contributions to the campaign funds needed to win the next election," wrote Edwin Sutherland in his 1949 classic, *White Collar Crime*. This explanation still seems relevant today.

"Probably much more important than fear, however, is the cultural homogeneity of legislators, judges and administrators with businessmen," Sutherland goes on to explain. "Legislators admire and respect businessmen and cannot conceive of them as criminals; businessmen do not conform to the popular stereotype of 'the criminal.' The legislators are confident that these respectable gentlemen will conform to the law as a result of very mild pressures."[76]

Meanwhile, the investigation of corporate crime is often slower, more difficult, and less successful because relatively sophisticated people capable of covering their tracks usually commit the crimes. As Robert Morgenthau, the U.S. attorney for New York City, put it, white-collar crime is "not even discoverable without substantial investigation," and even when detected it leaves a trail of evidence that "is difficult, if not impossible to follow."[77] Also, as we have discussed, large corporations have many layers of authority and decision making, which can make it difficult to hold anybody in particular responsible. Corporate crimes can involve complex chains of command, and it is difficult to pin criminal culpability on any single individual.[78] As Justice Department investigators have suggested, "executives at the higher levels can absolve themselves of responsibility by rationalizing that the operationalization of their broadly stated goals has been carried out without their knowledge."[79]

Additionally, corporate and white-collar crimes tend to be somewhat complex in nature. For example, price fixing is a lot more difficult to prove than burglary. Definitively tracing a fatal cancer to a particular corporate polluter or product can be much more difficult than the ballistic tracking of a murder to a specific gun and its owner. And financial fraud in particular (which can involve a byzantine series of transactions) is often so difficult to prosecute successfully that most federal prosecutors are reluctant to take on such cases, usually preferring to fill their dockets with high-profile drug or burglary cases that are easier to prosecute or to focus on obstruction of justice violations or other indirectly related charges.[80]

These difficulties are amplified by the fact that corporations and individual executives can often afford the best legal defense, whereas street criminals typically can't. As Professors Michael Benson and Francis Cullen note in *Combating Corporate Crime*, "with virtually unlimited financial and legal personnel resources at their disposal, corporate criminals can erect stiff legal obstacles for prosecutors to overcome."[81] Former Enron CEO Jeffrey Skilling, for example, reportedly spent $23 million

198 | THE PEOPLE'S BUSINESS

(a little more than 1 percent of the budget for the entire Department of Justice) on his defense before the government froze his assets.[82]

In terms of resources, government prosecutors are clearly outgunned. The Securities and Fraud Task Force for the Southern District of New York, the nation's leading team of securities fraud prosecutors, has a staff of only twenty-five attorneys, much smaller than the typical corporate defense firm, the biggest of which have several hundred partners and more than a thousand lawyers on staff.

Unless they have enough evidence and the statutory authority to pursue a criminal case, prosecutors will usually settle for civil violations resulting in a modest fine, often less than the profit the company made breaking the law and rarely big enough to serve as a meaningful deterrent. Knowing this, many companies have decided it is worth risking a fine rather than complying with the law. Even when fines are applied, it is often part of a settlement in which the company neither admits nor denies wrongdoing. "By relying on the civil injunction," says Russell Mokhiber, editor of the *Corporate Crime Reporter,* "federal police avoid branding the defendant corporation with the symbols of crime, thus crippling the intended punitive and deterrent effects of the criminal sanction."[83] Corporations often prefer to settle quietly as opposed to noisily contesting and risking reputational damage.

DEVOTING MORE JUSTICE DEPARTMENT RESOURCES TO CORPORATE CRIME

Perhaps the most straightforward way to crack down on corporate crime would be for the Department of Justice to devote more resources and more attention to the problem. Sadly, the Justice Department for years has been understaffed, underfunded, and undermotivated when it comes to this issue.

As a result, corporations and executives have been emboldened to break the law, knowing that it is unlikely that they will be caught. As law professor John Coffee has explained, "The consensus of criminologists is that the likelihood of apprehension is far more important than the severity of punishment. . . . From a policy perspective, this means that the passage of tough mandatory sentences on white collar offenders will do less to achieve deterrence than investment in enforcement and detection."[84]

The Department of Justice's inattention to corporate crime is long-standing. But the last two decades have been especially bleak, going back to the early years of the Reagan administration, when the Justice Department abolished both the department's Law Enforcement Assistance Administration (which conducted the most comprehensive study of corporate crime in history and began to make research funds available for studies on corporate crime) and the Economic Crime Enforcement Division (which provided specialized staff support to local offices).[85]

As David Burnham, a long-term Justice Department observer, notes, "Even a cursory examination of the Justice Department's recent record uncovers weak-kneed, politics-ridden enforcement activities that almost always concentrate on the small fish while allowing the big ones to get away."[86]

After interviewing dozens of current and former federal prosecutors, regulatory officials, defense lawyers, criminologists, and high-ranking corporate executives, *Fortune* magazine concluded in March 2002 that "the U.S. regulatory and judiciary systems do little if anything to deter the most damaging Wall Street crimes. . . . The already stretched "white-collar" task forces of the FBI focus on wide-ranging schemes like Internet, insurance, and Medicare fraud, abandoning traditional securities and accounting offenses to the SEC."[87]

For example, of the 6,876 defendants convicted for white-collar crimes in 2000, most were likely to be penny-stock, "boiler room," and other low-rent scams. As for the more sophisticated forms of accounting fraud, "the data suggest . . . the government lacks the will to bring these people to justice," concludes Kip Schlegel, a Justice Department criminologist who has studied securities fraud.[88]

In response to all the outrage in 2002, the Justice Department established a new Corporate Fraud Task Force in July of 2002.[89] Nominally responsible for coordinating financial fraud investigations among federal, state, and local authorities, the task force included top officials from the DOJ, the FBI, the SEC, and other government agencies, as well as U.S. attorneys for New York, California, and other major business hubs.[90] But the task force was greeted with well-deserved skepticism, since it initially had no budget or staff.[91]

Apart from the hapless Corporate Fraud Task Force, there were few indications that the Justice Department saw corporate crime as a new enforcement priority. The overall increase in the budget to fight white-collar crime in 2003 was just 3 percent—barely keeping up with inflation.[92] The department's 2003 budget highlights document didn't even mention corporate crime; nor was it listed as a "critical management issue" in the department's 2001–2006 strategic plan.[93] Other emerging forms of crime, such as cybercrime, have received significantly greater attention and resources in recent years.[94]

The Department of Justice also failed to convert the Corporate Fraud Task Force into a permanent corporate crime division. Such a division was proposed back in 1990 in response to the savings-and-loan scandal, but it has since received little support in Congress.[95]

A new corporate crime division, if it had adequate staffing, could also track the incidence of corporate crime and develop a longitudinal analysis of the effectiveness of different sanctions and policies (including some of those suggested here). The new department's mandate could also include producing an annual report on corporate crime as an analogue to the FBI's annual Crime in America report, which is essentially a compendium of statistics related to street crimes such as assault, robbery, and burglary. The FBI should also provide a searchable database on corporate crime.[96]

Collecting and disseminating data on corporate crime would be a logical starting point for building awareness and understanding of the problem.

Were the FBI to monitor the extent of corporate crime and its cost, law enforcement officials would be better able to analyze patterns and direct resources.[97] Though the FBI has taken no steps to collect such data, the 2004 appropriations bill for the Justice Department did contain committee report language (though no specific funding) directing the FBI to "to provide the Committee with information about the resources that it would take to produce a comprehensive report that includes all criminal, civil and administrative actions brought against a company, including resolution of the case."[98]

A corporate crime division could also markedly improve efforts to crack down on corporate crime by providing specialized technical personnel (including accountants, engineers, and lab technicians) and by creating a national legal brief bank, which would allow all prosecutors across the country to share strategies and other resources in pursuing corporate criminals. "In effect," suggest Professors Michael L. Benson and Francis T. Cullen, "a brief bank would level the playing field between large corporate law firms and individual local prosecutors. Corporate law firms would have to contend with the collective experience of local prosecutors nationwide instead of just an isolated and overworked assistant district attorney."[99]

OTHER FEDERAL AGENCIES

Corporate activity is regulated by a number of laws designed to control specific illegal acts such as restraint of trade (e.g., price fixing and monopolistic practices), false advertising, tax evasion, unsafe work conditions, the manufacture of unsafe foods and drugs, illegal rebates and foreign payoffs, unfair labor practices, discriminatory employment practices, and environmental pollution. The bulk of the regulations designed to implement these laws are enforced through administrative governmental agencies, including the Federal Trade Commission (FTC), the Food and Drug Administration (FDA), the Securities and Exchange Commission (SEC), the Environmental Protection Agency (EPA), and the Consumer Product Safety Commission (CPSC), as well as law enforcement departments like the Antitrust Division of the Department of Justice.

All of these agencies have the power to fine violators and file civil complaints. But with the exception of the EPA, all criminal complaints brought by these agencies are handled by the Justice Department. Thus, effectively policing corporate crime depends

not just on the Justice Department prosecuting corporate criminals, but also on the enforcement divisions of various regulatory
agencies uncovering different corporate crimes.

However, corporations have had great success in influencing
these regulatory agencies and rendering their enforcements and
regulations largely ineffective.

At the Securities and Exchange Commission, for example,
business interests succeeded in keeping the agency grossly underfunded in the 1990s, thus handcuffing its ability to police
the market. Between 1993 and 2001, the number of public companies skyrocketed and stock market trading volume went up
600 percent, while the agency's overall budget went up just 67
percent and its enforcement staff grew by just 15 percent.[100] The
SEC's total 2001 budget—$422.8 million—was smaller than the
gross annual income of any of the top twenty U.S. corporate law
firms.[101]

As a result, the backlog of pending enforcement cases grew
77 percent between 1991 and 2000, from 1,264 to 2,240. The
SEC's failure to keep pace forced it "to become selective in its enforcement activities," according to the GAO, and hampered its
ability to detect and prevent new kinds of fraud. Meanwhile, tort
"reforms" such as the Private Securities Litigation Reform Act
(PSLRA) of 1995 and the Securities Litigation Uniform Standards
Act (SLUSA) of 1998 removed the threat of punishment when
the securities markets' "gatekeepers" (particularly the auditors,
who signed off on the books) failed to fulfill their duties. At the
same time, the SEC's lack of resources left it virtually powerless
to prevent the ensuing tidal wave of fraud. "What emerged," in
the words of one congressional committee that investigated the
Enron scandal, "was a story of systemic and arguably catastrophic
failure, a failure of all the watchdogs to properly discharge their
appointed roles."[102]

After the Sarbanes-Oxley Act, the SEC's budget was gradually
expanded to $841 million in 2004, an amount that would even-
tually enable the commission to add 710 new jobs to its staff of
3,100.[103] Yet the increase was unlikely to put much of a dent in
the huge backload of enforcement cases. By 2003, there were
2,200 ongoing investigations of corporate fraud, including some

very large and complicated ones, and the SEC's enforcement and compliance divisions indicated in 2003 that they were still unable to open new investigations that they believe are necessary.[104]

At the Environmental Protection Agency, meanwhile, a series of senior career enforcement officials have resigned in recent years, accusing the Bush administration of weakening EPA enforcement, undermining existing enforcement cases, and reducing enforcement personnel. Public Employees for Environmental Responsibility (PEER) discovered that the EPA was referring fewer cases for prosecution and that EPA's criminal field agents (which only number about 120 in the entire country) were being called away to "serve on contingency teams of what they call national security events—big events like the Super Bowl and the Winter Olympics, and the Major League Baseball All-Star Game—to providing a security escort and doing personal errands for then-administrator Christine Todd Whitman." PEER documented a 40 percent dropoff of new cases referred to the Justice Department by EPA under the Bush administration. Jeff Ruch, the founder and executive director of PEER, described an atmosphere of total regulatory capture at EPA: "Generally speaking, the [Bush] administration's agenda is corporate control of the environmental agencies. Corporate control consists of putting lobbyists and lawyers from the corporations in high positions and re-writing the regulations, undermining enforcement and, in the case of outsourcing, replacing the agency's civil staff with corporate consultants."[105]

The Occupational Safety and Health Administration (OSHA), which is responsible for making sure that workplaces remain safe, has also been extremely lackluster in its enforcement, especially in recent years. Between 1972 (when OSHA was created) and 2001, there have been at least 200,000 deaths on the job, but only 151 referrals for criminal investigation and just 8 cases resulting in jail time.[106]

Under the Occupational Safety and Health Act, OSHA is empowered to conduct workplace inspections and issue citations for violations and recommend (to the Occupational Safety and Health Review Commission) civil penalties (up to $10,000 per violation) and jail terms (up to six months per violation).

In practice, however, the average OSHA penalty is embarrassingly insubstantial. Of the 170,000 workplace deaths since 1982, only 16 convictions have resulted in jail time (under the OSH Act, killing a worker is only a misdemeanor with a maximum prison term of six months). Even for willful violations (in which the employer knew that workers' lives were being put at risk), the typical fine is less than $25,000. Since 1982, there have been 1,242 deaths determined by OSHA to be willful violations.[107]

Meanwhile, OSHA has less than 1,000 inspectors for the more than 4 million workplaces that it is responsible for (state agencies are responsible for the rest). One observer calculates that it would take OSHA 119 years to inspect every workplace.[108] Responding to a series of workplace safety debacles under President Bush, Margaret Seminario, AFL-CIO's director of occupational safety and health, has concluded that "it's fair to say that the administration has just shut down the regulatory operation at OSHA."[109]

However, in June 2003, Senators Jon Corzine (D-N.J.) and Edward Kennedy (D-Mass.) proposed increasing the maximum prison sentence for workplace deaths that result from willfully ignoring workplace safety regulations from six months to ten years.[110]

THE ROLE OF WHISTLEBLOWERS

A crucial and often undervalued aspect of effectively cracking down on corporate crime is whistleblowing. In many cases, employees who witness the crime firsthand can do a far better job of detecting and exposing corporate crimes simply because of their insider knowledge. And because corporate crime cases can be relatively complex, sophisticated, and difficult to detect, the use of whistleblowers is often indispensable to discovery and successful prosecution.

Unfortunately, whistleblowing protections in this country are largely inadequate. Whistleblowers usually have to endure significant personal adversities. They often experience physical or psychological retaliation. In most cases their careers suffer great damage. Of three hundred whistleblowers interviewed by researchers for the Conference Board, 69 percent said they had lost their jobs or were forced to retire.[111] As a result, many employees who witness criminal activities may simply decide that the personal risks are too great and keep their mouths shut. As the story of Jeffrey Weigand (the Brown & Williamson tobacco scientist-turned-whistleblower whose life is depicted in the film *The Insider*) revealed, once an employee decides to blow the whistle, there is virtually no turning back.

In spite of these enormous risks, whistleblowers have come forward and been instrumental to the identification and prosecution of certain forms of corporate crime, including product safety violations and fraud by government contractors. As Tom Devine of the Government Accountability Project (GAP) notes:

> Corporate whistleblowers have exposed and stopped countless instances of the food industry trying to make money off of products likely to sicken consumers, such as contaminated government-approved meat and poultry, or illegal drugs in the supply of animal feed that ends up in milk or other products. They have forced the shutdown of nuclear power plants that were 97 and 82 percent complete, by demonstrating that the companies have either colluded with or hoodwinked the Nuclear Regulatory Commission into rubber-stamping facilities that were accidents waiting to happen. . . . They have exposed numerous incidents where incinerators were illegally burning mercury, arsenic, or other heavy metals near residential sites and black churches in the South or even near or next to schoolyards. Those disclosures forced the shutdown of toxic [waste] incinerators.[112]

Congress included a new whistleblower provision in the Sarbanes-Oxley Act that protects corporate employees from retaliation when they report information that they reasonably believe shareholders should know, most notably accounting fraud. How far the law's protective reach actually extends remains to be seen. In theory, at least, it would apply to just about any illegal business activity, since it applies to any violation of law that has the potential to materially affect the company's stock value. Unfortunately, the law does not cover others who might blow the whistle, including government employees and employees who

206 | THE PEOPLE'S BUSINESS

work for corporate subcontractors. As a result, whistleblower laws remain a patchwork of provisions that leave many employees unprotected.[113]

Whistleblowers can and should be rewarded financially so that they are encouraged to speak up. One model for this is the False Claims Act (FCA), which empowers individuals with evidence of fraud committed by government contractors to sue the offending contractor and receive a percentage of the damages as a reward. The federal government is given the first option to litigate the suit once the fraud is brought to its attention. Yet if it chooses not to, the original plaintiff can still pursue the case on his or her own, much like a private attorney general. If the plaintiff prevails, the government wins three times the amount that it was defrauded (triple damages), from which the plaintiff is rewarded a percentage.[114]

Because of the law's success, Congress has periodically seen fit to broaden the reach of the False Claims Act. President Reagan, for instance, initiated amendments to the FCA in 1986 after reports revealed now-legendary stories of $600 toilet seats, $400 hammers, and $7,622 coffeemakers.

GAP's Tom Devine considers the FCA to be "the most effective whistleblower statute on the books," because it provides enough financial incentive for whistleblowers to overcome the institutional pressures that normally squelch any desire to report illegal business activity.[115] When the law (which dates back to the Civil War) was modernized in 1986, annual government fraud collections from the FCA averaged about $6 million a year. In the ten years that followed, this increased to roughly $200 million a year.[116] According to Professor William L. Stringer of the University of Pennsylvania, from 1986 through 1996, taxpayers saved from $35.6 to $71.3 billion thanks to the deterrent impact of the act.[117]

Unfortunately, the FCA addresses only corporate fraud in relation to government contracts. Yet, if the FCA is any example, individuals who witness corporate crime will speak out given proper incentives. Such incentives should be extended to all corporate crimes. Given such incentives, one could imagine that somebody like Enron's Sherron Watkins or WorldCom's Cynthia

Cooper (whistleblowers who were named *Time* magazine's Persons of the Year in 2002) might have spoken up sooner and could have helped mitigate the effects of the fraud at their corporations.

THE ROLE OF PRIVATE LAWSUITS

Where government criminal enforcement and regulation fails to keep corporations in line, private lawsuits can fill the gap, allowing victims of corporate wrongdoing to hold corporations accountable, often through the use of class-action lawsuits.

Although civil lawsuits are an imperfect and sometimes expensive means of seeking justice, when all else fails, for many of the victims of corporate wrongdoing they are an important last opportunity for justice. As Joanne Doroshow of the Center for Justice and Democracy explains, "Our legal system protects us all from injury and disease, whether or not we ever go to court. This is because the prospect of tort liability deters manufacturers, builders, chemical companies, hospitals and other potential wrongdoers from repeating their negligent behavior and provides them with an economic incentive to make their practices safer."[118]

Yet, a corporate-driven "tort reform" movement has succeeded in driving Congress to pass a series of new laws that limit the ability of victims to seek redress for their injuries and harms, emboldening corporate managers to put potential victims of corporate wrongdoing at greater risk. Changes in securities laws in the 1990s offer a useful case study.[119]

In 1993, the Supreme Court effectively gutted the Racketeering In Corrupt Organizations (RICO) statute as it applied to accountants and lawyers for their participation in securities fraud.[120] Then, in *Central Bank of Denver v. First Interstate Bank of Denver* (1994), the Court (in a 5–4 decision) overturned half a century of precedent by issuing a ruling that law firms, accountants, banks, and others who knowingly "aid and abet" securities fraud are not liable, at least under federal law.[121]

In 1995 a multimillion dollar corporate lobbying campaign succeeded in convincing Congress to pass the Private Securities Litigation Reform Act (PSLRA), the only law that passed over a presidential veto during President Clinton's eight years in office.[122] The PSLRA imposed a series of close-to-impossible hurdles for investors seeking to hold corporate executives and accountants liable. For instance, the law imposed a freeze on plaintiffs' ability to discover evidence until much later in the legal process, requiring victims of fraud to first demonstrate a "strong inference" that the defendants acted with the intent to defraud. It replaced "joint and several" liability with "proportionate" liability, which meant that accountants and bankers would not have to open up their "deep pockets" to compensate the victims of corporate fraud.[123] (At the time, the *New York Times* warned that once the deterrent threat of civil lawsuits was taken away, "companies and their agents could make false projections and estimates of future performance, even if they were deliberate lies, without fear of lawsuits by those defrauded."[124])

Three years later, Congress passed the Securities Litigation Uniform Standards Act (SLUSA), which forced small investors bound together in class-action lawsuits to take their case to federal court instead of state courts. As a result, they were subject to the draconian terms and reduced remedies established by the PSLRA, instead of the often more investor-friendly laws of their own states.[125]

A massive upsurge in securities fraud began shortly after these "reforms" were passed.[126] The number of earnings restatements rose steadily and dramatically, from 158 in 1998 to 233 in 2000.[127] In 2001, 270 public companies restated their earnings. In 2002, the number rose even further to 330.[128] Back in 1981, the number was just 3.[129]

Shortly after Enron collapsed, law professor John Coffee advised Congress that these "securities reform" laws and court decisions were the greatest single structural and psychological cause of the corporate crime wave, since they weakened the potential threat that civil lawsuits traditionally posed to the accountants, lawyers, and bankers who are supposed to serve as the market system's "gatekeepers" and internal watchdogs. "For [Arthur] Andersen and Merrill Lynch—and for all auditors, analysts and other gatekeepers—these ongoing cases reveal the fallacy of a concept that had become enshrined in judicial orthodoxy by the early 1990's: the idea that it would be irrational for professional gatekeepers to engage in fraud because they are pledging their reputations, built over years or decades, in vouching for the financial statements or management strategies of their clients," Coffee explained.[130]

As we conclude this chapter, it's worth repeating that there are a variety of actions that will be necessary to adequately address and deter corporate crime. Though some of the suggestions we make here are relatively straightforward, such as more resources, more enforcement, and tougher penalties, others are not.

As a starting point, we need a broader understanding of the true extent of corporate crime. One logical way to accomplish this would be through a corporate crime database and annual report that would remind the press, policymakers, and the public that corporate crime is a major problem that does exponentially more damage to our society, both physical and financial, than street crime. Such a report would also reveal which particular industries should be prioritized for targeted enforcement actions.

Giving government enforcement agencies the mandate and resources to go after corporate crime would also result in more successful prosecution efforts, which would generate more attention for corporate crime, which would stir public interest and outrage, which would produce more public pressure, which would produce tougher enforcement, and so on. Unfortunately, the wheels have been spinning the other way for decades: less enforcement has provoked more crime, which has overwhelmed agencies and produced more powerful corporations more capable of pressuring regulators and legislators into backing off from regulations and their enforcement.

Finally, we need to be smart about sanctions. Different corporate crimes call for different responses, and we need to be smart in deciding how, when, and where to punish individuals, corporations, or both. Corporate crime has many facets and hence many appropriate responses.

In cases where corporate officers and directors are clearly negligent or where they are personally profiting, it makes sense to charge officers and directors. However, we believe that going after the corporation is very important, since in many cases the crime is the result of an institutional bureaucracy and responsibility is spread out among multiple decision makers. But sanctions for corporations are tricky, since corporations are not people and do not think and feel (or, as an old saying goes, they have "no body to kick and no soul to damn"). Though big fines can send a message to corporations that crime doesn't pay, fines alone are rarely enough. Often, internal reforms are necessary to prevent corporations from breaking the law again. In cases where reform seems hopeless, we should consider such sanctions as forced divestitures, license revocations, and even charter revocation.

If we want to crack down on corporate crime, we will have to organize around a set of demands. Since powerful and entrenched business interests will fight even the slightest attempt to alter their activities, sustained political pressure from a public sick of being ripped off, poisoned, and taken advantage of by large corporations is necessary to bring about any reform.

One example of what can happen if a persistent campaign is waged is Canada's new corporate crime law for workplace manslaughter (which makes corporations, their directors, and their executives each criminally accountable for putting workers' lives at risk). In that case, a coalition composed of the victims' families, union locals, and supportive lawyers and academics worked with legislators and federal policymakers to draft and pass the new law.[131]

Of course, to some extent we can only accomplish so much through tougher regulations and sanctions. As we discuss elsewhere, a lot of the guiding pressures that create a criminogenic culture within so many corporations is inherent to the nature of the corporate form. No matter how thorough the enforcement of regulations and how tough the penalties, as long as the incentives and pressures remain, corporate crime will continue to occur, and tougher penalties for breaking the law will only serve as an afterthought, unable to deter the internal decision making that leads to corporate crime the same way that end-of-pipe regulations fail to significantly prevent toxic pollution.

Yet, given that these changes are long-term changes and the threat that corporate crime poses in our daily lives is immediate, we cannot wait for the long term. We must address the problem of corporate crime given the existing version of the corporate form the best way we know how: through tough enforcement and meaningful penalties and sanctions.

We believe that there are few people who believe that corporations should be allowed to get away with criminal behavior, and a broader public understanding of how widespread the problem is will lay the groundwork for building an organized constituency to address some of these more fundamental causes. Cracking down on corporate crime will also weaken the corporations' standing both financially and politically, which will in turn make other, stronger measures more feasible. For these reasons, efforts to crack down on corporate crime are particularly important in the larger struggle to eliminate excessive corporate power.

6 | Saving Our Democracy from a Corporate Takeover

"There are two things that are important in politics. The first is money, and I can't remember what the second one is."

—U.S. Senator Mark Hanna (1895)

In April 2000, future President George W. Bush was shoring up support for his first run for the White House, jumping from fundraiser to fundraiser. But some fundraisers are better than others, and on April 26 a particularly profitable fundraiser brought in a record-setting $21 million in a single evening. One of the cochairs of the event was then Enron chairman Kenneth Lay.[1]

At the time, Enron was still flying high. "Kenny Boy" Lay and Bush were old family friends who had gotten to know each other in Texas, where Bush was governor and Lay operated a natural gas trading outfit whose business model primarily depended on removing government oversight of the energy sector. Lay had donated dutifully to Bush's two gubernatorial campaigns and had encouraged his fellow executives to do the same (in 1994

Enron and its executives gave Bush $146,500, making Enron the largest donor in Bush's first gubernatorial campaign). Later, Bush signed a state energy deregulation bill that Lay had asked him to support. Bush also took Lay's recommendation and named utility deregulation supporter Pat Wood III to the state Public Utility Commission.[2] And, when Enron lobbyists were stymied in the legislature or even with the governor's staff, they would often turn to what was known as "plan B," as in B for Bush. It meant telling their boss to call Bush personally. "We knew he would take Ken Lay's call," recalled one of Enron's chief lobbyists.[3]

Given the access he had received in Texas, Lay appeared to think that supporting Bush's presidential run would be an equally good investment. So he went out and helped to raise $112,000 for Bush's White House bid. Lay arranged for Bush campaign aides and family members to use Enron jets, and he even helped to underwrite the 2000 GOP convention, the Florida recount, and the inauguration. Lay also sent a letter to two hundred executives at the company encouraging them to "voluntarily" give money to Bush. (As one former executive later recalled, "It was more or less required that you participate in the political action committee if you were an officer.") Enron and Enron employees donated $736,800 to Bush in political and related contributions during his political career, making Enron Bush's largest single career funding source until the company's collapse.[4]

And sure enough, upon Bush's victory, the White House doors swung wide open for Enron. Company executives enjoyed at least forty meetings with White House officials in 2001 and met a total of seventy-two times with officials from various federal departments and agencies, including the Commerce Department, the Treasury Department, the Commodity Futures Trading Commission, the Federal Energy Regulatory Commission, the Export-Import Bank, and the Overseas Private Investment Corporation (OPIC).[5] Lay and other Enron officials privately advised Vice President Cheney in six closed-door energy policy meetings, exerting influence on an energy policy that read like an Enron wish-list with its commitments to further deregulation of the electricity industry.[6]

Enron also got its man from Texas, Pat Wood III, nominated as head of the Federal Energy Regulatory Commission (FERC), which is responsible for overseeing the energy sector. Wood replaced the former FERC chair Curtis Hebert Jr. In an early 2001 telephone call, Lay told Hebert that Enron would support him only if he backed a national push for further deregulation. "When I told [Lay] that I didn't think it was the right thing to do and also that there was no legal basis for it under the federal power act, he told me that he and his company, Enron, could no longer support me as chairman," Hebert told the *New York Times*. By August 2001, Hebert was gone.[7]

Enron also obtained favors from the Bush administration for its operations around the world. Top officials from the National Security Council, as well as Vice Precident Dick Cheney and Secretary of State Colin Powell, pressured high government officials in India on behalf of Enron's Dabhol electricity plant, which even the World Bank had concluded was "not economically viable" because it would produce too much power at too high a price for the Indian state of Maharashtra. In total, Enron received more than $7 billion in subsidies and loans from taxpayer-financed international finance institutions such as OPIC.[8]

All in all, more than fifty administration officials had some kind of connection to Enron, including Lawrence Lindsey, a former Enron consultant turned top Bush economic advisor; Robert Zoellick, a former paid consultant to Enron who was appointed as U.S. Trade Representative; and Thomas White, former head of Enron Electricity Services (EES), who was appointed Secretary of the Army.[9] Even after leaving EES (which was accused of manipulating electricity rates in California) for the Army, White had seventy-seven documented phone calls with company insiders and sold millions in Enron stock shortly before the company's collapse.[10] Lindsey and White both resigned two years after being sworn in, dogged by their own controversies and feuds.

Of course, Enron didn't donate only to the Bush administration. The company showered plenty of money on senators and congressmen, too. One of the company's best investments was former Texas senator Phil Gramm (R), the man behind the 2000 Commodities Futures Modernization Act. This act was attached as a little-scrutinized rider to a 1,100-page appropriations bill. The provision essentially enabled Enron to operate an energy trading subsidiary without federal oversight, which allowed Enron to use whatever pricing model it felt like using in its energy derivatives business. This was one of many techniques that Enron used to inflate its earnings.[11] Gramm received $97,350 of Enron money between 1989 and Enron's collapse.[12]

Enron also gave $11,000 to former president Bill Clinton's presidential campaign, and Clinton's ambassador to India regularly reported on the Dahbol situation to Lay.[13] According to *Time* magazine, "long before Cheney's task force met with Enron officials and included their ideas in Bush's energy plan, Clinton's energy team was doing much the same thing."[14]

Enron also spent more than $3 million on thirty-six registered lobbyists at fourteen different lobbying firms.[15] The last report the Enron Political Action Committee filed with the Federal Election Commission is 967 pages long.[16]

To measure the effect of government regulation on its business, Enron set up a computer program that would calculate the cost of federal rule changes. Employees called it "the matrix." When the cost of a rule change was too high, that was the signal for Enron to mobilize its lobbyists and for executives to make some key phone calls. It was the epitome of cost-benefit analysis applied to political influence peddling.[17]

Though Enron was a particularly egregious tale of corporate influence peddling, it was, and is, far from an anomaly. The same story has been played out time and again in Washington before and since Enron's demise. It doesn't matter what industry's interests are at stake—the archetypal story is the same over and over. Big corporation donates lots of money to campaign of a senator. The senator, knowing that the corporation's money is needed to help win the election, cozies up to the corporation and makes all kinds of promises about how he or she will support policies that benefit the corporation. Once elected, the senator is bombarded with calls and requests for meetings with lobbyists representing the corporation. So, the senator listens to the corporate lobbyists, and absent a compelling reason to do otherwise, goes along with the corporate position, knowing that doing so means more support in the next election. Sometimes, a senator will even introduce a bill whose text is written by corporate lobbyists.

At the risk of stating the obvious, this is a serious problem for our democracy. This corporate stranglehold on the electoral process means that corporate voices are drowning out citizen voices and explains why legislation coming out of Washington often reads like it was ripped straight out of a playbook written by the Business Roundtable. It also means that any serious attempt to regulate corporations and curb corporate abuses is up against incredible odds, since politicians generally don't like to upset their biggest donors.

As we continue this chapter, we will probe deeper into this basic storyline in order to understand what can be done. We will look at how corporate money helps determine who gets elected and what they do when elected. We will also look at some of the more complicated and insidious ways that corporations influence and shape the political debate in Washington. Finally, we will examine how we can take back our democracy, evaluating different approaches to campaign finance and lobbying reform.

GETTING ELECTED

Over the years, the process of getting elected has become distorted by the introduction of massive amounts of money into political campaigns, particularly in the case of candidates for federal office. Between 1990 and 2000, combined congressional campaign spending per election cycle doubled in real dollars, from $445.2 million to $998.5 million.[18] And that doesn't include the money invested in national parties and special interest groups, which was estimated to bring total election spending in

2000 to $4 billion. For a House race in 2002, the average cost was $966,000. For a Senate race in 2002, the average cost was more than $5 million.[19] The candidate who raises the most money almost always wins. In the 2002 Congressional elections, for example, the candidate who raised the most money won a whopping 94% of all races. This is a rate that has held steady for the last three election cycles.[20]

What this means, essentially, is that candidates who want to run for political office need to be able to raise an awful lot of money, particularly if they are challenging an incumbent. Money is necessary to get their message out. It buys television and radio ads. It buys mailings and signs. It buys staff for a campaign office. It buys credibility with the media. In short, without sufficient funding, it is usually impossible to reach enough voters to win an election. And though we would all like to think that voters are smart enough to see through misleading propaganda, the sad truth is that most voters do not spend much time thoroughly examining all of the candidates.

As the cost of running for federal office continues to skyrocket, the ability of a candidate to raise the kind of money needed to be competitive from small, grassroots donors becomes less and less. Though Howard Dean's bid to win the Democratic Party nomination for the 2004 presidential election did demonstrate that candidates could successfully raise lots of money through small individual donations, the fact that Dean's small donor success was such big news demonstrates just how dominant big corporate money has become in the political process.

In the 2000 election cycle, for example, business interests contributed $1.23 billion to all races, accounting for 75.3 percent of all money spent on elections. In 2002 (with no presidential election at stake), business contributed $1.03 billion, accounting for 73.3 percent of all donations.[21] No other group comes close. Labor, the next biggest interest group, accounted for only about 7 percent of all donations.[22]

The consequences of this are that, in most cases, in order for a candidate to have a shot at winning a federal election, he or she must be able to appeal to Big Business. Thus, large corporations act as a sort of gatekeeper, anointing only those candidates who can demonstrate that their agendas sufficiently overlap with the agendas of big-money corporate donors. Though there are still some congressional districts in the country where it is possible to get elected without selling one's soul to Big Business, big corporate money still makes a big difference.

Of course, there is one other way to get elected to Congress besides having to appeal to Big Business. And that is to provide the money yourself. In 2000, for example, former Goldman Sachs CEO Jon Corzine shattered all campaign finance records by spending about $63 million of his own money to win election to the Senate as a New Jersey Democrat. Other self-financed (and winning) candidates in 2000 included Minnesota Democrat Mark Dayton ($8.6 million), Washington Democrat Maria Cantwell ($7.5 million), and Wisconsin Democrat Herb Kohl ($4 million).[23] One result of this is that the Senate is becoming more and more of a millionaires' club. In 2002, at least forty of the one hundred U.S. senators had more than $1 million in assets. That was up from twenty-eight Senate millionaires in 1994 and thirty-four in 1996.[24]

It stands to reason that, on the whole, the thinking of millionaires will be more friendly to the agendas of large corporations than to the agenda of the working poor (though there are exceptions like Corzine, who is one of the more liberal senators). In fact, many of the Senate millionaires earned their money working for (and sometimes owning) large corporations. At the very least, a Senate that is forty percent millionaires is certainly not a representative sample of the population at large.

AND ONCE ELECTED . . .

The importance of money, of course, does not end on Election Day for most politicians. The focus just shifts to the next election. Indeed, many politicians are now involved in a kind of perpetual campaign in which it's often hard to tell where the fundraising for one election ends and the fundraising for the next one begins. Because these politicians know how costly campaigns are and want to ward off potential challengers, they are continually raising money.

Raising money once elected is a different ballgame than getting elected in the first place. Actually, it's a lot easier, because once a lawmaker is in power, he or she has votes to cast, bills to introduce, and influence to peddle. There are always pending matters of great concern to some industry or another, and there are always opportunities to influence policy.

Do campaign contributions buy votes? Not directly. That would amount to illegal bribery. But, in the aggregate, take any major vote for which an industry's interest is at stake and tally up how much that industry gave to both the nays and yeas and a pattern of influence will inevitably emerge

For example, in March 2002, the Senate voted on a proposal to raise the Corporate Average Fuel Economy (CAFE) standard to 36 miles per gallon by 2015, up from the current level of 20.4 miles per gallon, the lowest level since 1980. Though the proposal would have been a clear way to reduce pollution and dependence on foreign oil, powerful automakers opposed it, claiming that investing in the technology required for improved fuel economy would prove too costly. The proposal was defeated by a 62 to 38 margin. The 62 senators who voted against raising standards had received an average of $18,800 from auto companies. The 38 senators who supported the proposal averaged $5,590.[25]

Or consider the July 2002 Senate vote on whether to ship 77,000 metric tons of nuclear waste to Nevada's Yucca Mountain despite serious safety questions both about the site (on an earthquake fault zone) and the transportation of the waste (even one minor accident could have disastrous consequences). Shipping the waste to Nevada was a priority for the nuclear industry because finding a disposal site meant that nuclear facilities could keep generating toxic waste and not have to worry about storing it on site. The proposal passed 60–39, with a lot of grease provided by the nuclear industry. The 60 yea voters on average received $46,913 from the nuclear industry. The 39 senators who voted nay received an average of $17,687.[26]

Obviously, the list could go on, and it does.[27] But trying to detect a pattern of quid pro quo corruption only tells part of the story.

There is a saying in Washington that money doesn't buy votes; it buys access. After all, a legislator is a lot more likely to accept a meeting with a representative of a large corporation that has been a generous campaign donor over the years than he or she would be to accept a meeting with an ordinary citizen who has no real money or influence to offer. Legislators are generally busy people concerned with maintaining their position of power. They tend to prioritize meetings with the people who can help them most.

The representatives of these corporations, usually registered lobbyists, work hard to get those meetings. That is their job. And though they use a variety of tactics to get face time with lawmakers, the best tactic of all is being the representative of a client who has given money in the past and is likely to do so again in the future. As Howard Marlowe, the former president of the American League for Lobbyists, has put it, "We don't get access due to our ability or our knowledge of the issues, we get it with money. As a result, we spend way too much time trying to figure out how to buy access."[28]

Once access has been purchased, the lobbyist has an opportunity to convince the legislator and/or his or her staff why they should support the position advocated by the corporation that the lobbyist represents. These lobbyists, of course, are professionals at persuading elected officials and their staff. They often come armed with customized supporting documents, such as studies generated by corporate-funded think tanks to back up their positions or "grassroots" petitions generated by phony corporate-funded "citizens" groups. Sometimes corporate executives join lobbyists in these meetings.

Journalist Jeffrey H. Birnbaum offers this explanation of lobbying in his 1992 classic on Washington lobbying, *The Lobbyists:*

> The lobbyists' trade bears close similarity to the ancient board game Go, the object of which is to surround the

enemy completely, cut him off from any avenue of escape, and thus defeat him. Blocking the decision-maker at every turn is the object of any successful lobbying campaign. Equally important is not to allow the decision maker to know he or she is being entrapped. . . .

. . . The fact that lobbyists are everywhere, all the time, has led official Washington to become increasingly sympathetic to the corporate cause. This is true among Democrats as well as among Republicans. . . .

Lawmakers' workdays are filled with meetings with lobbyists, many of whom represent giant corporations. And their weekends are stocked with similar encounters. . . . Contends one congressional aide: "Who do these guys hang out with? Rich people. If you spend your time with millionaires, you begin to think like them." Lobbyists provide the prism through which government officials often make decisions.[29]

Though money is the main tool of lobbyists, there are also other means of gaining access and influence.

One way is through personal connections. A look at the top lobbying firms in Washington reveals a who's who of former congressmen, ex-congressional staffers, and the family and friends of current elected officials. Prominent lobbyists include former Senate majority leader Bob Dole (R-Kans.) and former representative Bob Livingston (R-La.), who was once almost Speaker of the House. According to the *Wall Street Journal*, 40 percent of the members of Congress who were defeated in the 1992 elections went on to work for lobbying firms. Between 1988 and 1993, 42 percent of all permanent Senate committee staff directors became lobbyists. For the House side, the rate was 34 percent.[30] According to the Center for Public Integrity, at least twenty-seven of the top one hundred Clinton administration officials have either lobbied on behalf of corporate or individual clients or joined law firms that also lobby.[31]

Meanwhile, a growing number of lobbyists these days are relatives of current members of Congress. A recent *Los Angeles Times* examination of lobbyist reports, financial disclosure forms, and dozens of other state and federal records found that "at least 17 senators and 11 members of the House have family members who lobby or work as consultants on government relations, most in Washington and often for clients who rely on the related lawmakers' goodwill."[32] For example, John Breaux Jr., son of Senator John Breaux (D-La.), reported nearly $1 million in lobbying and consulting fees during his first two years of being in business, including $160,000 from DaimlerChrysler to lobby against higher fuel-efficiency rules, among other things. Sen. Breaux, initially undecided, wound up voting against the fuel-efficiency rules.[33]

Spouses are also increasingly playing the role of lobbyist. As the *Washington Monthly* described it in a recent article, "You don't hear much about these spousal contretemps anymore, but not because they've disappeared. Rather, such symbiotic relationships have simply become institutionalized. No longer peddling cosmetics, many congressional wives are now full-fledged members of D.C.'s access business."[34]

Lobbyists and their corporate clients also provide plenty of weekend getaways for members of Congress and their staff. Though a 1996 lobbying reform bill banned lawmakers and their staffers from accepting privately financed junket vacations, corporate donors get around this with a loophole that allows for elected officials to attend "fact-finding" missions or conferences where they are to be a speaker or a panelist.[35]

Corporations also employ an army of trade associations, public relations specialists, and consultants who work to generate phone calls and letters and manipulate public opinion on issues. As Birnbaum explains, "Thanks to Washington-based direct-mail and telemarketing wizardry, corporations can solicit letters and phone calls from voters in any district in the nation. And clever Washington-based lobbyists know the best way to guarantee their point of view will be heard is to take constituents with them when they go to speak to members of Congress."[36]

Corporations also fund countless think tanks to generate research to legitimize otherwise outlandish positions. As *TomPaine.Com* reports, "The Economic Strategy Institute (funding from UPS) opposes foreign competition in the express-mail market. The Alexis de Tocqueville Institute (money from Microsoft)

says open source-code for software is a threat to national security. And a favorite of the Bush administration, the Competitive
Enterprise Institute (big bucks from Big Tobacco), actually ad-
vises Americans to 'Light up,' giving a filter-tipped finger, as it
were, to a health-obsessed government."[37] In a city that thrives
on information and spin, Washington corporate lobbyists are
providing plenty of both.

How big is the Washington, D.C., lobbying and influence industry? Though many people follow the industry, few have a
good handle on how big it actually is. This is primarily because
lobbying and influence constitute such a sprawling enterprise
that it is difficult to determine who should count as part of it
and even more difficult to then actually count them.

One could begin with a list of registered lobbyists. Between
1998 and 2002, the number of lobbyists registered with the secretary of the Senate averaged 19,100.[38] That amounts to almost
36 full-time lobbyists for each member of Congress, far more
than most members have on their own staff.

But that only tells part of the story. That ignores the staffs of
these lobbyists, as well as massive grassroots lobbying and public relations operations set up to influence federal policy, which
are not included under the reporting requirements of the the
Lobbying Disclosure Act.

Then there are the Washington, D.C., law firms, many of
whom also have lobbying practices. There are 8,000 law firms in
the Washington capital area, and 77,000 lawyers registered with
the Washington, D.C., bar.[39] Again, how much time lawyers
spend doing lobbying-related work is not always clear, but certainly they play a key role.

In 1994, Kevin Phillips, a former Republican strategist, estimated that about 91,000 people were connected with the lobbying business in Washington.[40] In 2003, political scientists
Burdett Loomis and Michael Struemph estimated that the number probably exceeded 100,000.[41]

What about the financial size of the industry? Low estimates
put it at $1.5 billion to $2 billion a year. A higher estimate
comes from former representative Dick Armey (R-Texas), who

asserted in 1999 that "Washington's lobbying industry, which is the largest private employer in the nation's capital, generates $8.4 billion in revenue each year. If the lobbying industry were its own economy, it would be larger than the economies of 57 countries."[42] Kevin Phillips suggested in 1994 that "the capital region's combined public and private politico-legal payrolls, consulting, brokerage and transfer fees" might be as much as $50 to $75 billion.[43]

How much of that money is corporate? Again, it is hard to tell. Certainly, corporations are not the only interest group that lobbies the federal government. Citizens' groups, labor unions, foreign governments, and other groups all lobby the government as well. Still, the vast majority is certainly corporate. After all, three-quarters of campaign contributions come from business donors. And unlike campaign contributions, there are no limits on lobbying expenditures, which favors those with more money to spend, such as corporations.

UNDERMINING REGULATION

Though much analysis of corporate money in politics has a tendency to focus on elected officials, such a focus ignores a vast alphabet soup of regulatory agencies that are constantly being influenced by sophisticated corporate lobbyists and lawyers.

The regulatory process is often a complicated, byzantine bureaucracy in which a dogged business lobbyist has multiple opportunities to affect the process and in which the average citizen lacks the time and know-how to make sense of the mind-numbing details. And though various regulatory laws may look good on paper, their execution is another subject altogether. Journalist William Greider explains in *Who Will Tell the People?*:

> While the news media focus on the conventional political drama of enacting new laws, another less obvious question preoccupies Washington: Will the government enforce the law? Does the new law enacted by Congress really have to

mean what the public thinks it means? Or is there a way to change its terms and dilute its impact on private interests? Lawyers inquire whether exceptions can be arranged for important clients. Major corporations warn enforcement officers of dire economic consequences if the legal deadlines are not postponed for a few more years. Senators badger federal agencies to make sure the law is treating their clients and constituents with due regard.

Washington, in other words, engages in another realm of continuing politics that the public rarely sees. . . . This is where the supposedly agreed-upon public objectives are regularly subverted, stalled or ignored, where the law is literally diverted to different purposes, where citizens' victories are regularly rendered moot.[44]

The more than 100,000 lawyers and lobbyists who work inside the Washington, D.C., beltway dominate the regulatory system, often supplying the language for proposed regulations themselves. Bolstered by manufactured think-thank reports and "astroturf" (fake grassroots) lobbying pressure, industry lawyers and lobbyists are consistently at the table when it comes to the development, drafting, public comment, and administrative review of consumer, labor, environmental, and other forms of regulation, dominating public comment and public hearings and often supplying their own science and studies.

Corporations also spend directly to influence the decisions of regulators, paying for junkets and other door openers that can help ensure a favorable decision. For example, in June 2003, the Federal Communications Commission voted to ease ownership limits on radio, television, and newspapers, just as the broadcast industry wanted. As it turns out, industry groups and companies had, during the prior eight years, paid for more than 2,500 junkets—providing travel, lodging, and entertainment here and abroad worth $2.8 million—for FCC commissioners and top staff.[45] In the eight months prior to the proposal, FCC officials met with top broadcasters seventy-one times, but only met with consumer and public interest groups five times.[46] The

Wall Street Journal reported on the day of the decision that a Bear Stearns media analyst had helped to write the new media ownership regulations.[47]

Corporations also work hard to get their people into regulatory leadership positions though a business-government revolving door that often puts former industry officials in the peculiar position of regulating their former industry colleagues. For example, Harvey Pitt, who came to head the SEC under President Bush in 2001 after serving as a lawyer to all of the Big Five accounting firms, proved embarrassingly incapable of understanding that the accounting firms might bear significant responsibility for the wave of corporate scandals in 2002.

Or consider George W. Bush's Food and Drug Administration, where chief counsel Daniel E. Troy has been an outspoken advocate of commercial free speech for clients that have included tobacco and pharmaceutical companies. Troy even filed one case on behalf of the probusiness Washington Legal Foundation[48] to challenge the FDA's restriction on the drug companies' ability to tell doctors how their medicines could be used for conditions the drugs were not approved to treat. Troy contended that regulators were violating the First Amendment. Peter Barton Hutt, a lawyer for the pharmaceutical and other industries, told the *New York Times* that Troy was doing "superbly" in his new job. Hutt, who was the FDA's chief counsel during the Nixon administration, told the *Times* that he believed the agency has a new policy, although unwritten, to limit its enforcement actions so as to minimize the risk that a court could find that it had violated the First Amendment.[49]

In fact, under Bush, the FDA invited the public and "interested parties" to submit comments "to ensure that its regulations, guidance policies, and practices continue to comply with the governing First Amendment case law" and do not impose "unnecessary restrictions on speech."[50] Meanwhile, the pharmaceutical industry spent $2.6 billion on consumer ads in 2002 in the United States—more than double the amount spent in 1998. But while the FDA sent 158 regulatory letters in 1998 to companies about ads the agency found to be false or misleading, it sent only 26 in 2002. "Ads are running now that would not be allowed to run in 1998," says Dr. Sidney Wolfe of Public Citizen's Health Research Group. "The amount of damage done to consumers by these false and misleading ads is enormous."[51]

All told, the Bush administration has 100 top officials who in their prior lives were lobbyists, attorneys, or spokespeople in industries they now oversee.[52]

Obviously, the greatest hurdle to effective government regulation of corporations is that Washington has increasingly become corporate-occupied territory. Corporate money and corporate lobbyists are everywhere one turns, and this overwhelming presence makes it very difficult to get anything done without the blessing of corporate special interests.

Still, there are certain ways that the regulatory process could function better to ensure that citizen voices are heard in the absence of comprehensive campaign finance and lobbying reforms. One way to rebalance the process is to institutionalize and strengthen citizen voices in the process. Essentially, the goal would be to somehow make sure that there is always some kind of citizens' group present at regulatory proceedings and hearings and that the public actually comments when regulatory rules go out for public comment (as opposed to what happens now, when public comments are almost always dominated by corporate lawyers, lobbyists, and corporate front groups).

This could be accomplished by creating government or government-sponsored agencies that would be tasked with the explicit purpose of making sure that various public interest voices were represented in the regulatory process. One long-standing idea in this vein is that of a Consumer Protection Agency. Originally conceived in 1959 by Sen. Estes Kefauver to secure effective representation for the consumer (whom he called the "forgotten man in our Government structure"), such an agency could be designed to investigate, develop facts, and present consumer interests to legislators, regulators, and courts. It would also participate in federal agency proceedings and challenge agencies that neglect to enforce statutes passed by Congress. Though such an agency was championed by Ralph Nader and others in the 1970s, the legislation to create it never managed to pass both the House and the Senate at the same time. Eventually, after a House defeat in 1978, the proposal was shelved. We propose to pull it off the shelf and give it another look. The obvious concern in creating such an agency is that it, too, would be overwhelmed by corporate interests. This is certainly a risk, given the current atmosphere in Washington. Still, such an agency, managed with a clear mission to represent the public interest and connected to grassroots citizen groups and interested citizens, could work to elevate those important voices that have consistently been underrepresented in the regulatory process.

THE 1970S: FECA, SUN-PAC, AND *BUCKLEY v. VALEO*

Though the issue of money corrupting politics has been a problem throughout U.S. history, in order to understand today's situation, we can begin in 1972, when Congress responded to a series of campaign finance outrages with the landmark Federal Election Campaign Act (FECA), which mandated extensive disclosure of campaign contributions and expenditures, filling in a long-standing gap in information on who was paying for federal elections. In 1974, Congress responded to the Watergate scandal by strengthening FECA, putting limits on both contributions and expenditures and creating a Federal Election Commission to monitor and enforce the law.

But just when it looked like Congress was finally getting a handle on the money problem, a couple of key rulings changed things.

First came the SUN-PAC decision of 1975, a little-known Federal Election Commission ruling that had profound effects on the ability of corporations to participate in federal elections. Under the ruling, corporations were for the first time allowed to solicit PAC contributions from their employees, which in practice has generally meant something a bit more forceful than mere solicitation. The decision also allowed corporations to use their own treasury funds to manage their PACs. Prior to SUN-PAC, corporate PACs had depended on stockholder approval.[53]

Predictably, the number of corporate PACs exploded. Though labor PACs outnumbered corporate PACs 202 to 89 in 1974, by 1984, corporate PACs outnumbered labor PACs 1,862 to 394.[54]

The next year, campaign finance reform suffered a significant defeat that has both crippled efforts to reform the law and opened the floodgates for big corporate money to dominate politics for almost three decades. That defeat was the January 1976 Supreme Court decision in *Buckley v. Valeo*, in which the Court ruled that limits on campaign expenditures were unconstitutional. The reasoning was that spending money is essential to most ways of getting information to the public during a campaign; therefore, placing limits on how much money a candidate can spend was tantamount to placing limits on a candidate's free speech. As the Court majority explained:

> A restriction on the amount of money a person or group can spend on political communication during a campaign necessarily reduces the quantity of expression by restricting the number of issues discussed, the depth of their exploration, and the size of the audience reached. This is because virtually every means of communicating ideas in today's mass society requires the expenditure of money.
>
> The concept that government may restrict the speech of some elements of our society in order to enhance the relative voice of others is wholly foreign to the First Amendment, which was designed to secure "the widest possible dissemination of information from diverse and antagonistic sources," and "to assure unfettered interchange of ideas for the bringing about of political and social changes desired by the people."[55]

The Supreme Court did rule that limits on individual campaign contributions, however, were acceptable, because the state did have a compelling interest in preventing the kind of quid pro quo corruption that could conceivably arise from unlimited donations. However, since a candidate presumably could not corrupt himself or herself by spending massive amounts of money on his or her own campaign, such personal spending limits were deemed unconstitutional. The Court, however, missed a broader understanding of corruption. In clearing the way for unlimited spending, it corrupted politics by essentially creating an electoral process whereby candidates must fight to attract boatloads of mostly corporate money to even be competitive.

Though the decision itself was a confused opinion that spans 143 pages and lacks a coherent unifying vision, it has stood as a significant legal bulwark against all who might attempt to fix the problem of campaign finance by going after the most obvious problem: the out-of-control expenditures that have turned elections into fundraising horse races.

"This single legal decision has shaped the thinking and stymied the enactment of campaign finance reform. Left unchallenged, this ruling has single-handedly distorted our thinking about reform options," write Jamin Raskin and John Bonifaz in *The Wealth Primary: Campaign Fundraising and the Constitution*, a look at the antidemocratic force of money in politics.[56]

Without effective limitations, campaign expenditures have exploded in the last three decades. Congressional campaign spending has increased 500 percent since 1972.[57] The results for representative democracy have been predictably disastrous, and the countless anecdotes of outrages could and do fill volumes.[58]

Two years after *Buckley v. Valeo*, the Supreme Court ruled in *First National Bank of Boston v. Bellotti* (1978) that a Massachusetts law preventing corporations from spending money to influence the outcome of a citizen initiative was an unconstitutional free speech restriction, further eroding the ability of governments to limit the increasingly dominant role that big corporate money has had on elections.[59]

The rise of corporate money in politics, however, is not solely a consequence of Supreme Court decisions. One of the important developments in the 1970s was that Big Business, feeling increasingly besieged by a growing anticorporate sentiment and a rise in the number of regulations and regulatory agencies, suddenly became much more involved in politics.

Between 1968 and 1978, the number of corporations with public affairs offices in Washington grew from one hundred to more than five hundred.[60] According to a 1979 Conference

Board study, "Ninety-two percent of government relations executives polled said that over the past three years, their companies' concern with and involvement in federal government relations had gone up. Of these respondents, 61 percent said that this increase has been extremely strong."[61] A 1976 study found that 92 percent of CEOs were spending more time on external relations than they were in 1972 or 1970, and a 1978 survey found that CEOs of *Fortune* 1000 companies were spending 40 percent of their time on "public issues"—more than double what they were spending just two years prior.[62] As political scientist David Vogel described it, corporations in the 1970s took on many new strategies for affecting the political process, including:

> increasing the physical presence of corporate officials in Washington, using lawsuits as a device to influence the implementation of government regulatory policy, grooming chief executives to be comfortable when dealing with the public, organizing citizens at the grass roots, making more extensive use of coalitions and ad hoc alliances, enhancing the awareness of common interests among diverse organizations and constituencies.[63]

Corporations continue to employ these strategies today with even more force, as we have seen. Each year, it seems, corporate interests are only growing more entrenched in Washington.

If there is any bright spot, it is that abuses have grown so outrageous that public opinion has begun to crystallize on the issue of money in politics. Poll after poll shows that the majority of people think that wealthy special interests (mostly corporations) have too much influence over the political process and that they want to see some reform. For example, a 2002 CBS News poll found that 72 percent of Americans think that "many public officials make or change policy decisions as a direct result of money they receive from major campaign contributors," compared to 13 percent who did not think so.[64] Meanwhile, a 2001 ABC News/*Washington Post* poll that found that 93 percent of Americans "think politicians do special favors for people and groups who give them campaign contributions." Of those polled,

87 percent found this to be a problem and 67 percent said it was "a big problem."[65]

It is this public sentiment, spurred by the Enron scandal, that finally helped propel the McCain-Feingold campaign finance bill into law in March 2002 after seven years and countless revisions. But McCain-Feingold (which banned unregulated "soft-money" donations to national parties) was only a first step. For the remainder of this chapter, we will look at the next steps to get corporations out of politics and to establishing a true democracy of the people, by the people, and for the people.

CAMPAIGN FINANCE REFORM, McCAIN-FEINGOLD STYLE

The story of McCain-Feingold goes back to 1995, when Senators John McCain (R-Ariz.), Russell Feingold (D-Wisc.), and Fred Thompson (R-Tenn.) realized that something needed to be done about the corrupting influence of money in politics. So they put together an ambitious bill that would have tackled campaign finance from a number of angles. The bill banned PACs, which allow individual donors representing the same corporation or special interest to bundle their individual contributions into one substantial donation. It banned soft money, the large, unregulated donations that could be made to national parties and to lawmakers for "party-building activities." It required that Senate candidates raise 60 percent of their funds from their home states. It promised free TV airtime and discount mailing rates for candidates who abided by spending limits. But it failed to get past a Republican filibuster in June 1996.[66]

Each subsequent year brought a new version of the campaign finance bill and a heated floor battle. In the House, the Republican leadership tried putting various "poison pills" in different versions to sink the bill. But by August 2001, the House had resoundingly passed the Shays-Meehan bill, which banned soft money, on a 252–179 vote. Now it was up to the Senate.

On March 20, 2002, sixty senators voted to pass the McCain-Feingold campaign reform bill, and President Bush promised to sign the bill into law.[67] Public interest groups who had been working for years to enact some kind of campaign finance reform cheered. "Americans have won an historic victory to help bring our government back to the people," said Scott Harshbarger, president of Common Cause, one of the major groups behind the campaign finance legislation.[68]

The bill that was ultimately approved by both houses of Congress closed the "soft money" loophole, which had allowed large and unregulated donations to flow to political parties. Soft money donations to the two parties had grown dramatically in the 1990s, jumping from $86.1 million in 1992 to $262 million just four years later.[69] The law also banned organizations such as corporations, unions, nonprofits, and other interest groups from airing so-called "issue ads" using soft money within thirty days of a primary or sixty days of a general election.

However, the law doubled the limits on individual "hard money" donations to candidates from $1,000 to $2,000. And since only 0.11 percent of political donors gave the $1,000 maximum in 2002 and these donations accounted for 55.5 percent of candidates' individual fundraising, raising these limits only made these $1,000 donors (most of whom are connected to corporations) more influential.[70] The law also raised the limit on what an individual can give to all federal candidates and political parties from $25,000 a year to $95,000 per two-year election cycle, another generous nod to the wealthiest and generally corporate-connected donors. PACs were left to live another day.

On March 27, President Bush signed the Bipartisan Campaign Reform Act (BCRA) into law with little fanfare. There was no ceremony, and no cameras were present. Shortly after signing the bill, Bush boarded Air Force One and began a two-day, three-state tour to raise $4 million for Republican candidates and his party. When asked later that day in Greenville, South Carolina, if it was inappropriate to be engaging in soft money fundraising that would soon become illegal, Bush retorted, "I'm not going to lay down my arms."[71]

The Democrats, meanwhile, took in $12 million in soft money contributions of their own on March 22—two days after the Senate passed the bill. The money came from two Hollywood executives. Haim Saban, the creator of the *Teenage Mutant Ninja Turtles*, donated $7 million; Steve Bing, a writer and producer responsible for such Hollywood blockbusters as *Kangaroo Jack*, gave $5 million.[72]

On November 6, 2002, the BCRA and its ban on soft money went into effect. But so far, there has been little noticeable decline in money in politics. With the soft money loophole closed, special interests have simply found new ways of using money to influence electoral outcomes. One was through so-called "527" groups (named for a section in the tax code), which engage in election-related activities such as issue ads or get-out-the-vote drives, essentially accomplishing activities that had previously been funded by soft money. Public Citizen found that in the 2002 midterm congressional elections, the 170 leading 527 groups had raised at least $115.5 million between them.[73] The Center for Public Integrity, meanwhile, reported in September 2003 that 527 groups had accounted for almost $450 million in spending since 2000.[74] Though initially dominated by Democratic-leaning organizations, Republicans quickly caught on. According to the Center for Public Integrity, in 2003 the Republican Governors Association, a 527 group, "attracted six-figure donations from drug companies Pfizer Inc., Bristol Myers Squibb Co., and GlaxoSmithKline . . . along with tens of thousands from financial services firms and energy companies."[75] As we write this, the Federal Elections Commission (FEC) is still deciding what rules should apply to 527 groups.

Additionally, since the passage of the BCRA, the Federal Elections Commission (which enforces this new law) has issued rulings that undermine parts of the law. According to Rep. Shays, who filed a lawsuit in October 2002 along with other sponsors of BCRA to overturn the FEC's rulings, the agency allowed national parties to set up sham affiliates and spend soft money as "independent" groups, narrowed the ban on soft money solicitations by parties and candidates so that the ban covers only explicit "asks," and issued regulations that "open the door to candidate and officeholder Leadership PACs continuing to receive and spend soft money."[76]

Another change that helped candidates raise more money came in January 2003, when House Majority Leader Tom DeLay (R-Texas) pushed through changes to ethics restrictions that had prevented members from accepting free trips and lodging in connection with charity events. In April 2003, after some bad publicity, DeLay and other representatives spent their congressional spring break on a corporate-sponsored vacation to Key Largo's exclusive Ocean Reef Club as part of an ostensible fundraising event for the DeLay Foundation for Kids.[77] In 2004, DeLay went a step further when another of his charities, Celebrations for Children Inc., sent out brochures advertising that the organization's "marquee" event would be the Republican National Convention in New York. For $500,000, donors would get a private dinner before and after the convention with DeLay and colleagues, as well as with high-level staffers.[78] However, Delay ultimately decided to cancel the New York City event, claiming that the city was too expensive.[79]

Events since the 2002 passage of the BCRA indicate that dealing with campaign finance one loophole at a time will not be a particularly effective strategy to significantly reduce the amount of money out of politics. As Justices John Paul Stevens and Sandra Day O'Connor noted in upholding the constitutionality of the BCRA, "Money, like water, will always find an outlet. What problems will arise, and how Congress will respond, are concerns for another day."[80]

The simple truth seems to be that the BCRA was a mere band-aid for a wounded democracy in need of major surgery. As long as the cost of getting elected remains exorbitant, only candidates who pander to wealthy corporations or are rich themselves stand a good chance of getting elected. In order to fix that problem, we need to enact rules that ensure a fair funding fight and allow candidates whose political positions do not align nicely with big money donors to have a fair chance.

There are basically two complementary approaches to solving this problem. One is to limit the amount of money that can be spent on a campaign. Reasonable limits on expenditures would level the playing field, eliminate the fundraising and advertising wars that dominate current campaigns, and restore the importance of stump speeches, debates, and other more substantive modes of campaigning. The other approach is to provide a publicly funded substitute for the big corporate money that currently dominates elections. If qualifying candidates could receive public funding for their campaigns, they wouldn't need to raise loads of money to be competitive. As a result, they would be less tied to corporate or other special interests when elected, and less dependent on them to get reelected.

CAPS ON EXPENDITURES: REVERSING *BUCKLEY v. VALEO*

Probably the surest way to limit the influence of money in politics is to limit the money in politics. After all, if there were spending limits on elections, candidates would raise less money. If candidates raised less money, they would have less need to pander to big corporate interests. And if they had less need to pander to big corporate interests, they would be better able (and qualified) to legislate in the public interest.

But although the solution seems simple, there is a formidable obstacle: namely, the standing Supreme Court interpretation of the First Amendment. As we discussed earlier, in the 1976 *Buckley v. Valeo* decision, the Court majority ruled that a federal election law that capped political campaign expenditures (including independent expenditures) was an unconstitutional restriction on free speech. The reasoning was that since spending money is an essential part of disseminating political messages, the First Amendment prevents such expenditures from being regulated unless there is an overwhelming public interest reason to do so.

But as the *New York Times* observed in a 1998 editorial entitled "Time to Rethink *Buckley v. Valeo*," "the nation's political system has suffered ever since from that decision, which . . . did much to promote the explosive growth of campaign contributions from special interests and to enhance the advantage incumbents enjoy over underfunded challengers. . . . In deciding

Buckley, the Court's aim was to protect free speech. What it produced in practice is an untenable distortion of the First Amendment and the democratic process."[81]

It doesn't take much to see that the explosion of campaign cash since *Buckley* has severely diminished the ability of most citizens to engage in meaningful political expression. Meanwhile, the influence of large corporations and other big money donors has enjoyed a tremendous boost.

Though it should be clear that the Supreme Court made a tremendous mistake in *Buckley v. Valeo*, how likely is it that the Court will actually reverse this decision? The National Voting Rights Institute (NVRI), which is working to overturn *Buckley*, believes that there is a decent possibility: "*Buckley* was decided on a limited factual record, and the case leaves the door open for courts to consider new state interests that justify spending limits. A quarter century of skyrocketing spending and deepening public cynicism have paved the way for *Buckley* to be reexamined."[82] According to the NVRI, more than two hundred constitutional scholars, twenty-six state attorneys general, and twenty-one secretaries of state or chief state election officials have called for *Buckley* to be overturned.

Both Justices Stephen Breyer and Ruth Bader Ginsburg have expressed a desire to revisit *Buckley*. For example, in *Nixon v. Shrink Missouri Government PAC* (2000), Breyer wrote that "money is property; it is not speech."[83] In that decision, both Breyer and Ginsburg also called into question the distinction between contributions and expenditures, and why limits on contributions were acceptable but limits on expenditures were not. And in *Austin v. Michigan State Chamber of Commerce* (1990), Chief Justice William Rehnquist joined a majority in upholding restrictions on a corporation's electoral activities to prevent "the corrosive and distorting effects of immense aggregations of wealth that are accumulated with the help of the corporate form and that have little or no correlation to the public's support for the corporation's political ideas."[84]

Another encouraging sign comes from Vermont. In 1997, Vermont enacted spending limits on state campaigns as part of a comprehensive campaign finance reform package that also limited contributions and enacted public funding. Predictably, the law was challenged by numerous plaintiffs, including the Vermont Right to Life Committee and the Vermont Republican State Committee. The case *(Landell v. Sorrell)* made its way to the Second Circuit U.S. Court of Appeals, and on August 7, 2002, a three-judge panel ruled that contrary to the logic of *Buckley v. Valeo*, contribution spending limits were okay:

> Fundamentally, Vermont has shown that, without expenditure limits, its elected officials have been forced to provide privileged access to contributors in exchange for campaign money. Vermont's interest in ending this state of affairs is compelling: the basic democratic requirements of accessibility, and thus accountability, are imperiled when the time of public officials is dominated by those who pay for such access with campaign contributions.[85]

Plaintiffs have appealed to the Supreme Court. If the Court decides to hear this case, it would offer an opportunity to reverse *Buckley v. Valeo*.

Another case that could one day head to the Supreme Court comes out of Albuquerque, New Mexico, where a challenge to a 1974 city law limiting spending and contributions in mayoral and city council races spurred the Tenth Circuit Court of Appeals to halt enforcement of Albuquerque's spending limits for the 2001 elections.[86] A third case of interest is *Kruse v. City of Cincinnati*, in which the Sixth Circuit Court ruled that a 1995 city law that limited spending in council races was unconstitutional. However, one member of the three-judge panel argued that "it may be that the interest in freeing officeholders from the pressures of fundraising so they can perform their duties, or the interest in preserving faith in our democracy, is compelling, and that campaign expenditure limits are a narrowly tailored means of serving such an interest."[87] Unfortunately, the Supreme Court refused to hear an appeal of this case.

If *Buckley* were overturned, it would mean that state, local, and federal governments could place limits on campaign expenditures, which would effectively free candidates from having to raise huge sums of money. This would allow more candidates from a broader political spectrum an opportunity to compete and allow candidates to free themselves from the influence of big corporate money.

PUBLIC FUNDING OF ELECTIONS

As long as *Buckley* remains the law of the land, any attempts to directly limit the money involved in races will unfortunately be unconstitutional. But there is another solution to making races competitive and giving a wide selection of candidates a fair chance at defeating big money corporate candidates. That solution is public funding of elections.

Though there are numerous permutations of public funding proposals, the basic concept is that any candidate who can demonstrate widespread support (substantial signatures or substantial small donations, for example) would be entitled to a public subsidy to run his or her campaign. Typically, receipt of the public subsidy entails a promise that the candidate will abide by spending limits and will reject special-interest contributions. As a *USA Today* editorial calling for full public funding of elections put it: "The simple truth is that campaigning is expensive, and candidates will get the money someplace. Far better that the public, not the special interests, put up the bucks."[88] Candidates in "clean elections" spend more time with voters and devote more attention to the issues, while spending less time "dialing for dollars" and schmoozing at $1,000-a-plate fundraisers.

So far, four states—Arizona, Maine, Massachusetts, and Vermont—have experimented with public financing of elections. By and large, the experiment has been a success.

Maine was the first to take the plunge. In 1996 Maine voters approved a Clean Elections initiative by a 56 to 44 percent margin, providing full public financing for candidates who agreed to abide by spending limits and reject special-interest contributions. In 2000, Maine had its first "Clean Election." The results were impressive. Private spending per candidate dropped 51 percent. The number of contested primaries rose 40 percent. All told, one-third of the elected representatives to the Maine

House participated in the Clean Elections system, and 54 percent of Clean Elections candidates won their races against privately financed candidates.[89]

Arizona and Vermont also held their first Clean Elections in 2000. In Arizona, the number of candidates running for state legislature increased from 135 to 214, with 60 of those 214 candidates running as Clean Election candidates. Private spending per candidate dropped 17 percent, and the majority of elected representatives on the Arizona Corporations Commission (which regulates public utilities and facilitates business incorporation and securities regulation) were elected without donations from the corporations they are elected to regulate. By 2002, approximately three-quarters of candidates running for office in Maine and Arizona were participating in Clean Election programs.[90]

The results from Arizona, Maine, and Vermont have been encouraging. For one, there were simply more competitive races. There were more challengers, more women and people of color, and candidates spent more time doing grassroots organizing and less time fundraising. Public Campaign, a nonprofit organization that advocates for public funding of elections, described the results as "inspiring." The success in Massachusetts, however, was far less inspiring, primarily because incumbent leaders in the state legislature failed to properly fund the system. But the success of Maine, Vermont, and Arizona has inspired other states, including Connecticut, Illinois, Maryland, Minnesota, New Mexico, North Carolina, and Wisconsin, to explore public financing of elections.[91]

Another approach is to use matching funds. For example, in New York City, qualifying candidates for city offices can receive $4 in public funds for every $1 they raise for contributions of $250 or less (based on this model, a $100 contribution would actually be worth $500). The idea is to reward candidates who raise lots of money in small donations. New York City first tried this approach in 2001, and a record number of candidates ran for office. As 2001 New York City mayoral candidate Mark Green reported, "the campaign finance program energized the city's elections—quite a few of the City Council races featured five or more legitimate candidates—and enabled many challengers to defeat party favorites."[92]

On the federal level, presidential candidates who abide by certain spending limits can access millions of dollars in public funds. Ronald Reagan, for example, accepted more than $90 million in public funding in three presidential bids.[93] However, by 2004, both presidential candidates had opted out of public funding altogether, as the cost of running for president topped $200 million per candidate.

The one obvious critique of public funding of elections is that it is a system of "foodstamps for politicians," a system whereby those with the power to tax and spend get to choose how much public money they should be able to spend on their own campaigns. Full public funding of elections also leads to the obvious question of who should qualify and who should get to decide who qualifies.

One way to democratize the process of public funding is through a system of tax credits, such as the initiative that passed in Arkansas in 1996 by an impressive 66 percent to 34 percent margin. Under the system, every Arkansas taxpayer gets $50 that he or she can allocate to a candidate, to a political party, or to a political committee. "Candidates, parties, and organized groups will thus compete with each other for these public funds by working to convince voters that they should direct their share of public financing in that candidate's or that group's direction," explains Zach Polett, director of political operations for the Association of Community Organizations for Reform Now (ACORN). "All Arkansans will be equal in this process, since all will have the same $50 to allocate. And non-Arkansans will not be able to make an allocation since they are not Arkansas taxpayers."[94]

Though there are some admitted kinks in public funding still left to be worked out, such a system would be a definite improvement over the system that we have now, where candidates who can't appeal to big donors right off the bat are often prevented from running serious campaigns and where candidates who do get elected often find themselves owing much to their corporate donors. We believe that if citizens are to gain control over their democracy, it is crucial that more and more states follow the example of Maine, Vermont, Arizona, and Massachusetts and move to Clean Elections.

FREE AIRTIME

Though we would like to see full public funding for all federal elections, we recognize that, considering the mammoth effort it took to get the modest BCRA passed through Congress, such a reform seems far off. However, one intermediate step that shows promise is requiring broadcast networks to provide free airtime for candidates in the weeks leading up to the elections.[95]

One of the reasons for the high cost of elections is the high cost of advertising, particularly television advertising. In 2000, an estimated $1 billion of approximately $4 billion in campaign spending by candidates, parties, and interest groups went to television stations, up from $250 million in TV political ads in 1990. As former senator Bill Bradley (D-N.J.) put it while seeking the Democratic Party nomination in 2000, "Today's political campaigns function as collection agencies for broadcasters. You simply transfer money from contributors to television stations."[96]

In order for candidates to reach a wide audience, they need to get on television. But in order to get on television, candidates need to spend a lot of money. Television stations love it. In 2000, the profit margin of television stations in the top ten media markets was an enormous 46.2 percent (as compared to an average of 6.8 percent for the *Fortune* 500).[97] The next ten markets had a 32.7 percent profit margin, and the ten after that a 24.1 percent profit margin.

At the same time, television stations continue to reduce their election coverage. For example, the three major national networks devoted 28 percent less time to coverage of the presidential election in nightly news programs in 2000 than they had in 1988.[98] And the average televised excerpt from a candidate's remarks fell to 7.8 seconds in 2000, a record low. In 1968 it was 43 seconds.[99]

As Paul Taylor, former executive director of the Alliance for Better Campaigns (which advocates for free airtime), puts it:

> Let's follow the bouncing ball. Our government gives broadcasters free licenses to operate on the public airwaves on condition that they serve the public interest. During the campaign season, broadcasters turn around and sell access to these airwaves to candidates at inflated prices. Meanwhile, many candidates sell access to the government in order to raise special interest money to purchase access to the airwaves. It's a wonderful arrangement for the broadcasters, who reap windfall profits from political campaigns. It's a good system for incumbents, who prosper in the big-dollar, high-ante political culture of paid speech. But it's a lousy deal for the rest of us.[100]

Advocates of free airtime have pointed to the fact that the public actually owns the airwaves. Broadcasters get federal licenses for free on one condition—that they serve "the public interest, convenience, and necessity."[101] But as anybody who has watched TV lately can attest to, the broadcasters do a dismal job.

As part of their duty to serve the public interest, the argument goes, broadcasters should be required to give candidates free airtime in the weeks leading up to the election. The current version of the proposal, encapsulated in a bill introduced by Senators John McCain (R-Ariz.), Russell Feingold (D-Wisc.), and Richard Durbin (D-Ill.),[102] requires that all radio and television broadcast stations air a minimum of two hours per week of candidate-centered or issue-centered programming for six weeks preceding a primary or general federal elections. Half of the segments must air between 5 P.M. and 11:35 P.M. Programming that airs between midnight and 6 A.M. does not count.

According to McCain, "this legislation will slow the political money chase. It will help to ensure that citizens receive the information they need to function in a self-governing democracy. And it will help open up the political marketplace to those currently priced out of it—including candidates who are not wealthy."[103]

McCain and other reformers recognize that free airtime is only an intermediate step toward more comprehensive campaign finance reform. Still, it is an intermediate step worth pursuing.

WHAT ABOUT THE LOBBYISTS?

As we have discussed, campaign finance reform is only part of the battle. Money can purchase access, but a Washington, D.C., lobbying community estimated at 100,000 has many other ways of getting lawmakers and regulators to pay attention to the concerns of their clients. Though campaign finance reform would obviously take some of the wind out of lobbyists' sails, it certainly would not eliminate their influence. And if serious campaign finance reform were successful and corporate donations to elections were curtailed, it stands to reason that corporations might put even more effort into other methods of lobbying.

Lobbying today is a sophisticated mix of tricks and tactics, of think tanks and public relations and phony grassroots groups and weekend getaways and personal connections. This makes it all the more difficult to deal with effectively.

The most basic reform would be full disclosure. Though lobbyists who meet directly with members of Congress and their staffs do have to register with the secretary of the Senate and the clerk of the House, the ancillary mix of public relations and think tank and phony grassroots activity goes almost entirely unreported. All of these activities should be covered by the Lobbying Disclosure Act if they are related to specific legislative goals. Additionally, all groups that do advocacy work on behalf of corporate clients should be required to disclose who their corporate backers are each time they present a survey or a study. Corporations shouldn't be able to hide behind sham grassroots organizations, public relations firms, and research-for-sale think tanks in their efforts to influence public policy.

Another distressing imbalance between citizens and corporations in the lobbying arena is that while corporations can deduct their lobbying expenses on their income tax returns as necessary business expenses, members of the public who want to make their voices heard in Washington (or their state capitals) must pay their own way with no tax break provided. Thus, it would make sense either to eliminate the business tax deduction for lobbying, give citizens a tax deduction for civic participation expenses, or both.

One final problem is the revolving door. Swinging from government to business, it means that many lobbyists are former members of Congress, former congressional staffers, or former White House staffers. One way to solve this problem is to slow the "revolving door" between the halls of government and the halls of "K Street" (the lobbying corridor in Washington). For example, laws could be passed that mandate "cooling off" periods of five or even ten years before deposed lawmakers and/or their staffers can join a firm that lobbies their former colleagues or employers. President Clinton actually enacted such a five-year "cooling off" period for the executive branch shortly after he took office, only to reinstate the one-year "cooling off" period that existed prior to his presidency and that remains in force today.[104] And, as the Center for Public Integrity documents, at least twenty-seven of the top one hundred Clinton administration officials have either lobbied on behalf of corporate or individual clients or joined law firms that also lobby.[105]

Swinging from business to government, the revolving door means that many regulators and staffers come from the private sector. These former corporate executives who suddenly find themselves in Washington often have a hard time separating their duty to the public with their duty to their former colleagues, as Harvey Pitt's recent tenure at the SEC demonstrated so well. It is important to mention here because it is another key way that corporations influence the government—by getting their people in positions of power. This is not to suggest that corporate officials should be prohibited from using their experience to serve the public. However, to make sure their decision making is impartial, we should mandate a cooling-off period that would prohibit government regulators from making decisions that directly affect any corporation for which they had worked in the prior five, or even ten, years.

AT THE STATE LEVEL

Though this chapter has focused primarily on the corporate capture of the federal government, much of what we have said goes for state-level governments as well. Of course, there are differences. Running for state-level offices is typically a less costly affair than running for federal office, which means that candidates are not as acutely dependent on big corporate donors to get elected. On the other hand, in many states there are few limits on corporate support for state and local candidates. So the possibility for stronger democracy in state legislatures does exist, though typically state legislatures are far more corrupt.

In larger states, there is plenty of money floating around state elections. In Texas, for example, statewide and legislative candidates raised $195 million in 2002. And of the fifty largest individual contributors, all but four were business executives. (The others were two lobbyists and two attorneys.)[106]

One key factor about state legislatures is that they typically don't pay very well, which means that for many state-level lawmakers, doing the people's business is a second job. Naturally, this can result in myriad conflicts of interest. According to the Center for Public Integrity, in 1999 more than one in five state legislators sat on a legislative committee that "regulated their professional or business interest," and at least 18 percent had "financial ties to businesses or organizations that lobby state government."[107]

> State legislatures are also far less likely to provide their poorly paid lawmakers with competent, experienced staff. Groups armed with cash throw money into state campaigns, pay millions to lobby lawmakers, and take advantage when lawmakers are underpaid, understaffed, overworked, and overwhelmed. Lax ethics laws and toothless enforcement agencies can't track wrongdoing and, too many times fail to uncover instances of abuse.[108]

One group that takes advantage of the fact that state legislators sometimes need outside help is the American Legislative Exchange Council (ALEC), which serves a kind of clearinghouse for conservative, free-market state legislation that does a lot of the work already for state lawmakers.

The group sponsors conferences and meetings for state legislators, where they are given "model" legislation developed by and for corporate special interests on "issues that range from rolling back environmental and consumer protections to privatizing government services such as prisons and schools."[109] A recent Natural Resource Defense Council (NRDC) report described ALEC as "Corporate America's Trojan Horse in the States."[110]

Though the group touts Jeffersonian principles of freedom, "ALEC is nothing less than a tax-exempt facade for the country's largest corporations and kindred entities. Companies like Enron, Amoco, Chevron, Shell, Texaco, Coors Brewing, Koch Industries, Nationwide Insurance, Pfizer, National Energy Group, Philip Morris, and RJ Reynolds pay for essentially all of ALEC's expenses," NRDC reports. "They funnel cash through ALEC to curry favor with state lawmakers through junkets and other largesse in the hopes of enacting special-interest legislation—all the while keeping safely outside the public eye . . . most Americans undoubtedly would be shocked to learn that many of the state laws under which they live and work have actually been written by major U.S. corporations—not by the state legislators they have elected to represent them."[111]

ALEC members sponsored more than 3,100 pieces of legislation during 1999–2000; more than 400 of these bills passed.[112] ALEC boasts that more than one hundred members hold senior leadership positions in state legislatures and that several governors, including Republican George Pataki (N.Y.), are members. Additionally, more than eighty Members of Congress are former ALEC members, including Speaker J. Dennis Hastert (R-Ill.), House Majority Leader Tom Delay (R-Texas), and Senate Budget Committee Chairman Don Nickles (R-Okla.), which makes ALEC seem a little bit like a corporate "farm team" for federal legislators.[113]

Unfortunately, similar groups organized to support state lawmakers who want to challenge corporate dominance are not nearly as large or well funded. Therefore, one step that progressives could take would be to set up a network of state-level legislators to support legislation to challenge corporate power and counter the influence of the ALEC.[114]

The most promising reform on the state level is publicly funded elections, as we discussed above. Additionally, the various conflicts of interest that proliferate at the state level because of the lax ethics rules and the need for many state legislators to supplement their public service with a second income pose a difficult problem, but the fixes will vary from state to state. In general, though, lawmakers should be forced to recuse themselves when discussing an issue in which they have a personal or financial stake.[115]

Another important issue on the state level is judicial elections, where the amount of money has grown dramatically in recent years. In the 38 states that conduct elections for their supreme courts, the amount of money raised by those candidates hit $45.6 million in 2000, a 61 percent increase from 1998 and double the amount raised in 1994. The funding was dominated by two groups: lawyers and business interests.[116] As we discussed in Chapter 2, corporate interests have become particularly involved in the judicial arena in recent years as they have realized just how important the judiciary is. In January 2004, Tom Donohue, president of the United States Chamber of Commerce, announced that the chamber "will put its clout and dollars into a number of state judicial and attorney general races this year. We're going to pick the ones where we think the American business community is getting an unfair shake because of the behavior of either the governor or the state attorney general or the justices of the state Supreme Court."[117]

State judicial elections are becoming an increasingly important battleground, and the growing money reflects this. We believe that states should implement full public funding of judicial elections so that judicial candidates do not have to rely on the support of the Chamber of Commerce in order to be elected. Additionally, we believe that many states need to improve disclosure laws for judicial elections.

BANNING CORPORATIONS FROM POLITICS

Most of the reforms presented so far offer various ways to chip away at this problem, primarily by reducing the influence of money in politics. But what about an outright ban against corporate participation in politics? Could we enact such a law? Actually, we already did, almost one hundred years ago. The 1907 Tillman Act, still on the books, says that it is "unlawful for any national bank, or any corporation . . . to make a contribution or expenditure in connection" with a federal election. Unfortunately, the act was full of loopholes, and corporations have found many ways around the Tillman Act over the years, including now-illegal soft money contributions to federal candidates, PACs, and the bundling of individual donations from multiple employees and executives. In addition to the federal government, there are eighteen states that ban direct contributions from corporations to candidates.[118] However, as we have learned, there are plenty of indirect ways that corporations can contribute, too.

Still, it stands to reason that if we are really serious about getting corporations out of politics, we should enact a comprehensive ban on any corporate involvement in politics, something that would apply not just to campaign contributions, but also to lobbying and the other influence-peddling activities we have described. Such a law would have to be written carefully to avoid the possibility of loopholes and back channels, as well as withstand the inevitable legal challenges.

Though we recognize that any attempt to ban corporations from political participation would be unfeasible in today's political climate, such a fundamental reform should be the ultimate goal. Indeed, in order for citizens to truly assert their sovereign authority to govern themselves, we must be sure that corporations, as mere creatures of the state, have only those rights and privileges granted to them by citizen governments. Corporations should enjoy no rights of participation in a citizen democracy.

One ray of hope in this area came in April 2002, when BP/Amoco CEO Lord John Browne announced that BP was voluntarily ending all contributions to political candidates around the world. "We must be particularly careful about the political process—not because it is unimportant—quite the reverse—but because the legitimacy of that process is crucial both for society and for us as a company working in that society," Browne announced. "That's why we've decided, as a global policy, that from now on we will make no political contributions from corporate funds anywhere in the world."[119]

Then again, BP still maintains an employee PAC. And when Ralph Nader and Citizen Works followed up and asked all *Fortune* 500 companies in Spring 2003 if they would join BP in agreeing to suspend donations to all candidates, only three even bothered to respond. All three said no.

One of the great problems of our era is the decline in political and civic involvement in this country. Every year, the populace seems to grow ever more disinterested and disengaged in politics. Voter turnout continues to drop and public cynicism about the government continues to rise, placing the very legitimacy of our participatory democracy in increasing doubt.

Though our government has indeed been corrupted and weakened, we do not believe that this corruption is an inherent quality of democratic self-rule. Rather, it is the consequence of misguided policies that must be corrected. We believe that the most effective way to control corporations is to take back our government and restore citizen democracy. The only true power that citizens have over corporations is through the very governments that created corporations in the first place. Though we can affect corporations in our various roles as consumers, workers, and investors, the only sphere where we can legitimately achieve meaningful control over corporations is the sphere of government.

252 | THE PEOPLE'S BUSINESS

If corporations can effectively choose who gets elected and then exert undue influence over elected lawmakers' decisions, as they do today, it is safe to say that the laws will be written and enforced in ways that benefit corporations above all. Meaningful attempts to control corporate behavior have little chance of becoming law when lawmakers are largely beholden to corporate influences.

Therefore, it seems to us that the most fundamental first step to making corporations accountable is limiting their influence over the political process. Only when the people can effectively control their democracy will their democracy effectively control corporations.

Wresting our democracy from corporate control will obviously be a difficult task. Still, we believe that there are some solid starting points that an organized movement of citizens can strive toward as guideposts in the long process of restoring true democracy. Reducing the amount of money in politics is crucial, since most of the money comes from corporations or wealthy donors who are connected with corporations. Our democracy rests on a principle of one person, one vote. This is grossly distorted by the ability of certain factions to spend inordinately more on political campaigns than others.

We recognize that reducing the influence of corporations and their money in politics may likely be a gradual process. Yet, rapid advances can come when large, organized groups of citizens work simultaneously for laws like Clean Elections on the local and state level. Over time, Clean Elections can help to create legislatures that have the courage to control corporations in a meaningful way because they are not dependent on them for campaign donations and not overwhelmed by them in other ways. However, these battles will be hard fought, as we saw with even the exceedingly modest BCRA, and will take well-organized citizen-led movements to push for them.

Ultimately, we believe that effective campaign finance reform is one of the keystones in building a citizen-led movement to take back our democracy. Political activity has been a great motivating force in our country's history, and many of the great social movements in this country have been centered around political parties and political involvement. We believe that restoring the political process to the citizens and making politics relevant once again is a crucial conduit for the broader movement to challenge corporate power.

Though we recognize the obvious chicken-and-egg dilemma—we must free our democracy from corporate influence to build a broad-based movement to challenge corporate influence—we believe the two objectives go hand-in-hand. Campaign finance reform creates the conditions for more citizen political involvement, which creates the conditions for more campaign finance reform. In fact, campaign finance reform is an excellent motivating tool for getting citizens involved in politics in the first place, as we have seen from the hundreds of citizen groups across the country that are already working on campaign finance reform. Like media reform (which we discuss in the conclusion), campaign finance reform is an essential part of the struggle to control corporations. Without it, many of the other reforms we have discussed in this book will not be possible.

CONCLUSION: BUILDING THE MOVEMENT TO CHALLENGE CORPORATE POWER

For the past six chapters, we've explored some of the ways that large corporations have come to dominate our society and our politics, and we have recommended specific reforms along the way.

Now, as we come to the conclusion, we think it is worth stepping back and assessing what our priorities should be, and perhaps most importantly, what it will take to bring about the many reforms we've discussed.

These are difficult questions, and we don't pretend to have definitive answers. But we believe that one thing is certain. None of the reforms we have proposed will come about without strong organizing efforts, continuous on-the-ground experimentation, and an ever-evolving assessment of the strengths and weaknesses of each particular approach. To free our economy, culture, and politics from the grip of giant corporations, we will have to organize a large, diverse, and well-organized movement.

In this chapter, we offer some thoughts on how we can organize such a movement to challenge corporate power, what the obstacles to building such a movement might be, and also what some of the most promising starting points may be.

THINKING AND ACTING LOCALLY AND GLOBALLY

As we begin to sketch out a plan of action, we believe it is appropriate to start by asking at what level we should focus our efforts: local, state, national, or global? The answer, we believe, is a balance of all four. Too much focus on the local level loses sight of the fact that much political power is centered in Washington, D.C. (both within the federal government and within the institutions of corporate globalization); but too much focus on Washington, D.C., loses sight of the fact that there are more opportunities for democracy when decision-making power is exercised at the local level. Though many of the reforms in this book are framed in terms of national policy proposals, few will occur without strong grassroots pressure. And many could and should be adapted to the local and state levels.

Across the country, many local communities continue to organize in resistance to giant chain stores like Wal-Mart, predatory lenders, factory farms, private prisons, incinerators and landfills, the planting of genetically modified organisms, and nuclear power plants. Local communities are continuously organizing to strengthen local businesses,[1] raise the living wage,[2] resist predatory marketing in schools,[3] cut off corporate welfare,[4] and protect essential services such as water from privatization.[5] Local struggles are crucial for recruiting citizens to the broader struggle against corporate rule.

However, it's often quite easy to get caught up in the demands of local organizing without connecting with other communities or building a deeper movement that confronts the same corporations elsewhere. Many local victories have simply pushed corporate developers upon neighboring communities or have been overturned because citizens were unprepared to defend their decision-making rights in the courts. Corporations are well positioned to defend their rights at whatever level the struggle takes them. Are we?

Housing rights activist and movement historian Randy Shaw has suggested that the most successful campaigns of the 1990s were fought at both the local and national level, with solid coordination between the two. Many struggles were undermined, however, by the lack of a multidimensional organizing strategy. As "the constituencies central to reclaiming America's progressive ideals bypass national fights to pursue local issues, their adversaries have faced surprisingly little opposition in dismantling federal programs achieved by six decades of national grassroots struggle," writes Shaw. "Citizen activists and organizations have steadfastly maintained their local focus even as national policy making drastically cut the resources flowing to communities. From 1979 to 1997, for example, federal aid to local communities for job training, housing, mass transit, environmental protection, and economic development fell by almost one trillion dollars. . . . I believe citizen activists and organizations cannot reclaim America's progressive ideals by pouring all their efforts into local issues."[6]

Robert Fisher, in his analysis of neighborhood organizing in America, has similarly cautioned that unless local activism is connected to a national movement, it "will win limited reforms but not address the continued incidence of powerlessness, prejudice and poverty in the United States."[7] Fisher hoped for the emergence of a federated national organization that could unify grassroots activity in local communities. But this entity never developed.

Local community struggles are most successful when they unite around state or national policies that place structural restraints on corporations. One example of a multidimensional campaign that combined local, national, and even global activism for many victories is the grassroots environmental movement's struggle to fight waste disposal facilities. Among the many successes of this multi-decade struggle is a U.S. moratorium on the construction of new hazardous waste incinerators. This victory came only after communities across the country banded together in the early 1990s into a loose-knit alliance, using specific struggles, such as the battle of the people of East Liverpool, Ohio, against the WTI hazardous waste incinerator, to highlight the dangers of these dioxin-spewing machines, the disproportionate targeting of low-income communities (especially communities of color), and the failure of government regulators. With support from groups like Greenpeace and Lois Gibbs' Center for Health, Environment & Justice, the campaign peaked in a joint act of civil disobedience in front of the White House in May of 2003. The day after the protest, the EPA enacted an eighteen-month moratorium on the construction of these "death machines."[8]

Another example of how citizens can cement local victories in government policy comes from Nebraska's farmers, who in 1982 succeeded in passing a statewide ban on corporate farms that has stood ever since, despite corporate challenges. The law came into effect after the Nebraska Farmers Union used the citizen initiative process to gather more than 57,000 signatures in support of the state prohibiting nonfamily farm corporations from owning farmland or livestock. The citizens of Nebraska have beaten back numerous attempts to weaken this structural barrier to corporate control over the state's farms in the years since.[9] South Dakota also succeeded in placing anticorporate farming restrictions in its constitution in 1998, not only forbidding corporations from owning or controlling farmland, but also paying farmers to raise crops or livestock on their behalf. And seven other states—Iowa, Kansas, Missouri, Minnesota, Oklahoma, North Dakota, and Wisconsin—also have statutes restricting corporate involvement in agriculture, though most include loopholes that dilute the impact of the ban.[10]

Unfortunately, examples like these—where grassroots movements have succeeded in placing structural restraints on corporations—are not as common as they should be. One of the ways we can accelerate the process is by organizing a large-scale national network of state and local lawmakers who are interested in enacting policies that address specific issues or place broader restraints on corporate power. Such a network could help legislators share information and build off each other's success with laws and policies that strengthen community struggles against corporate predators and that proactively control corporations.

Just as the corporations have the powerful American Legislative Exchange Council (ALEC) to distribute and support model legislation in the states,[11] so we need our own networks to experiment with and advance different policies that can curb and limit corporate power. The National Caucus of Environmental Legislators, a low-budget coalition of state lawmakers established in 1994 in response to the Republican takeover of Congress and several state legislatures, is a model that could be used to introduce and advance innovative legislative ideas at the state level.[12] The New Rules Project has also begun to analyze and compile information on these kinds of laws.[13] Additionally, the US PIRG network of state public interest research groups[14] and the Center for Policy Alternatives (CPA)[15] have also worked to promote model progressive legislation, as has the newly founded American Legislative Issue Campaign Exchange (ALICE).[16]

However, as journalist John Nichols has noted, "there is still a general agreement that progressives need more organized muscle . . . if they want to counter ALEC's multistate, multi-issue thrust."[17] Additionally, these groups need to get more aggressive when it comes to challenging corporate power head on.

In addition to developing an organization to orchestrate state-level laws, we also believe we need a national clearinghouse and institute for scholars and activists who wish to study corporate power and develop innovative solutions to controlling corporations. Such a clearinghouse could also support the movement-building process, develop new organizing strategies and model legislation, and continuously develop new ways to connect local struggles with national policy questions.

MOVING THE MOVEMENT

Despite their many strengths, many major movements of the past few decades (labor, environmental, consumer) have suffered from internal fractures and, increasingly, a lack of connection to the broader society. The result is that they have been increasingly boxed into "special interest" roles, often with little connection to the broader society, despite the fact that the policies they advocate generally benefit the vast majority of people.

Though sometimes these different groups come together in coalitions for specific issues or to support certain candidates, there is no unifying vision. As Professor George Lakoff has suggested, "coalitions with different interest-based messages for different voting blocks [are] without a general moral vision. Movements, on the other hand, are based on shared values, values that define who we are. They have a better chance of being broad-based and lasting. In short, progressives need to

be thinking in terms of a broad-based progressive-values movement, not in terms of issue coalitions."[18]

Such a broad-based movement, we believe, should be focused around the one pressing concern that we all share regardless of whether we see ourselves as tied to labor, environmental,
consumer, or other specific causes: that we all want a just and
sustainable economy and a functioning democracy and that the
dominant power of large corporations poses a fundamental
threat to these goals.

So, what will it take to bring us out of our divided special-interest roles and into a coherent and unified movement? Lawrence
Goodwyn, a historian of the populist movement, has suggested
that the "flowering of the largest democratic movement in
American history" went through a four-stage sequential process
of democratic movement building:

> (1) The creation of an autonomous institution where new in-
> terpretations can materialize that run counter to those of
> prevailing authority—a development which, for the sake of
> simplicity, we will describe as "the movement forming";
> (2) the creation of a tactical means to attract masses of
> people—"the movement recruiting"; (3) the achievement
> of a heretofore culturally unsanctioned level of social
> analysis—"the movement educating"; and (4) the creation
> of an institutional means whereby the new ideas, shared
> now by the rank and file of the mass movement, can be ex-
> pressed in an autonomous political way—"the movement
> politicized."[19]

Right now, we appear to be variously operating in stages one
through three. The mosaic of movements that came together en
masse to shut down the World Trade Organization's ministerial
meeting in Seattle in 1999—labor, environmentalists, indige-
nous people, farmers, consumers, animal rights activists, small
business owners, and many others—demonstrated both that it is
possible to unite in opposition to corporate rule and that there
is no shortage of passionate people concerned about corporate
power and willing to do much about it. As one journalist observed, "Through the teargas and among the forest of picket
signs and banners, one could finally glimpse at least the rough

but real outlines of the much-sought-after progressive coalition, an American version of a green alliance. Hard hats and long-shoremen standing with granola crunchers and tree huggers, bus drivers and carpenters with snake dancers and organic food activists. Or as one hand-painted sign smartly put it: Teamsters and Turtles Together at Last."[20]

Yet the coalition that came together in Seattle to defend our democracy against the many-faceted threat of the World Trade Organization (WTO) has yet to be transformed into the kind of mainstream national movement that can mount a sustained challenge to corporate dominance here in the United States. To do this, we will need to nurture and develop the synergies between the many different and distinct strands of the movement against corporate rule. We need to recognize that, while most of us are focused on one or another specific issue, all of our causes are equally threatened by corporate rule.

If there is one group that is at the center of a struggle to challenge corporate power, it is organized labor. Though today's labor movement may not be the political force that it once was (the percentage of the workforce belonging to a union has fallen from a peak of 35 percent of nonagricultural jobs in 1954 to just about 13 percent today, including under 9 percent of non-government workers), organized labor still represents 16 million Americans,[21] most of whom quite clearly understand the dangerous consequences of corporate power.

As a Century Foundation Task Force *Report on the Future of Unions* concluded, "labor unions have been the single most important agent for social justice in the United States. They have played a vital role in originating a national debate over the sharing of the riches of economic growth, and they have been a leading force in opening up opportunity to all working people."[22]

The labor movement, as we noted, was a key participant in the Seattle protests. And unions have already been leading advocates of some of the reforms we have discussed in this book. Labor is at the forefront of efforts to challenge excessive CEO pay, corporate attempts to move their headquarters offshore to avoid paying their fair share of taxes, and the outsourcing of jobs. Labor also has played a leading role in opposing the war in Iraq and exposing war profiteers benefiting from Iraq reconstruction contracts. And local labor councils played a decisive role in establishing the Cities for Peace network (which began as a coalition of more than one hundred cities that passed resolutions opposing the war in Iraq but has since expanded to address other issues, including health care, education, jobs, and housing) and have also begun to organize a socially diverse network of resistance to corporate assaults upon the social welfare sector.[23] These groups, as well as the anticorporate globalization networks (such as the Mobilization for Global Justice), have demonstrated how local activism can connect to a broader policy agenda.[24] As AFL-CIO president John Sweeney has written, unions need to start "building social movements that reach beyond the workplace into the entire community and offer working people beyond our ranks the opportunity to improve their lives and livelihood."[25] This is beginning to occur more frequently. Union locals and national labor support groups like Jobs With Justice have been a key force in building cross-town alliances around economic justice battles such as living wage campaigns and the new Fair Taxes for All campaign.[26] Another key labor-supported group, the National Interfaith Committee for Worker Justice, has anchored a multicity network of local interfaith groups concerned about worker rights and related issues.[27]

These union-led, cross-community alliances have in turn supported some of the strongest union organizing campaigns, including the nearly two-decades-old Justice for Janitors campaign that the Service Employees International Union (SEIU) and its allies successfully organized in Los Angeles and other cities across the country.[28]

Clearly, labor unions, along with community-based organizations and churches, will be central to the construction of lasting local coalitions that can serve as organizing clearinghouses to challenge corporate rule.

Meanwhile, other groups have also begun to articulate their struggles within the framework of democratic challenges to corporate rule. After Enron's collapse, more than two hundred groups released a Unity Platform on Corporate Accountability that called "for a fundamental transformation of the relationship between corporations and society." [29] And even though the platform was not immediately translated into new campaigns, it signaled the direction that many felt needs to be followed. Among many things, the platform called for "the phase-out of big business financing of electoral campaigns," the restoration of "public ownership of vital services such as energy and water," the establishment of "civil and criminal liability of a corporation's top management and directors," and "an overhaul of corporate governance laws, concerning both publicly and privately held corporations, to ensure that all the main stakeholders of a corporation—including its minor shareholders, workers, community, and customers—are represented in the exercise of authority and accountability." [30]

BUILDING A NEW POLITICS

Any movement that is serious about controlling corporations and restoring democracy must fully engage in political struggle. However, at a time when our democracy appears broken and politics is so thoroughly under the sway of large corporations, it is tempting to give up on politics. We must resist this temptation. Democracy offers the best solution to challenging corporate power. We must engage as citizens, not just as consumers. We must value and rebuild the public sphere. We must work to change the rules instead of agreeing to play with a stacked deck. And as a movement we must continue to openly debate the question of whether we need a third party (and what kind) or whether we can extricate either of the two major parties from their corporate paymasters.

THINKING AS CITIZENS, NOT CONSUMERS

One of the biggest challenges to effective political engagement is that in the hypercommercialized culture we inhabit, people spend far more time and energy thinking about what products they want to buy next than they spend thinking about how they can change their local community or affect the latest debates in Washington, D.C., or their state capitol. And when so much energy is spent on commercial and material pursuits

264 | THE PEOPLE'S BUSINESS

instead of on collective and political pursuits, people begin to see themselves as consumers, not citizens. As social scientist Carl Boggs has suggested, "Citizen participation, which once defined the very essence of liberal-democratic politics, now seems thoroughly undermined by a culture that glorifies the single-minded pursuit of (economic) self-interest."[31]

One indication of how strong the pressures have become to pursue our lives as consumers rather than as citizens is the ubiquitous reach of corporate advertising. In 2004, annual U.S. spending on advertising was projected to reach $266.4 billion[32] (enough to expose the average American to an estimated 2,000 commercial messages in a single day, or more than 100 per waking hour[33]). This is up from $212 billion in 2000, $33.3 billion in 1976, and just $450 million in 1900.[34] We now find corporate advertising and marketing virtually everywhere, even where we least expect it. Our local children's museum is sponsored by McDonald's,[35] our public radio broadcast is sponsored by Archer Daniels Midland,[36] and our national PTA now lists Coca-Cola as a proud sponsor.[37] Our presidential debates are sponsored by Phillip Morris and Anheuser-Busch,[38] and President Bill Clinton's inaugural parade featured a Budweiser float.[39] Everywhere, it seems, corporations are singing their siren song of consumerism, creating new wants and needs in order to keep their profits high and telling us that all we have to do to be happy is to buy new corporate products.

Another telling sign of the growing dominance of consumerism is how much time we spend shopping. As of October 2003, there were 46,438 shopping malls in the United States, covering 5.8 billion square feet of space, or about 20.2 square feet for every man, woman, and child in the United States. That's about 50 percent more than in 1986, when there were 28,496 shopping centers, covering 3.5 billion square feet (or about 14.7 square feet per capita).[40] Shopping has become a national pastime, and as economist Juliet Schor reports, "Americans spend three to four times as many hours a year shopping as their counterparts in Western European countries. Once a purely utilitarian chore, shopping has been elevated to the status of a national passion. Shopping has become a leisure activity in its own right. Going to the mall is a common Friday or Saturday night's entertainment, not only for the teens who seem to live in them, but also for adults."[41] After the tragedy of September 11, President George W. Bush told Americans that one of the best things they could do in response was to go shopping.[42]

When corporate-driven consumer culture becomes so pervasive, we increasingly come to expect that personal consumption will do more to satisfy us than civic engagement. Personal consumption is immediate. A new product can improve one's life in a tangible, measurable, and nearly instant way. Political engagement, by contrast, can be a source of endless frustration. There are usually no tangible, immediate results (and often few ultimate results) to organizing local citizens or writing a letter to your elected representatives or even voting. Experiences that cannot easily be commodified and therefore do not contribute to the GDP or to corporate bottom lines— including spiritual pursuits, personal engagement with the struggle to build community-level consciousness and civic-minded values, even informal friendships—are increasingly marginalized. In a culture driven by an insatiable appetite for money and material goods, these experiences are not valued in and of themselves.

Another consequence of the hypercommercialization of our culture is that instead of organizing collectively, we often buy into the market-based ideology of individual choice and responsibility and assume that we can change the world by changing our personal habits of consumption. Instead of connecting to large-scale democratic struggle, we often seek refuge from the destructive consequences of corporate power by isolating ourselves in personal or spiritual pursuits.

The politics of recycling offers a minor but telling example of how corporations manage to escape blame by utilizing the politics of personal responsibility. Ever since corporations joined the grassroots environmental movement in celebrating Earth Day, they began to spread the message that the best thing we can all do for the environment is to adopt a "Hints from Heloise" approach:

become environmentally conscious consumers and do our part by not littering and recycling. Although recycling is a decent habit, the message conveyed is that the onus for environmental sustainability largely rests upon the individual, that the solutions to pollution are not to be found further upstream in the industrial system. But the truth is that we have a far greater ability to bring about ecological sustainability through both industrial policies (including product design and procurement standards), and ecologically conscious community planning.

The personal choices we make are important. But we shouldn't assume that's the best we can do. We need to understand that it can't truly be a matter of choice until we get some more say in what our choices even are. We will not get very far by being passive consumers who respond to choices corporate marketers have selected for us. True power still resides in the ability to write, enforce, and judge the laws of the land, no matter what the corporations and their personal-choice, market-centered view of the world instructs us to believe. If we forsake these arenas and assume we can make a difference by just buying organic fair-trade products and recycling, we will not get very far.

Therefore, we believe that any movement to challenge corporate power will have to confront the relentless spread of commercialism and the cultural mindset it produces. One way to reduce the spread of advertising would simply be to eliminate the federal tax deduction that all corporations receive for their advertising expenses.[43] We should also begin reclaiming public institutions like schools, universities, and arts institutions as commercial-free zones where critiques of our current system of political economy can be free to develop. However, we should be prepared to defend our efforts to limit advertising against First Amendment challenges brought by corporations, who, as we discussed in Chapter 2, have greatly expanded the commercial speech doctrine in recent years to the point where even a law that prohibits tobacco billboards within 1,000 feet of a school or playground has been declared unconstitutional.

More generally, we simply need to understand just how savvy corporations have become at directing our attentions to the sphere of commercial consumerism and away from civic engagement. The first step of resisting is simply to understand what we are trying to resist.

REBUILDING THE PUBLIC SPHERE

Another challenge to political engagement is that corporations continue to wage a broad-based ideological and policy assault on the idea of both government regulation and the public sphere in general. Through both legislative and legal efforts, corporations and their allies have steadily reduced the government's involvement in a number of areas, including the provision of essential services. An aggressive series of recent tax cuts has weakened the government's ability to fund public education and other social services. Meanwhile, through a barrage of articles, policy papers, issue ads, and other forms of propaganda, corporations and their think-tank proxies have convinced us that government is an inherently corrupt and inefficient endeavor anyway, and that the hypermarketization of our society and culture is both natural and beneficial.

As a result, the space left to challenge the dominant power of corporations is rapidly vanishing. With increased corporate encroachment upon our schools and universities, our arts institutions, our houses of worship, and even our elections, we are losing the independent institutions that once nurtured and developed the values and beliefs necessary to challenge the market-centered view of the world fostered by corporations.

These and other institutions and public assets should be considered valuable parts of a public "commons" of our collective heritage and therefore off limits to for-profit corporations. "The idea of the commons helps us identify and describe the common values that lie beyond the marketplace," writes author David Bollier. "We can begin to develop a more textured appreciation for the importance of civic commitment, democratic norms, social equity, cultural and aesthetic concerns, and ecological needs. . . . A language of the commons also serves to restore humanistic, democratic concerns to their proper place in public policy-making. It insists that citizenship trumps ownership, that the democratic tradition be given an equal or superior footing vis-à-vis the economic categories of the market."[44]

We must reclaim this idea of the commons and refuse to buy into the corporate logic that tells us that the public sector is wasteful and inefficient. We must also understand that, in a democracy, governments fail when the people refuse to or are simply unable to participate as they should. The fundamental principles of democratic government remain sound, but only as long as We, The People participate in our own governance.

CHANGING THE RULES

Much citizen organizing today focuses on influencing administrative, legislative, and judicial processes that are set up to favor large corporations from the very start. As activist and historian Richard Grossman has noted, "at every step of the regulatory process, corporations are sitting there with due process and the capacity to threaten to sue. The people are outmaneuvered and outnumbered, and simply because of history, the corporation has enormous legal privilege at every step of the way."[45] Although we don't expect or advocate that activists stop fighting the battles that immediately confront so many communities, we do think it is essential to examine the many ways that the deck is stacked in favor of corporations and begin to develop campaigns and strategies that change the rules. Put simply, many of the rules are not fair, and until we can begin to collectively challenge this fundamental unfairness, we will continue to fight with one hand tied behind our backs.

This dynamic runs deep in our political culture. Countless community-based organizations have fallen into the mindset of accepting existing rules and policies. Instead of providing opportunities for people to organize collectively to demand real political solutions and start asking tough questions about how harmful policies become law in the first place, many community-based organizations seem content to merely clean up the mess left behind by failed economic policies and declining social services. And although we should not discount the difference that many of these organizations do make on a local level, we are concerned that the community service opportunities too often distract from organizing for meaningful change at a deeper level.

As sociologist David Wagner has suggested:

What if all the energy that went into volunteering and working at millions of positions in the nonprofit economy were
channeled elsewhere? What if these people were recruited as
organizers of social action that demanded more for the
needy? . . . If the poor and other consumers were more directly organized on their own behalf rather than being spoken for by social service, foundation officials, local public
officials, and advocacy groups, perhaps such deep cuts in social welfare benefits would not have occurred.[46]

Put another way, if there were a leak in your roof, would you
leave out a fresh bucket each time it rained to catch the water,
or would you fix the roof? Likely, you'd fix the roof. Yet, when it
comes to organizing, too many of us seem content to merely
put out a new bucket each time it rains.

DO WE NEED A THIRD PARTY?

Another important question in our attempts to engage politically revolves around party politics. Put simply, should we focus
our efforts on reforming either of the two major political parties
so that it can ably represent our concerns, or would we be better
off building a new party that will be more responsive to our
needs?

There are few people today who would dispute that both
major parties have increasingly cozied up to business interests
in order to stay competitive in the fundraising chase. In the
process, both parties have lost their will to do battle against
the powerful corporate lobbyists that regularly swarm their
conventions and the halls of Congress. As long as they remain
a willing partner in the corporate money game (which they will
likely continue to do until the broken campaign finance system
is fixed), politicians of both parties will continue to be beholden to corporate interests. And even though Howard Dean's
attempt to win the Democratic Party's 2004 presidential nomination demonstrated broad interest within the party for a
more populist agenda and showed that lots of money can be
raised from millions of small donors, his short-lived candidacy

was so striking because it has been far more the exception than the rule.

Today, both of the two major political parties are too entrenched in the corporate money chase to offer many fresh ideas. Instead, they debate a narrow set of issues in order to draw distinctions for the benefit of a narrow pool of centrist "swing" voters. As Ralph Nader has written, "These parties see their self-perpetuation in the narrowest of dimensions—largely by allowing business interests too great a say in local, state, and national agendas."[47]

The alternative, then, is independent political parties. Besides being a source of new political ideas (Nader is quick to note that third parties "were the first to raise the seminal issues of our past—from slavery's abolition to the status of women, minorities, labor and farmers"[48]), third parties can also serve as coordinating frameworks for larger social movements. As Carl Boggs notes:

> Through the 1990s the most ambitious and systematic effort to politicize new social movements and citizens' initiatives has been the European Green parties, which made their electoral breakthrough in West Germany during the early 1980s. . . . What made the European Greens so explosive, at least at their inception, was that, as an 'antiparty party' organically tied to citizen movements but committed to electoral politics they held to ideals of internal party democracy and grassroots participation while incorporating ecological and feminist sensibilities into their programs.[49]

Brazil's Workers Party (PT) is another example of a political party that turned close connections with an activist base into political success with the election of Luiz Inacio Lula de Silva (better known as Lula) as Brazil's president in October 2002. The PT, founded in the late 1970s by labor activists after a series of major strikes, "attracted traditionally incompatible groups, including Trotskyists, Leninists, Marxists, Catholics from the liberation wing of the Catholic Church, nearly illiterate workers, and renowned intellectuals."[50] As an open party, the PT was able to pull together many different groups looking for a political party to call home. As journalists Sue Branford and Bernardo Kucinski have written, "the 'attraction of opposites'—the coexistence of different tendencies and schools of thought within the same party, each one bowing to the decisions of the majority—is still a hallmark of the PT."[51] In order to maintain links to different social movements and involve smaller parties, the PT has a National Mass Movements Secretariat and created the National Forum of Democratic and Popular Organizations.[52] In short, the PT offers a good example of how a third party can provide an umbrella organization for a whole range of disaffected political constituencies who might agree on little more than the fact that the current political debate doesn't take their opinions into account.

Unfortunately, third-party politics in the United States suffers from a major obstacle: the winner-take-all design of the U.S. electoral system. Most other industrialized democratic nations have some kind of parliamentary system with proportional representation, the kind of system that can support several parties. But the winner-take-all U.S. system favors two parties, and as a result there are at any one time at best only a handful of Independents in Congress and in state capitols. And though the U.S. has no shortage of third parties (at least seventy-eight have run candidates for president since 1992),[53] the last third party to successfully upset the established political order was the Republican Party of Abraham Lincoln.

Efforts to reform the electoral system in a way that opens up space for diverse political opinions are increasing as citizens organize for instant runoff voting, proportional representation, fusion balloting, open primaries, free airtime for candidates, and other electoral reforms.[54] Without these reforms, it will be difficult for third parties to win office. And even then, the enactment of these reforms is no guarantee of any party's success. For the foreseeable future, third-party efforts are likely to gain their greatest success in local and state governments, particularly in areas such as New York City, where fusion balloting and public funding of elections allow greater access for third-party candidates. Third party challenges will be much more viable in states with Clean Elections, such as Arizona and Maine.

Though independent parties offer an appealing alternative to the corporate-controlled two-party system, it is conceivable that if we are able to thoroughly reform the campaign finance system and remove the polluting consequences of corporate money and influence peddling, the two major parties would be more open to insurgent campaigns from the grassroots and their leaders more responsive to the needs of their constituents.

The great unresolved question, then, is, which will be more difficult: reclaiming one of the two major political parties so that it offers a political voice to the millions of Americans who currently feel they have no voice in Washington, or successfully building a third party that can draw its strength from these millions of disaffected voters? Neither will be easy.

Without any clear resolution of this question, our sense is that the movement must continue to push and prod the major political parties to be more responsive and, where major parties are thoroughly unresponsive, organize third-party challenges. Meanwhile, as the movement to challenge corporate power continues to grow, we hope that it will eventually become large enough to either wrestle one of the major political parties from the grips of leaders tied to the corporate sector or form a significant base for a third-party challenge in different areas of the country.

FIRST STEPS

Since we believe that the most successful organizing happens when it is focused on specific demands, we suggest two crucial reforms that we believe have great potential to aid the movement's ability to grow and that could serve as a compelling foundation for a mass movement that challenges corporate power more broadly: campaign finance reform and media reform.

Fundamental changes in our political system will clearly be necessary to drive corporations out of direct involvement in our elections and restore the people's faith in representative democracy. As long as our elected officials are beholden to large corporations, and as long as big business continues to set the policy agenda in Washington, D.C. and state capitals, attempts to make meaningful changes through the levers of government are likely to fail. The movement for campaign finance reform, organized at the local level with support from national groups such as the Center for Voting and Democracy and Public Campaign, provides a useful framework for action for the broad spectrum of people who currently feel shut out of politics.

Media reform is also essential. Much of our understanding of the world and politics is filtered through the media. With growing government secrecy and a corporate-dominated two-party political system, the role of independent media is more critical than ever. As Bill Moyers suggested in his keynote address at the National Conference on Media Reform last year, "if free and independent journalism committed to telling the truth without fear or favor is suffocated, the oxygen goes out of democracy."[55]

Without a media system that is accessible to movement organizers and not afraid to ask tough questions about our political economy and the dominant role of corporations, we will have a tough time communicating between ourselves and getting our ideas into the mainstream, no matter how much organizing we do. In November 2003, more than 1,400 activists from across the social and political spectrum convened in Madison, Wisconsin, for the largest-ever conference concerning corporate control of the media.[56] "Media reform is an issue whose time has come," noted journalist John Nichols, an organizer of the conference. "The fight over ownership marks the beginning of a new movement to ensure a diverse, independent and competitive media."[57]

Getting corporations out of politics was the subject of Chapter 6. Since we only briefly touched on media reform in Chapter 4, we will revisit that important question here.[58]

The media have always been and will continue to be the most important tool for communicating ideas and educating the public about ongoing problems. What Thomas Paine said more than two hundred years ago—"There is nothing that obtains so general an influence over the manners and morals of a people as the press; from that as from a fountain the streams of vice or virtue are poured forth over a nation."[59]—is still largely true today. Therefore, any movement serious about building democracy and challenging corporate power is going to have to understand the media and how to use it.

The power of the media to affect politics and public opinion cannot be understated. History is replete with examples that show how critical the media's role has been in addressing the injustices of our society. For example, many Progressive Era reforms came only in response to the investigative exposes of corporate abuses by muckraking journalists like Upton Sinclair (best known for his disturbing descriptions of the meat-packing industry, which helped create the public pressure that led to the Meat Inspection and Pure Food Drug Acts of 1906, the first consumer safety laws) and Ida Tarbell (who exposed the monopolistic practices of the Standard Oil Company, which was eventually broken up by the government), among others. Writing in popular magazines like *Collier's* and *McClure's*, these writers provided a powerful public challenge to the corruption of the Gilded Age.

Yet, as we discussed in Chapter 4, the vast majority of today's mainstream media (including television, radio, movies, books, and recorded music) is dominated by just a handful of large for-profit corporate conglomerates primarily interested in making money. [60]

Because of increased corporate consolidation of the media, coverage of all levels of government has been greatly reduced. At the local level, the *American Journalism Review* reports that "more community views are being lost" in local daily and weekly publications. Although the number of weekly journals has actually increased, more and more of them are being snapped up by newspaper chains that are filled with syndicated content as opposed to in-depth local coverage.[61] Meanwhile, at the state level, a 2002 study by the Project on the State of the American Newspaper found that "the number of reporters covering state capitols across the country full-time had fallen to just over 500, a figure the *American Journalism Review* described as 'the lowest number we have seen, and probably the lowest in at least the last quarter century.'"[62]

The view from Washington is no better. A 1999 survey of nineteen federal agencies by two longtime Washington journalists revealed that newspapers are jettisoning traditional beat coverage of the regulatory agencies, leaving many important developments uncovered in an era of increasing industry control over federal regulation. "Peek behind the numbers and you find other notable, and sometimes worrisome trends," notes the *American Journalism Review*. "For one, it can scarcely be reassuring how much the newspaper industry has come to rely on just four key outlets—the *New York Times*, the *Washington Post*, *Los Angeles Times* and *Associated Press*—to monitor vast portions of the federal government."[63]

As for coverage of the world at large, a 2000 industry study found that there were only 282 correspondents working abroad for all of the nation's newspapers combined. And a 1998 study by the University of California, San Diego, found that only 2 percent of total newspaper coverage focused on international news, down from 10 percent in 1983. Several prominent journalists have concluded that the cutbacks have contributed to Americans' lack of understanding about the rest of the world. "I think most Americans are clueless when it comes to the politics and ideology and religion in [the Muslim] world and, in that sense, I think we do bear some responsibility," concludes Martin Baron, editor of the *Boston Globe*.[64]

When people are kept ignorant of what is happening in their communities, in their states, in Washington, D.C., and in the world, it becomes much easier for large corporations to overwhelm the political process and control the economy without citizens understanding what is happening.

As Robert McChesney has written, "crucial public issues are barely covered by the corporate media, or else are warped to fit the confines of elite debate, stripping ordinary citizens of the tools they need to be informed, active participants."[65]

Though media reform is a complex subject, there are a few approaches that bear mentioning. One is to establish and strengthen nonprofit media outlets.

The Pacifica radio network, for example, has nonprofit, noncommercial, listener-supported stations in six cities, all of which are free to criticize corporate America and project an entirely different view of how the world is and ought to be. Its popular

Democracy Now! news program is heard on 160 different stations.[66] Another potential area of growth for independent media is the emergence of low-power FM radio (LPFM). In 2000, the FCC agreed to bring local radio to "underserved" communities by granting licenses for LPFM stations of up to 100 watts (which covers about 3.5 miles), though powerful broadcasting lobbyists forced the FCC to shrink back its proposal.[67] And although about 1,100 stations have had permits denied,[68] the 220 or so low-power radio stations that have made it on the air have in some cases been successful as community-organizing tools.

The Independent Media Center (IMC), meanwhile, is a Web-based network of collectively run nonprofit media outlets that exists in several dozen cities throughout the country and throughout the world. Originally established to provide a journalists' clearinghouse during the 1999 World Trade Organization (WTO) protests in Seattle, the IMC has blossomed into a grassroots, do-it-yourself, open-source publishing outlet for community activists who are eager to distribute the news and views that can't be found in the corporate media.[69] There are also numerous nonprofit national periodicals that provide a similar take on events.

Three policies have the potential to increase broad public support for a noncommercial, nonprofit media sector: (a) reducing mailing rates for nonprofit media with little or no advertising; (b) allowing taxpayers to check off some of their federal tax bill to donate the money to nonprofit news outlets; and (c) requiring for-profit radio and broadcast TV stations to cede a certain percentage of profit to noncommercial media as a condition of their license.

Meanwhile, as we discussed in Chapter 4, the structure of corporate media conglomerates is a major impediment to competition, variety, and depth of news coverage. The most effective way to ensure the diversity necessary for a vibrant democracy is to enact competition rules, such as limits on cross-media ownership and vertical integration that essentially mandate diversity by prohibiting media conglomerates. Targeting the media monopoly should be viewed as the first step to reviving a broad-based challenge to concentrated corporate ownership and control of a variety of business sectors, just as the late-nineteenth-century resistance by the Populists to banking and railroad concentration sparked a fire on the prairie that led to broad resistance to the other giant business trusts.

Additionally, we think that in addressing media reform, we must remember that one of the great secrets about television and radio is that the public actually owns the airwaves and the corporations rent them from us in exchange for a grossly under-enforced promise to serve "the public interest, convenience and necessity." Far more could be done to require broadcasters to live up to this standard. For example, the federal government could require stations to devote a certain portion of their broadcasts to commercial-free and/or independently produced local, national, and international news programs. Stations could also be required to produce noncommercial children's programming.

Also, we believe that it would be worthwhile to strengthen our public broadcasting system. Though networks like NPR and PBS offer good alternatives to the corporate-owned media, they still receive far too much corporate funding to be independent of the corporate sphere.

THE LONG-TERM VISION

Though campaign finance reform and media reform offer useful starting points, ultimately, there is much more to be done. We need to get tough on corporate crime. We need to make sure markets are properly competitive by breaking up the giant corporate monopolies and oligarchies. We need to make corporations more accountable to all stakeholders and less focused on maximizing shareholder profit above all. We need to stop allowing corporations to claim Bill of Rights protections to undermine citizen-enacted laws.

Ultimately, we need to restore the understanding that in a democracy the rights of citizens to govern themselves are more important than the rights of corporations to make money. Corporations are nothing more than a form of business organization, creatures of the state, given certain rights and privileges by state governments with an understanding that the public will benefit as a result. And since their charters and licenses are granted by citizen governments, it should be up to the people to decide how corporations can serve the public good and what should be done when they don't. As Justices Byron White, William Brennan, and Thurgood Marshall noted in 1978: "Corporations are artificial entities created by law for the purpose of furthering certain economic goals. . . . It has long been recognized, however, that the special status of corporations has placed them in a position to control vast amounts of economic power that may, if not regulated, dominate not only the economy but also the very heart of our democracy, the electoral process. . . . The State need not permit its own creation to consume it."[70]

We should always be on the watch for opportunities to call attention to these fundamental power dynamics. One recent example of the potential for organizing a large number of people around questions of corporate legal rights is the corporate challenge to the Federal Trade Commission's Do-Not-Call registry. Though the anti-telemarketing registry was hugely popular, with the users of at least 50 million telephone numbers signing up within weeks of its creation, telemarketing trade groups protested, claiming First Amendment protections for their corporate clients' commercial speech. Federal District Judge Edward W. Nottingham of Denver validated the telemarketers' claim in October 2003, but the Tenth Circuit Court of Appeals reversed Nottingham's decision and upheld the law in February 2004.[71] However, telemarketing groups have vowed to challenge the decision by appealing to the Supreme Court, posing the possibility that corporate claims to the First Amendment could undermine a law that was so popular that a Republican-controlled Congress moved quickly to support it after Nottingham's decision.[72]

Another good example is the way California groups advanced the Corporate Three Strikes law in 2003 to highlight the people's right to revoke corporate charters, proposing that the state revoke the charter of any corporation with three major felony convictions in ten years. Though the bill failed to get out of committee, it did help draw attention to the fact that all states have the power to put recidivist corporate criminals out of business if they choose to do so.

We should also continue to strive for effective ways to foster a national discussion about the consequences of corporate power. For instance, a congressionally appointed commission could assess the consequences of concentrated corporate ownership in specific sectors (we think media, energy, agriculture, and defense would be important industries to examine). Another question that a congressional or independent commission could examine is the threat that multinational corporations pose to our national security. Starting with any number of questions (e.g., offshore tax avoidance, war profiteering, outsourcing of jobs, dependence on foreign sources of energy, the threat that trade agreement provisions such as NAFTA's investor rights provision pose to sovereign governments), such a commission could be modeled after Senator Joseph O'Mahoney's Temporary National Economic Committee (TNEC; established in the late 1930s to examine issues of economic concentration, but derailed by World War II).[73]

The ability of any such commission to advance popular understanding of the dangers that corporate power poses to the public interest will depend on the willingness of such a commission to receive public input from concerned citizens, academics, and others and the readiness of these groups to raise their concerns in public hearings. At the same time that citizens are continuing to build organized networks around particular concerns, the commission would raise the profile of questions about corporate power to the level of national concern.

THE PEOPLE'S BUSINESS

The many constituencies concerned with the consequences of corporate power are indeed a diverse group, and although this diversity can be a source of strength, it also makes it difficult to clearly articulate a vision for the struggle.

What principles, then, can unite us?

As we noted in the introduction, we believe that a vast majority of people want to live in a world where they can earn a decent living, reside in a pleasant and safe community, and provide a good life for their children. They want a world where they can enjoy basic freedoms and basic privacies, where they are financially independent and spiritually fulfilled. They want clean water and clean air and safe food, both for themselves and for their children. They want a government that is responsive to their concerns.

Meanwhile, as poll after poll reveals, the majority of Americans believe that corporations have too much power over too many aspects of our lives. Most people are sick of being bombarded with constant corporate advertising and marketing, and as corporations continue to overextend themselves, people's image of big business is growing increasingly negative.

One abiding faith that almost all of us share is that of citizen democracy: that citizens should be able to decide how they wish to live through democratic processes and that big corporations should not be able to tell citizens how to live their lives and run their communities. As we have noted throughout this book, the most effective way to control corporations will be to restore citizen democracy and to reclaim the once widely accepted principle that corporations are but creatures of the state, chartered under the premise that they will serve the public good, and entitled to only those rights and privileges granted by citizen-controlled governments. And only by doing so will we be able to create the just and sustainable economy that we seek, an economy driven by the values of human life and community and democracy instead of the current suicide economy driven only by the relentless pursuit of financial profit at any cost.

Therefore, we must work assiduously to challenge the dominant role of the corporation in our lives and in our politics. We must reestablish citizen sovereignty, and we must restore the corporations to their proper role as the servants of the people, not our masters. This, we believe, is the people's business.

NOTES

INTRODUCTION

1. By large corporations, we mean more specifically large limited liability, publicly traded corporations. Though there are other forms of the corporation, this is the type that we mean throughout the book when we refer more generally to "corporations."
2. See the Bibliography beginning on page 318.
3. See p. xi for a list of commission members.
4. Corporations spent $212 billion on advertising in 2000 and were expected to spend $266 billion in advertising in 2004. Source: Mercedes M. Cardona, "Ad-Spending Soothsayers Optimistic on Year Ahead," *Advertising Age,* December 15, 2003.
5. Vincent P. Bzdek, "The Ad Subtractors, Making a Difference," *Washington Post,* July 29, 2003.
6. Quoted in Joel Bakan, *The Corporation* (New York: Free Press, 2004), p. 71.
7. Sarah Anderson and John Cavanagh, "Top 200: The Rise of Global Corporate Power," Institute for Policy Studies, 2000. http://www.ips-dc.org/reports/top200.htm)
8. "The Powell Memorandum" (a letter from Powell to U.S. Chamber of Commerce Education Committee chairman Eugene B. Syndor Jr., August 23, 1971, available at http://www.mediatransparency.org/stories/powellmanifesto.htm.)
9. Ibid.
10. For a detailed history, see Kim McQuaid, *Big Business and Presidential Power* (New York: William Morrow and Company, Inc., 1982), chap. 9.
11. Ted Nace, *Gangs of America* (San Francisco: Barrett-Koehler, 2003), p. 143.
12. David Vogel, "The Power of Business in America: A Re-appraisal," *British Journal of Political Science* 13 (1983): 35.
13. Nace, *Gangs of America,* p. 143.
14. Ibid.
15. Vogel, "The Power of Business in America," p. 38.
16. Jeff Krehely, Meegahan House, and Emily Kernan, "Axis of Ideology: Conservative Foundations and Public Policy," March 2004, available at http://www.ncrp.org.
17. Ibid.
18. Mark Dowie, *American Foundations: An Investigative History* (Boston: MIT Press, 2002).
19. *Business Week,* September 11, 2000.

20. Ronald Alsop, "Corporate Scandals Hit Home: Regulations of Big Companies Tumble in Consumer Survey: 'Money Can Rob the Goodness,'" *Wall Street Journal*, February 19, 2004.

21. Quoted in Bakan, *The Corporation*, p. 71.

22. Medard Gabel and Henry Bruner, *Globalinc.: An Atlas of the Multinational Corporation* (New York: The New Press, 2003).

23. *Alternatives to Economic Globalization*, available at http://www.ifg.org.

24. For a good book on corporate campaigns, see Kevin Danaher and Jason Mark, *Insurrection* (London: Routledge, 2003). Also see *Multinational Monitor*, Jan/Feb 2004 and Jan/Feb 2001; and http://www.corporatecampaign.org.

CHAPTER 1

1. http://www.licensedtokill.biz.

2. "New Tobacco Company, Licensed to Kill, Inc, Incorporated in the State of Virginia; Aims to Kill Over 400,000 Americans and 4.5 Million Other People Worldwide Annually," Licensed to Kill press release, April 17, 2003, available at http://www.licensedtokill.biz/media/pr030417.html. All the people "quoted" in the press release, including Gary Vastone, are made-up people with names meant to sound like symbols of death (Gary Vastone, for example, sounds a bit like "Gravestone").

3. For more on the violations of tobacco companies, see *Global Aggression: The Case for World Standards and Bold US Action Challenging Philip Morris and RJR Nabisco*, Infact (New York: Apex Press, 1998).

4. Harry Glasbeek, *Wealth by Stealth* (Toronto: Between the Lines Press, 2002), p. 7.

5. Ted Nace, *Gangs of America* (San Francisco: Berrett-Koehler, 2003), p. 24.

6. John D. Davis, *Corporations: A Study of the Origin and Development of Great Business Combinations and Their Relations to the Authority of the State*, vol. 2 (New York: Capricorn Books, 1961), p. 186.

7. Charles Perrow, *Organizing America* (Princeton: Princeton University Press, 2002), p. 32.

8. Louis Hartz, *Economic Policy and Democratic Thought, 1776–1860* (Cambridge: Harvard University Press, 1948), p. 69.

9. Smith, Book V, Chapter I, Part III (as quoted in Nace, *Gangs of America*, p. 40).

10. Glasbeek, *Wealth by Stealth*, pp. 72–73.

11. The process involves a legislative proceeding known as *quo warranto* (by what authority).

12. Frank Adams and Richard Grossman, "Taking Care of Business," in *Defying Corporations, Defining Democracy* (New York: Apex Press, 2001), pp. 64–65.

13. Ralph Nader, Marc Green, and Joel Seligman, *Taming the Giant Corporation* (New York: Norton, 1976), p. 34.

14. From Henry Carter Adams 1896 presidential address to the American Economic Association, as quoted in ibid., p. 63.

15. Thomas Jefferson to George Logan, letter, 1816. [Nov. 1816, in Paul Leicester Ford, *The Writings of Thomas Jefferson, Vol. 10* (New York, 1892–1899), p. 69.]

16. Daniel Raymond, "Wealth and Democracy," pp. 208–9 of *Thoughts on Political Economy* (Baltimore: F. Lucas Jr., 1820), which discusses favoritism in early chartering.

17. Arthur Schlesinger Jr., *The Age of Jackson* (Boston: Little, Brown and Company, 1946), p. 74.
18. Ibid., p. 76.
19. Ibid., pp. 123–24.
20. Andrew Jackson, "Why the United States Bank Was Closed," July 10, 1832.
21. Schlesinger, *Age of Jackson,* p. 105.
22. Richard Hofstadter, *The American Political Tradition* (New York, Alfred A. Knopf, 1948), p. 58.
23. Schlesinger, *Age of Jackson,* p. 337.
24. Ibid.
25. Christopher D. Stone, *Where the Law Ends: The Social Control of Corporate Behavior* (New York: HarperCollins, 1975), p. 20.
26. Abram Chayes, "Introduction," in *Corporations*, by John P. Davis (New York: Capricorn Books, 1961), pp. ix–xi.
27. *The Trustees of Dartmouth College v. Woodward 17 U.S. 518 (1819).*
28. Adams and Grossman, "Taking Care of Business," pp. 64–65.
29. Louis Menand, *The Metaphysical Club: A Story of Ideas in America* (New York: Farrar, Straus and Giroux, 2002), p. 243.
30. Nader et al., *Taming the Giant Corporation*, p. 42.
31. Ibid., p. 43.
32. Ibid., p. 45.
33. Ibid., p. 46.
34. Ibid.
35. Ibid.
36. Richard B. DuBoff, *Accumulation and Power* (Armonk, N.Y.: M.E. Sharpe Inc., 1989), p. 57.
37. Nader et al., *Taming the Giant Corporation*, p. 49.
38. Quoted in *Liggett Co. v. Lee*, 288 U.S. 517, 560, n. 37 (1933) (Brandeis dissent).
39. Nader et al., *Taming the Giant Corporation*, p. 52.
40. The Delaware Division of Corporations boasts: "Businesses choose Delaware because we provide a complete package of incorporation services including modern and flexible corporate laws, our highly-respected Court of Chancery, a business-friendly State Government, and the customer service oriented Staff of the Delaware Division of Corporations." See: http://www.state.de.us/corp/default.shtml.
41. William W. Cook, *The Corporation Problem: The Public Phases of Corporations, Their Uses, Abuses* (New York: Putnam's, 1891), p. 288.
42. Adams and Grossman, "Taking Care of Business," p. 63.
43. Shaw Livermore, "Unlimited Liability in Early American Corporations," *Journal of Political Economy* 43 (1935):674–8.
44. Adams and Grossman, "Taking Care of Business," p. 63.
45. William G. Roy, *Socializing Capital* (Princeton: Princeton University Press, 1997), pp. 161–63.
46. Ibid., p. 163.
47. 77th Cong., 1st Sess., S. Doc 35, TNEC, *Final Report and Recommendations* 28 (1941).
48. Community Environmental Legal Defense Fund, "A Citizen's Guide to Corporate Charter Revocation Under State Law." Available at http://www.celdf.org/cdp/cdp1.asp.

49. The statutes essentially codify the common law writ of *quo warranto* (by what authority), which allows an attorney general to demand that a corporation show by what authority it continues to exist.

50. "Environmental, Human Rights, Women's and Pro-Democracy Groups Petition Attorney General of California to Revoke Unocal's Charter," September 10, 1998, press release, available at http://heed.home.igc. org/charter/doc2.html.

51. Complaint lodged with the Attorney General of California under California Code of Civil Procedure § 803, California Corporations Code § 801, To Revoke the Corporate Charter of the Union Oil Company of California, September 10, 1998, available at http://heed.home. igc.org.

52. Bob Benson, "Soft on Crime?" *The Recorder,* October 14, 1998.

53. For details, see http://www.corporate3strikes.org/.

54. SB 335, California 2003–2004 session.

55. Charlie Cray, "Chartering a New Course," *Multinational Monitor*, October–November 2002.

56. Quoted in John Cavanagh and Jerry Mander, "Fixing the Rotten Corporate Barrel," *The Nation*, December 23, 2002.

57. "Environmental, Human Rights, . . .," September 10, 1998, press release.

58. Jonathan Chait, "Rogue State," *New Republic*, August 19, 2002.

59. William Cary, "Delaware Supreme Court Dominated by Corporate Bar," *Yale Law Review* 83 (1974):690–92.

60. Daniel J. H. Greenwood, "Democracy and Delaware: The Puzzle of Corporate Law," available at http://www.law.utah.edu/faculty/websites/greenwood/.

61. Ibid.

62. Ibid.

63. Ibid.

64. Nader et al., *Taming the Giant Corporation*, p. 70.

65. Ibid., p. 67.

66. Quoted in Gabriel Kolko, *The Triumph of Conservatism* (New York: The Free Press, 1963), p. 176.

67. Temporary National Economic Committee, Final Statement of Senator Joseph C. O'Mahoney, "The Preservation of Economic Freedom," 10 (March 11, 1941). Cited in *Taming the Giant Corporation*, p. 70.

68. Nader et al., *Taming the Giant Corporation*, p. 71.

69. *First National Bank of Boston v. Belotti*, 435 U.S. 765 (1978).

70. David Kessler, *A Question of Intent* (New York: PublicAffairs, 2001), pp. 392–93.

71. Ibid., p. 392.

CHAPTER 2

1. Original complaint of Marc Kasky, Case #994446, Superior Court of California, San Francisco Count, available at http://reclaimdemocracy. org/nike/kasky_original_complaint.pdf.

2. Carl J. Mayer, "Personalizing the Impersonal: Corporations and the Bill of Rights," *Hastings Law Journal* 41 (March 1990):582.

3. Ibid., p. 580.

4. Ibid., p. 583.

5. David Millon, "The Ambiguous Significance of Corporate Personhood," *Stanford Agora* 1, no. 2. available at: http://agora.stanford.edu/agora/cgi-bin/article2_corp.cgi?library=millon.
6. http://www.wlf.org/Litigating/litprojects.asp.
7. The Supreme Court has upheld restrictions on certain forms of commercial speech, including advertising (*Zauderer v. Office of Disciplinary Counsel*, 471 U.S. 626 [1985] [upholding reduced First Amendment rights for advertisements]; and *Posadas de Puerto Rico Assoc. v. Tourism Co.*, 478 U.S. 328 [1986] [upholding advertising restrictions on gambling against claim of prior restraint on commercial speech]).
8. See, e.g., *Riley v. Nat'l Fed'n of the Blind*, 487 U.S. 781 (1988) (refusing to apply First Amendment to securities area); *Mills v. Elec. Auto-Lite Co.*, 396 U.S. 375 (1970) (First Amendment does not apply to corporate proxy statements).
9. Bruce Ledewitz, "Corporate Advertising's Democracy," *Boston Public Interest Law Journal* (Spring/Summer 2003) (12 B.U. Pub Int. L.J. 389). p. 444.
10. John Kenneth Galbraith, *The New Industrial State*, 2nd ed. (Boston: Houghton Mifflin Co., 1971). P. xviii.
11. Ledewitz, "Corporate Advertising's Democracy." p. 444.
12. *Central Hudson Gas & Electric Corporation v. Public Service Commission of New York*, 447 U.S. 557 (1980).
13. Ibid.
14. *44 Liquor Mart v. Rhode Island*, 517 U.S. 484 (1996).
15. Linda Greenhouse, "High Court Says Liquor Price Ads Can't Be Banned," *New York Times*, May 14, 1996.
16. *Lorillard Tobacco Co. v. Reilly*, 84 F. Supp.2d 180 (D. Mass. 2000).
17. *Pacific Gas & Electric v. Public Utilities Commission*, 475 U.S. 1 (1986).
18. Mercedes M. Cardona, "Ad-Spending Soothsayers Optimistic on Year Ahead," *Advertising Age*, December 15, 2003.
19. Vincent P. Bzdek, "The Ad Subtractors, Making a Difference," *Washington Post*, July 29, 2003.
20. Lawrence Soley, *Censorship Inc.: The Corporate Threat to Free Speech in the United States* (New York: Monthly Review Press, 2002), p. 9.
21. The case involved four animal rights activists, who were arrested at the mall on May 19, 1996, for handing out literature opposing fur garments in front of Macy's. See Mike Kaszuba, "Judge Lambasts State Supreme Court over Ruling," *Minnesota Star Tribune*, January 13, 2000.
22. *First National Bank of Boston v. Bellotti*, 435 U.S. 765 (1978).
23. Ibid.
24. *Montana Chamber of Commerce v. Argenbright*, U.S. 9th 98-36256 (2000).
25. *First National Bank of Boston v. Bellotti*. 435 U.S. 765 (1978).
26. *Trustees of Dartmouth College v. Woodward*, 17 U.S. 518 (1819).
27. *Austin v. Michigan State Chamber of Commerce*, 494 U.S. 652 (1990).
28. Daniel J. H. Greenwood, "Essential Speech: Why Corporate Speech Is Not Free," *Iowa Law Review* 83 (August 1998): 995.
29. Charles Lindblom, *The Market System* (New Haven: Yale University Press, 2001), p. 239.
30. For a discussion on media conglomerates, see Chapter 4.
31. *Marshall v. Barlow's*, 436 U.S. 307 (1977).

32. *Dow Chemical v. United States,* 476 U.S. 227 (1986).

33. This doctrine has been most famously espoused by University of Chicago law professor Richard Epstein, in his 1989 book *Takings: Private Property and the Power of Eminent Domain* (Cambridge: Harvard University Press).

34. *Pennsylvania Coal Co. v. Mahon,* 260 U.S. 393, 415 (1922).

35. *Mugler v. Kansas,* 123 U.S. 623, 668–69 (1887).

36. *Penn Central Transp. Co. v. City of New York,* 438 U.S. 104, 124 (1978).

37. *Philip Morris, Inc. v. Reilly,* 312 F.3d 24 (2002).

38. William Greider, "The Right and US Trade Law: Invalidating the 20th Century," *The Nation,* October 15, 2001. p. 21; For more specific examples of how corporations have used NAFTA's Chapter 11 provisions, see Michelle Swenarchuk, "Chapter 11 Dossier: Corporations Exercise Their Investor 'Rights,'" *Multinational Monitor,* April 2001; Mary Bottari, "NAFTA's Investor Rights: A Corporate Dream, a Citizen Nightmare," *Multinational Monitor,* April 2001.

39. Scott R. Bowman, *The Modern Corporation and American Political Thought* (University Park: Pennsylvania State University Press, 1996), pp. 54–55.

40. Thom Hartmann, *Unequal Protection* (Rodale, Pa.: Rodale Press, 2002), pp. 95–119.

41. Charles Wallace Collins, *The Fourteenth Amendment and the States* (New York: Perseus Books; 1974)

42. *Chicago, Milwaukee and St. Paul Railway v. Minnesota,* 134 U.S. 418 (1890).

43. John Holland, "Wal-Mart Sues Turlock over Ban," *Modesto Bee,* February 12, 2004.

44. John Ritter, "California Tries to Slam Lid on Big-Boxed Wal-Mart," *USA Today,* March 2, 2004.

45. Holland, "Wal-Mart Sues Turlock over Ban."

46. John Holland, "Turlock Council Puts Up Funds for Wal-Mart Fight," *Modesto Bee,* February 25, 2004.

47. "The Powell Memorandum."

48. "NCLC Celebrates 25 Years of Service to the Business Community," available at http://www.uschamber.com/nclc/.

49. Ibid.

50. "About NCLC," available at http://www.uschamber.com/nclc/.

51. http://www.wlf.org/Litigating/litprojects.asp#1.

52. William G. Castagnoli, "What Is the WLF and Why Is It Challenging the FDA?" Medical Marketing & Media, April 1995, Vol. 30 ; No. 4, p. 26

53. From IRS Form 990, available from www.greenwatch.org.

54. http://www.wlf.org.

55. Christopher A. Brown, "FDA 'Trans Fat' Labeling Proposal Treads on Commercial Free Speech," WLF Legal Opinion Letter, June 6, 2003.

56. "EPA Enforcement Actions Would Tread on Constitutional Rights," WLF Legal Opinion Letter, August 23, 2002.

57. John Carey, "The FDA's Big . . . Free-Speech Challenge?" *Business Week,* November 15, 2002.

58. "Kasky v. Nike: U.S. Supreme Court Review Can Protect Free Public Debate," WLF Legal Opinion Letter, April 20, 2001.

59. Leslie Gordon Fagen, "Courts Must Refrain from Chilling Corporate Speech Rights," WLF Legal Backgrounder, July 21, 1995.

60. Elizabeth Vella Moeller, "DOJ Tobacco Suit Threatens Commercial Speech Rights," WLF Legal Opinion Letter, April 26, 2002.

61. "Campaign Finance Reform Silences Protected Free Speech," WLF Legal Opinion Letter, June 21, 2002.

62. John W. Bode, "Mandated Biotech Food Labeling Ineffective and Legally Suspect," WLF Legal Opinion Letter, March 3, 2000.

63. Richard M. Corner, "Free Flow of Commercial Speech Essential to World Market," WLF Legal Backgrounder, August 20, 1999.

64. Jeffrey P. Cunard and Rebecca Tushnet, "Landmark Speech Ruling Curtails FCC Cable Regulation," WLF Backgrounder, June 15, 2001.

65. Henry Weinstein, "Court Upholds Law Restricting 'Green' Labeling," *Los Angeles Times*, November 19, 1994.

66. Daniel E. Troy, "City Ordinances Banning Tobacco and Alcohol Advertising Are Unconstitutional," Washington Legal Foundation Legal Opinion Letter, July 29, 1994.

67. Robert S. Peck, "Proposal to Eliminate Tax Deduction for Advertising Expenses Is Unconstitutional," WLF Legal Opinion Letter, March 19, 1993.

68. Alan M. Slobodin, "Anti-Industry Propaganda Is Constitutionally Suspect," WLF Legal Opinion Letter, March 5, 1993.

69. Jeffrey R. Chanin and James E. Boasberg, "Product Placement in Movies Cannot Be Regulated as Commercial Speech Under the First Amendment," WLF Legal Backgrounder, January 8, 1993.

70. "Washington Outlook," *Business Week,* July 5, 1993.

71. Alan M. Slobodin, "Recent Commercial Speech Decision Casts Doubt on Advertising Names or Images," WLF Legal Opinion Letter. May 14, 1993.

72. Robert A. Levy, "Federal Agencies' Attacks on Ads Offend Commercial Speech," WLF Legal Opinion Letter, September 26, 1997.

73. "Excessive FDA Scrutiny of DTC Ads Undermines Speech Rights," WLF Legal Backgrounder, May 18, 2001.

74. Jonathan Massey, "FCC Interferes with Businesses' Free Speech and Property Rights," WLF Legal Backgrounder, March 31, 2000.

75. Mark Curriden, "Court Tackles Issue of Free Speech in Advertising," *Dallas Morning News*, April 25, 2001.

76. "FDA Must Clarify Drug Makers' Ability to Publicly Defend Products," WLF Legal Opinion Letter, February 28, 2003.

77. "Interview with Paul Kamenar, WLF, Washington DC," *Corporate Crime Reporter*, November 24, 2003.

78. Tony Mauro, "Escrow Fight: Is It Principle or Politics? $200 Million in Legal Aid Funds at Risk in High Court Showdown," *Legal Times*, December 2, 2002.

79. *Washington Legal Foundation v. Legal Foundation of Washington*, No. 01– 1325 (2003).

80. Linda Greenhouse, "The Supreme Court: Legal Aid for Indigents," *New York Times*, March 27, 2003.; see also Jerry Crimmins, "Key Legal Aid Finding Program Now Two Decades Old," *Chicago Daily Law Bulletin*, June 12, 2003.

81. Steve Barnett, "Local Citizen Inspection Law: Taking 'Right-to-Know' Too Far?" WLF Legal Backgrounder, April 30, 1999.

82. The Federalist Society, "Our Background," available at http://www.fed-soc.org/ourbackground.htm.

83. "The Federalist Society and the Challenge to a Democratic Jurisprudence," *Institute for Democracy Studies*, January 2001. Available at: http://www.institute-fordemocracy.org/fedsoc.html.

84. Neil A. Lewis, "A Conservative Legal Group Thrives in Bush's Washington," *New York Times,* April 18, 2001.

85. David Helvarg, *The War Against the Greens* (San Francisco: Sierra Club Books, 1994).

86. Community Rights Counsel, "Nothing for Free: How Private Judicial Seminars Are Undermining Environmental Protections and Breaking the Public's Trust," July 2000. Available at: http://www.tripsforjudges. org/crc.pdf.

87. Ibid.

88. Michael Scherer, "The Making of the Corporate Judiciary: How Big Business Is Quietly Funding a Legal Revolution," *Mother Jones,* November 2003.

89. Jonathan Groner, "Mississippi: Battleground for Tort Reform," *Legal Times,* January 26, 2004.

90. Laura A. Bischoff, "Races for Top Court Raised Millions," *Dayton Daily News,* March 4, 2003.

91. Brent Kendall, "Chamber of Commerce Plans State Judicial-Race Campaigns." *Los Angeles DailyJournal,* January 8, 2004.

92. http://www.acslaw.org.

93. Morton J. Horwitz, *The Transformation of American Law, 1870–1960* (Oxford: Oxford University Press, 1992), p. 72.

94. Christopher Stone, *Where the Law Ends* (New York: Harper Colophon, 1975), p. 28.

95. Roland Marchand, *Creating the Corporate Soul: The Rise of Public Relations and Corporate Imagery in American Big Business* (Berkeley: University of California Press, 1998).

96. Quoted in Joel Bakan, *The Corporation: The Pathological Pursuit of Profit and Power* (New York: Free Press, 2004), p. 26.

97. Ibid., pp. 56–57.

98. For contact information for these groups, see the Appendix.

99. Author interview with Jeff Milchen, June 16, 2003.

100. Hartmann, *Unequal Protection,* p. 281.

101. http://www.celdf.org.

102. For a exhaustive resource connecting *Nike v. Kasky* to the question of corporate constitutional rights, see http://www.reclaimdemocracy. org/nike/.

103. David Stout, "Court Upholds Telemarketing Restrictions," *New York Times,* February 18, 2004.

CHAPTER 3

1. Robert Monks, "The Curse of the Corporate State: Saving Capitalism from Itself," *New York Center for the Study of Financial Innovation*, No. 65, January 2004. p. 11, available at: http://www.ragm.com/library/topics/Corporate-StateReportCSFI.pdf.

2. Ibid. p. 12.

3. "ExxonMobil Shareholder Vote on Climate a Wake Up Call," Greenpeace press release, May 29, 2003.

4. Exxon Mobil, Summary of Proposal Votes, 2003.

5. Exxon Mobil 2003 proxy statement, available at http://www.sec.gov/ Archives/edgar/data/34088/000104746903013719/a2103052zdef14a.htm#dl1 092_shareholder_proposal_4ank.
6. Monks, "The Curse of the Corporate State." p. 12.
7. For scientific reports on the problem of climate change, see the Intergovernmental Panel on Climate Change: http://www.ipcc.ch/.
8. ExxonMobil's directors wrote that "current technologies have not demonstrated an ability to compete effectively on a large scale with fossil fuels. Despite cost reductions in recent years, the costs of generating electricity from wind and solar power are still two and eight times, respectively, more than those from a modern natural gas-fired plant. As a result, these technologies continue to rely on significant government subsidies to support their implementation and resulting strong growth projection. As a result, we do not believe that wind and solar energy represents a prudent near-term investment for ExxonMobil." See Exxon Mobil, Summary of Proposal Votes, 2003.
9. However, the SEC did allow Christian Brothers Investment Services Inc. to introduce a resolution that called on the company to provide the data to justify its failure to protect shareholder interests against the risks posed by climate change. That resolution won 8.8 percent of the shareholder vote. See "Shareholders Turn Up Global Warming Heat on ExxonMobil with New Resolution," Christian Brothers press release, May 26, 2004, available at http://www.cbisonline.com/headlines/headline_xom_victory.asp.
10. Russell Mokhiber, *Corporate Crime and Violence: Big Business Power and the Abuse of the Public Trust* (San Francisco: Sierra Club Books, 1994), chap. 30.
11. Jamie Court, *Corporateering* (New York: Tarcher-Putnam, 2003), pp. 16–17.
12. Sigrid U. Esser, "Reaching Out: Devising Individual Shareholder Programs," *The Conference Board Report*, March 2003, The Conference Board, New York. http://www.conference-board.org/publications/describe. cfm?id=654.
13. Social Investment Forum, "2003 Report on Socially Responsible Investing Trends in the United States," December 2003, available at http://www.social-invest.org/areas/research/trends/sri_trends_report_ 2003.pdf.
14. 8 Del. C.§141(a); Model Business Corporation Act §8.01(b).
15. Robert Monks and Nell Minow, *Power and Accountability* (New York: HarperCollins, 1991) pp. 87–88.
16. Ibid. Since the 1980s, some states have also enacted "exculpation statutes" which allow corporations to provide in their charters that directors are not liable for breaches of the duty of care involving simple negligence. Even in cases when a director might be held liable for a breach of the duty of care or loyalty, he or she may be entitled to indemnification from the corporation or covered by liability insurance provided by the company to directors and officers (except in cases of fraud). See: Senate Committee on Governmental Affairs, "Financial Oversight of Enron: The SEC and Private-Sector Watchdogs" (Staff Report), October 7, 2002.
17. Monks and Minow, *Power and Accountability*, p. 75.
18. Graef Crystal, "Pay to U.S. Directors Reveals Back-Scratching," *Bloomberg News*, August 6, 2003.
19. For a more complete history of the rise of limited liability, see Chapter 1.
20. Monks and Minow, *Power and Accountability*, p. 10.

21. John Micklethwait and Adrian Wooldridge, *The Company: A Short History of a Revolutionary Idea* (New York: Random House, 2003), p. 61. One key contributor to the increasing ownership of stock was the rise of large railroad companies, whose "voracious requirement for capital did more than anything else to create the modern New York Stock Exchange."

22. Ibid., pp. 103–11.

23. Adolf Berle and Gardiner Means, *The Modern Corporation and Private Property* (New York: MacMillan, 1932).

24. Esser, "Reaching Out."

25. Michael E. Murphy, "Dispelling TINA's Ghost from the Post-Enron Corporate Governance Debate," *Santa Clara Law Review* 43 (2002):3.

26. Monks and Minow, *Power and Accountability*, p. 31.

27. *Statistical Abstract of the United States, 2000.* U.S. Census Bureau, 2001, http://www.census.gov/prod/www/statistical-abstract-us.html, p. 523.

28. Investment Company Institute, Mutual Fund Fact Book, 2000. Available at: http://www.ici.org/pdf/factbooks3.html#2000%20Fact%20Book.

29. *Statistical Abstract of the United States, 2000.* p. 523.

30. Ibid.

31. Pensions & Investments/Watson Wyatt Global 300 Survey, 2003.

32. "Ten Major Investors Issue 10-Point 'Call For Action' on Global Warming Risks," INCR Press release, November 21, 2003, available at http://www.incr.com/news_release.htm.

33. Ibid.

34. Social Investment Forum, "2003 Report."

35. Barry B. Burr, "Corporate Governance: Activist Shareholders are 'Cabbing It' to 2004 Proxy Season; Previous Changes Haven't Been Enough to Satisfy Investors," *Pensions and Investments,* February 23, 2004.

36. In March 2004, the chairman of the board was also CEO at 378 of the *Fortune* 500 companies. For details, see "Split CEO/Chairman Roles," The Corporate Library,March 2004, available at http://www.thecorporatelibrary.org/Governance-Research/spotlight-topics/spotlight/boardsanddirectors/SplitChairs2004.html.

37. Jay W. Lorsch, *Pawns or Potentates: The Reality of America's Corporate Boards* (Boston: Harvard Business School Press, 1989), pp. 170–71.

38. Richard C. Breeden, "Restoring the Trust," Report to the Hon. Jed S. Rakoff, The United States District Court For the Southern District of New York on Corporate Governance for the Future of MCI, Inc.," August 2003 http://www.nysd.uscourts.gov/rulings/02cv4963_ 082603.pdf.

39. "The Barons of Bankruptcy," *Financial Times,* July 31–August 2, 2002.

40. "The Greedy Bunch—You Bought, They Sold," *Fortune Magazine,* September 2, 2002. p. 64.

41. Graef Crystal, "Pay to U.S. Directors Reveals Back-Scratching," *Bloomberg News,* August 6, 2003.

42. For a more detailed discussion on the pros and cons of holding directors responsible, see Chapter 5.

43. The Conference Board, "Part II: Corporate Governance," in *Commission on Public Trust and Private Enterprise,* January 9, 2003, p. 6.

44. Breeden, "Restoring the Trust."

45. The NYSE's new corporate governance listing requirements are available at http://www.nyse.com/pdfs/finalcorpgovrules.pdf. NASDAQ's corporate governance listing requirements are available at http://www. nasdaq.com/about/LegalComplianceFAQs.stm#corpgov.

46. Institute for Policy Studies and United for a Fair Economy, "Executive Excess 2003," p. 19. http://www.faireconomy.org/press/2003/EE2003.pdf .

47. Murphy, "Dispelling TINA's Ghost," p. 8.

48. See http://www.irrc.org for statistics on shareholder resolutions.

49. Edward Iwata, "Businesses Say corporate governance can go too far," *USA Today*, June 24, 2004.

50. Steve Jordon and Grace Shim, "Buffett, Munger Blast Scofflaws, Pair Say Scandals a Slap inShareholders' Faces," *Omaha World Herald*, May 5, 2003.

51. Institute for Policy Studies and United for a Fair Economy, "Executive Excess 2001."

52. Institute for Policy Studies and United for a Fair Economy, "Executive Excess 2003."

53. Ibid.

54. Amy Borus, "Executive Pay: Labor Strikes Back," *Business Week*, May 26, 2003. p. 46.

55. Will Bove, "Majority Votes on Shareholder Proposals Reach New High" Institutional Shareholder Services press release, August 8, 2003.

56. Andrew Countryman, "Investors Get Say on Equity Pay: SEC Mandates Stockholder Vote," *Chicago Tribune*, July 1, 2003.

57. Jill Treanor, "Rebels Humiliate Glaxo: The Shareholders' Message: You Won't Get Pounds 22m for Failure," *The Guardian*, May 20, 2003.

58. Jill Treanor, "Glaxo Appeases Investors with Boardroom Clean-up," *The Guardian*, June 6, 2003.

59. Between 1979 and 1989, the portion of the nation's wealth held by the top 1 percent nearly doubled, growing from 22 to 39 percent. In 1998, the top 1 percent of Americans controlled 38.1 percent of the country's wealth, the top 5 percent controlled 59.4 percent of the country's wealth, and the top 10 percent controlled 69.9 percent of the country's wealth. By comparison, the bottom 40 percent controlled just 0.2 percent of the country's wealth. See Edward N. Wolff, "Recent Trends in Wealth Ownership, 1983–1998," Levy Institute Working Paper No. 300, Table 2 (Levy Economics Institute, April 2000), available in a pie chart at http://www.faireconomy.org/research/wealth_charts.html.

60. http://www.domini.com.

61. Social Investment Forum, "2003 Report."

62. Ibid.

63. Daniel J. H. Greenwood, "Fictional Shareholders: For Whom Are Corporate Managers Trustees, Revisited," *Southern California Law Review* 69 (March 1996): 1021.

64. Costco employees earn $15.97 an hour, compared to $11.52 for Sam's Club employees and $9.64 for Wal-Mart employees. Costco also spends $5,735 a year on health benefits per employee versus $3,500 for Wal-Mart's Sam's Club. Source: Stanley Holmes and Wendy Zellner, "The Costco Way: Higher Wages Mean Higher Profits. But Try Telling Wall Street," *Business Week*, April 12, 2004.

65. Ibid.
66. Christine Frey, "Costco to Pay Quarterly Dividend," *Seattle Post-Intelligencer*, April 29, 2004.
67. Social Investment Forum, "2003 Report."
68. Ibid.
69. As the Social Investment Forum reports, "Community investing—capital from investors that is directed to communities that are underserved by traditional financial services—experienced tremendous growth from 2001 to 2003, despite difficult market conditions. In total, community investing expanded by 84 percent over the two-year period. Assets held and invested locally by community development financial institutions (CDFIs) based in the United States totaled $14 billion in 2003, up from $7.6 billion in 2001." The Social Investment Forum also notes that "community investing makes it possible for local organizations to provide financial services to low-income individuals, and to supply capital for small businesses and vital community services, such as child care, affordable housing, and healthcare. These local financial service organizations prioritize people who have been denied access to capital and provide them with opportunities to borrow, save, and invest in their own communities. In addition to supplying badly needed capital in underserved neighborhoods, community investment groups provide important services, such as education, mentoring, and technical support. They also build relationships between families, non-profits, small businesses, and conventional financial institutions and markets." Source: ibid.
70. For more on the Paper Campaign, see http://www.thepapercampaign. com/.
71. For a list of state corporate laws concerning corporate purpose, see http://www.citizenworks.org/enron/corp-states.php.
72. Greenwood, *Fictional Shareholders*, p. 1021.
73. Allan Kennedy, *The End of Shareholder Value* (Cambridge: Perseus Publishing, 2000), p. xi.
74. *Dodge v. Ford Motor Co.*, 204 Mich. 459, 170 N.W. 668 (1919).
75. Ibid.
76. Lawrence E. Mitchell, "A Theoretical and Practical Framework for Enforcing Corporate Constituency Studies," 70 *Texas Law Review* 579– 643 (1992). (February 1992): 601.
77. Robert Hinkley, "How Corporate Law Inhibits Social Responsibility," *Business Ethics Magazine*, January/February 2002. Available online at: http://www. divinerightofcapital.com/change.htm.
78. Peter C. Fusaro and Ross M. Miller, *What Went Wrong at Enron: Everyone's Guide to the Largest Bankruptcy in U.S. History* (Hoboken: John Wiley and Sons, 2002), p. 28.
79. Robert Estes, *The Tyranny of the Bottom Line* (San Francisco: Barrett-Koehler, 1996), p. 38.
80. As of April 2004, an average day on the stock exchange had witnessed 1.66 billion shares changing hands. That's more than double the volume of just five years ago; only 809 million shares changed hands a day in 1999. It's more than eight times the volume of 202 million daily share trades in 1992, which itself is almost twice the 109 million daily share trades in 1985, which is itself five times the 21 million daily share trades in 1977, which itself is seven

times the 3 million daily share trades in 1960. In 1983, 19 percent of American households owned stock, a number that had remained constant for twenty years prior. But over the last twenty years, it has grown substantially. In 1989, 31.6 percent of households owned corporate shares; in 1992 it was 36.6 percent; in 1995 it was 40.3 percent. Today it is almost half of all households, which includes 88 million individual investors (up from 69.3 million in 1995 and 52.3 million in 1989). Source: NYSE Overview Statistics, available at http://www.nyse.com.

81. While the number of investors with direct holding in stocks increased from 27.0 million to 33.8 million between 1989 and 1998, the number of investors with holdings in equity mutual funds rose from 4.5 million in 1989 to 14.7 million in 1998, and the number of individuals holding stock through retirement accounts or pension plans rose from 20.8 million in 1989 to 35.5 million in 1998. See NYSE Overview Statistics, available at http://www.nyse.com.

82. Lawrence Mitchell, *Corporate Irresponsibility* (New Haven: Yale University Press, 2001), p. 183.

83. http://www.nyse.com/marketinfo/1022221393023.html.

84. Alex Berenson, *The Number: How the Drive for Quarterly Earnings Corrupted Wall Street and Corporate America* (New York: Random House, 2003), p. xvi.

85. Marjorie Kelly, *The Divine Right of Capital* (San Francisco: Barrett-Koehler, 2002), p. 33.

86. Ibid.

87. Ibid., p. 13.

88. Aaron Bernstein, "Too Much Corporate Power?" *Business Week*, September 11, 2000 p. 148.

89. Hinkley, "How Corporate Law Inhibits Social Responsibility." Availabe at http://www.divinerightofcapital.com/change.htm.

90. Ibid.

91. In California, Senate Majority Whip Richard Alcaron is the chief author of the Code (Senate Bill 917). The Senate Judiciary Committee Staff notes: "Committee staff believes that this proposed standard is so vague as to make compliance impossible, and will result in layers of litigation to determine its meaning. . . . Society has yet to come to any sort of consensus on what constitutes fundamental human rights, community welfare, or appropriate labor and environmental standards, thereby inviting a subjective analysis by the judge or jury. As a matter of law and policy, the proponents' goals should not be accomplished simply by enacting a declaration of principles attached to a private right of action." For a full analysis, see http://info.sen.ca.gov/pub/bill/sen/sb_0901-0950/sb_917_cfa_20040121_120529_sen_ comm.html.

92. In Minnesota, Senator Sandy Pappas is chief author the Code (Senate File #1529) in the Senate. Representative Carlos Mariani is chief author in the House (House File #1534). See http://www.c4cr.org for details.

93. For a more complete discussion of holding directors and officers responsible, see Chapter 5.

94. Testimony to the California Senate Judiciary Committee, January 20, 2004.

95. *The Report of the American Bar Association Task Force on Corporate Responsibility,* March 31, 2003. available at: http://www.abanet.org/buslaw/corporateresponsibility/final_report.pdf

96. "German Corporate Governance and Management: An American's Perspective," in Zeitschrift für betriebswirtschaftliche Forschung (ZfbF), ed. Axel V. Weder (Dusseldorf: Verlagsgruppe Handelsblatt, 1996).

97. Korn/Ferry International, "Board Meeting in Session. European Board of Directors Study" (1996), p. 12.

98. Stefan Prigge, "A Survey of German Corporate Governance," in *Comparative Corporate Governance: The State of the Art and Emerging Research,* ed. Klaus J. Hopt (Oxford: Clarendon Press, 1998). p. 957.

99. Lawyer Jeff Gates, president of the Shared Capitalism Institute and a pioneer of federal Employee Stock Ownership Plan [ESOP] legislation, has argued that corporations will more broadly reflect the landscape of who is affected by the corporation when those who are affected gain an ownership stake: "The main 'systemic' deficiency in today's capitalism lies in its faulty 'feedback' system," writes Gates. "The system is not engineered—wired, if you will—to anticipate and respond to the needs of those who populate it. Rather, it is steadily being rewired to reflect the peculiar dictates of financial capital. However, the company could be financially reengineered so that a portion of its shares are owned by its consumers and its employees. Converting those stakeholders into shareholders could change things. For instance, where dissatisfied local residents now depend on a circuitous feedback system to register their concerns, an ownership stake would transform them from concerned (but disconnected) stakeholders into property-empowered owners. Even if local consumers and employees owned only a small quantity of the utility's total shares, this qualitative change in the composition of that ownership could transform the company's capacity to anticipate and respond to legitimate local concerns." From Jeffrey Gates, *The Ownership Solution: Toward a Shared Capitalism for the Twenty-First Century* (New York: Perseus Book Group, 1999). p. 8.

100. Murphy, "Dispelling TINA's Ghost," p. 19.

101. Kellye Y. Testy, "Linking Progressive Corporate Law with Progressive Social Movements," *Tulane Law Review* 76, nos. 5–6 (2002): 1237.

102. Margaret M. Blair and Lynn A. Stout, "A Team Production Theory of Corporate Law," *Virginia Law Review* 85, no. 2 (March 1999). pp. 247–328.

103. Margaret M. Blair, "Shareholder Value, Corporate Governance and Corporate Performance: A Post-Enron Reassessment of the Conventional Wisdom," available at: http://papers.ssrn.com/sol3/papers.cfm? abstract_id=334240.

104. Margaret Blair and Lynn Stout, "A Team Production Theory of Corporate Law," p. 303.

105. Blair and Stout, "Why 'Shareholder Primacy' Became the Dominant Paradigm in the Last Two Decades" http://www.teamproduction.us/dominantpradigm.htm.

106. Margaret Blair, "Shareholder Value, Corporate Governance and Corporate Performance," availablet at: http://papers.ssrn.com/sol3/papers.cfm?abstract_id=334240.

107. Mitchell, *Corporate Irresponsibility,* pp. 162–64.

108. Equity held in pension funds and other retirement accounts, such as 401(k)s and IRAs, as well as equity in trust funds and foundation and university endowments, is not subject to capital gains taxes.

109. See Chapter 1 for a short history of the rise of limited liability.
110. Estes, *Tyranny of the Bottom Line*, p. 208.
111. Ibid., p. 203.
112. Theodore Sonde and Harvey Pitt, "Utilizing the Federal Securities Laws to Clear the Air! Clean the Sky! Wash the Wind!" Howard Law Journal 16(1971): 16. p. 851.
113. http://www.corporatesunshine.org.
114. Joel Bakan, *The Corporation* (New York: Free Press, 2004), p. 70.

CHAPTER 4

1. "Enron Traders Caught On Tape," CBS News, June 1, 2004.

> In early June, transcripts of Enron traders were released, which revealed a contemptuous disdain for poor consumers who would pay much higher electricity rates as a result of the company's manipulation of the market:
>
> "They're f- - - - -g taking all the money back from you guys?" complains an Enron employee on the tapes. "All the money you guys stole from those poor grandmothers in California?"
>
> "Yeah, grandma Millie, man. But she's the one who couldn't figure out how to (expletive) vote on the butterfly ballot."
>
> "Yeah, now she wants her f- - - - -g money back for all the power you've charged right up, jammed right up her a- - - - - -for f- - - - -g $250 a megawatt/hour."
>
> Timothy Belden, a trader from the Portland office who plead guilty to charges in connection with energy manipulation, is caught on tape saying that the firm, "just (expletive) California . . . to the tune of a million bucks or two a day."
>
> Enron traders also fantasize about Ken Lay becoming Secretary of Energy, and when it comes to the debate over price caps (in 2000), they say that, "When this election comes Bush will f- - - - - -g whack this s—t, man. He won't play this price-cap b- - - - - -t."
>
> In regards to turning the power on and off, one Enron worker is caught saying, "If you took down the steamer, how long would it take to get it back up?"
>
> "Oh, it's not something you want to just be turning on and off every hour. Let's put it that way," replies another.

2. Jonathan Peterson and Nancy Rivera Brooks, "California Document Calls Energy Market Abuses the 'Tip of the Iceberg,'" *Los Angeles Times*, March 4, 2003.
3. Lowell Bergman and Jeff J. Gerth, "Power Trader Tied to Bush Finds Washington All Ears," *New York Times*, May 25, 2002.
4. Richard A. Oppel Jr., "Panel Finds Manipulation by Energy Companies," *New York Times*, March 26, 2003.
5. Adam D. Thierer, "Energizing America: A Blueprint for Deregulating the Electricity Market," Heritage Society Backgrounder 1100, January 23, 1997, available at http://www.heritage.org/Research/EnergyandEnvironment/BG1100.cfm.

6. Sharon Beder, "The Electricity Deregulation Con Game," *PR Watch* 10, no. 3 (2003).

7. Walter Adams and James W. Brock, *The Bigness Complex: Industry, Labor, and Government in the American Economy* (Second Edition), (Stanford, CA: Stanford University Press, 2004) p. 208.

8. American Prospect Debate: "Resolved: The Enron Affair is the Logical Result of Deregulation," March 20, 2002. Available at: http://www.ourfuture. org/onmessage/borosage/3_20_02_1.cfm

9. Tyson Slocum, "Electric Utility Deregulation and the Myths of the Energy Crisis," *Bulletin of Science, Technology and Society* 21, no. 6 (December 2001). p. 473.

10. For example, in Illinois, the Citizen Utility Board (CUB) (formed in 1983 by the state legislature) advocates for residential and small-business electricity, gas, and telephone rate payers before state regulatory agencies. The CUB generates its membership with monthly inserts into electricity, gas, and telephone bills, mandated by state law. Over the last twenty years, the CUB has saved consumers more than $5 billion by blocking rate hikes and winning consumer refunds. See http://www. citizensutilityboard.org/.

11. Greg Palast, Jerrold Oppenheim, and Theo MacGregror, *Democracy and Regulation: How the Public Can Govern Essential Services* (London: Pluto Press, 2003), p. 67 (for a broader discussion of the issues of setting prices, see pp. 56–87).

12. Public Citizen, "The Public Utility Holding Company Act and the Protection of Energy Consumers: An Examination of the Corporate Records of the Top Companies Pushing for PUHCA Repeal," September 2002. Available at: http://www.citizen.org/documents/cmeep15.pdf.

13. Public Citizen, "The Blackout Hearings High-Wire Act: Transmission for Households or More Profit for Corporate Profiteers," September 3, 2003. http://www.citizen.org/pressroom/release.cfm?ID=1535.

14. "State Approves Gas Rate Hikes for 3 Companies" *Associated Press*, August 18, 2003.

15. Peter Behr, "Utility Price Shock Coming in August," *Washington Post*, May 7, 2004.

16. Jonathan D. Glater, "Under Deregulation, Montana Power Price Soars," *New York Times*, August 21, 2003.

17. Slocum, "Electric Utility Deregulation and the Myths of the Energy Crisis." p. 473.

18. Public Citizen, "Blackout Hearings High-Wire Act. http://www.citizen. org/pressroom/release.cfm?ID=1535.

19. Ibid.

20. As we saw in Chapter 1, these limits could also be designed directly into the corporations' charters.

21. Rachel Gordon, "S.F. Voters Turn Off Public Power Bid," *San Francisco Chronicle*, November 10, 2001.

22. David Morris and Daniel Krarker, "Solutions to Electricity Crisis," *Oakland Tribune*, June 5, 2001.

23. New Rules Project, "Customer-Owned Electric Utilities: Generation, Transmission and Distribution," http://www.newrules.org/electricity/customerowned.html.

24. Amory Lovins and Hunter Lovins, *Brittle Power* (Andover, MA: Brick House Publishing Company, 1982).

25. Yochi J. Dreazen, "Fallacies of the Tech Boom," *Wall Street Journal*, September 26, 2002.

26. Karen Kaplan and Jon Healey, "Too Much, Too Soon for Telecom," *Los Angeles Times*, June 30, 2002.

27. Paul Starr, "The Great Telecom Implosion," *The American Prospect*, September 9, 2002.

28. Kaplan and Healey, "Too Much, Too Soon for Telecom."

29. Ibid.

30. Steven Rosenbush, "Inside the Telecom Game," *Business Week*, August 5, 2002.

31. Dreazen, "Fallacies of the Tech Boom."

32. "The Telecommunications Act: Consumers Still Waiting for Better Phone and Cable Services on the Sixth Anniversary of National Law," Consumers Union press release, February 6, 2002.

33. Ibid.

34. "Cooper, Kimmelman Remind Lawmakers of Warnings Made in Immediate Wake of Telecom Act's Passage," Telecom Policy Report, April 28, 2004.

35. Ibid.

36. Robert Kuttner, *Everything for Sale: The Virtues and Limits of Markets* (New York: Knopf, 1998), p. 175.

37. Stephen Pizzo et al., *Inside Job: The Looting of America's Savings and Loans* (New York: McGraw-Hill, 1989).

38. Kuttner, *Everything for Sale*, pp. 173–74.

39. "Oversight of Investment Banks' Response to the Lessons of Enron," Senate Permanent Subcommittee on Investigations, December 11, 2002.

40. "Report on Fishtail, Bacchus, Sundance, and Slapshot: Four Enron Transactions Funded and Facilitated by U.S. Financial Institutions," Senate Permanent Subcommittee on Investigations, January 2, 2003, available at http://levin.senate.gov/enronreport0102.pdf.

41. "Oversight of Investment Banks' Response to the Lessons of Enron," hearing of the Senate Permanent Investigations Subcommittee of the Government Affairs Committee," Senator Carl Levin, D-MI, Chair, December 11, 2002.

42. Weiss Ratings, "Crisis of Confidence on Wall Street," June 11, 2002, available at http://www.weissratings.com/crisis_of_confidence.asp.

43. "Interview with David Chacon," PBS Frontline, *The Wall Street Fix*, May 8, 2003, available at http://www.pbs.org/wgbh/pages/frontline/shows/wallstreet/interviews/chacon.html.

44. Anthony Bianco and Heather Timons, "Crisis at Citi," *Business Week*, September 9, 2003. p. 34.

45. "Ralph Nader, Citizen Works Criticize Wall Street Settlement as an Anemic Slap on the Wrist," Citizen Works press release, April 28, 2003, available at http://www.citizenworks.org/admin/press/secsettle-pr.php.

46. "Sad Chapter on Wall Street," *Washington Post*, editorial, April 30, 2003.

47. Bianco and Timmons, "Crisis at Citi." p. 34.

48. Quoted in William Greider, "Crime in the Suites," *The Nation*, February 4, 2002. p. 11.

49. U.S. General Accounting Office, "Financial Derivatives: Actions Needed to Protect the System," May 18, 1994.

50. Frank Partnoy, *Infectious Greed* (New York: Times Books, 2003) and U.S. House Committee on Banking Finance and Urban Affairs, "Safety and Soundness Issues Related to Bank Derivatives Activities," Minority Staff Report, October 1993.

51. For a detailed, step-by-step guide to corporate welfare and what to do about it, we suggest Ralph Nader, *Cutting Corporate Welfare* (New York: Seven Stories Press, 1999) (part of the Open Pamphlet Series).

52. The Cato Institute, *The Cato Handbook for Congress*, 108th Congress, Washington, DC. p. 337.

53. Nader, *Cutting Corporate Welfare*, p. 31.

54. Adams and Brock, *The Bigness Complex*, p. 325.

55. Ibid., p. 326.

56. David Korten, "Economies for Life," *Yes! Magazine*, Fall 2002.

57. Graeme K. Deans, Fritz Kroeger, Stefan Zeisel, *Winning the Merger Endgame: A Playbook for Profiting from Industry Consolidation* (New York: McGraw-Hill, 2002). FERC press release.

58. Richard B. DuBoff, *Accumulation and Power: An Economic History of the United States* (Armonk, N.Y.: M.E. Sharpe, 1989), p. 175.

59. Charles E. Mueller, "Antitrust Overview," *Antitrust Law and Economics Review* (GDP numbers adjusted for 2004), available at http://www. metrolink.net/~cmueller/i-overvw.html).

60. John Jewkes, *The Sources of Invention* (New York: W.W. Norton, 1971).

61. Ralph Nader, Mark Green, and Joel Seligman, *Taming the Giant Corporation* (New York: W.W. Norton, 1976), p. 221.

62. "Revitalizing Antitrust: An interview with Walter Adams and James Brock," *Multinational Monitor*, June 1996, available at: http://www.multinationalmonitor.com/hyper/mm0696.06.html.

63. Mercedes M. Cardona, "Ad-spending soothsayers optimistic on year ahead," *Advertising Age*, December 15, 2003.

64. Richard B. DuBoff and Edward S. Herman, "Mergers, Concentration, and the Erosion of Democracy," *Monthly Review*, May 2001. p. 26.

65. DuBoff, *Accumulation and Power*, p. 174.

66. Robert McChesney and John Nichols, *Our Media, Not Theirs* (New York: Seven Stories Press, 2002). p. 49.

67. Ibid., p. 49.

68. Ibid., p. 58–59.

69. A Philadelphia court of appeals delayed the FCC's rules from going into law in September 2003; the issue remains unresolved as of this writing. In January 2004, however, President Bush signed into law a compromise bill that allowed a media company to reach up to 39 percent of the national audience. For updates on the media ownership rules, see http://www.freepress.net/rules/.

70. "More than 1400 Gather in Madison, WI for National Conference on Media Reform," Mediareform.net press release, available at http://www.freepress.net/news/release.php?id=7.

71. Frank Ahrens, "Court Rejects Rules on Media Ownership," *Washington Post*, June 25, 2004.

72. Ted Turner, "Monopoly or Democracy?" *Washington Post,* May 30, 2003.
73. Ibid.
74. *Associated Press v. United States,* 326 U.S. 1, 20 (1945).
75. Robert Weissman, "Divide and Conquer: Restraining Vertical Integration and Cross-Industry Ownership," *Multinational Monitor,* October–November 2002.
76. Robert McChesney, *Rich Media, Poor Democracy* (Urbana, Ill: University of Illinois Press, 1999), p. 312.
77. DuBoff and Herman, "Mergers, Concentration, and the Erosion of Democracy."
78. New Rules Project, "Agribusiness Merger Moratorium," available at http://www.newrules.org/agri/merger.html.
79. Peter Carstensen, "Testimony on Concentration and Competition in Agriculture for the Senate Appropriations Subcommittee on Agriculture, Rural Development and Related Agencies," May 17, 2001. Presenting testimony on the consolidated nature of agriculture and suggesting policy and enforcement changes to address the inherent problems in this type of market.
80. http://www.competitivemarkets.com.
81. "Mergers and Acquisitions—Summary: 1985–1999," *Statistical Abstract of the United States 2000.*
82. DuBoff and Herman, "Mergers, Concentration, and the Erosion of Democracy."
83. Ibid.
84. Sam Natapoff, "Rogue Whale," *The American Prospect,* March 2004.
85. "Antitrust Regulators to Puzzle over Possible Merger of Tobacco Giants," *Winston-Salem Journal,* March 18, 2004.
86. Brock and Adams, *The Bigness Complex,* p. 45.
87. Bill Day, "Will the Trustbusters Ride Again?" *Des Moines Business Record,* November 21, 1998.
88. Charles Mueller, "Antitrust Overview," *Antitrust Law and Economics Review.* 1996, available at: http://www.metrolink.net/~cmueller/i-overvw.html?
89. For more about the Microsoft antitrust case, see the Consumer Project on Technology, available at http://www.cptech.org.
90. U.S. Senate Subcommittee on Antitrust, Business Rights and Competition Hearing on Antitrust Laws, September 19, 2002.
91. "Interview with Walter Adams and James Brock," *Multinational Monitor.*
92. *United States V. Aluminum Co. of America,* 148 F.2d 416, 432 (2nd Cir. 1945).
93. Nader et al., *Taming The Giant Corporation,* p. 199.
94. Ibid., p. 70.
95. Adams and Brock, *The Bigness Complex,* p. 321.
96. Robert W. Crandall, "The Failure of Structural Remedy in Sherman Act Monopolization Cases," in *Microsoft, Antitrust and the New Economy: Selected Essays,* ed. David S. Evans (Boston: Kluwer Academic Publishers, 2002).
97. Adams and Brock, *The Bigness Complex.,* p. 186.
98. Joseph Wilson, *Globalization and the Limits of National Merger Control Laws* (New York: Aspen Publishers, 2003).
99. Milton Friedman, "Public Schools: Make Them Private," *Washington Post,* February 19, 1955.
100. Barbara Miner, "Business Goes to School: The For-Profit Corporate Drive to Run Public Schools," *Multinational Monitor,* January–February 2002. p. 13.

101. Jeffrey Leverich, "Wisconsin Vouchers and the Bradley Foundation," October 3, 1998, available at http://www.weac.org.

102. Miner, "Business Goes to School."p. 13. See also Gerald W. Bracey, *The War Against America's Public Schools: Privatizing Schools, Commercializing Education* (Boston: Allyn & Bacon, 2002).

103. Erika Hobbs, "Low Rates, Needed Repairs Lure 'Big Water' to Uncle Sam's Plumbing," Center for Public Integrity, *The Water Barons*, available at http://www.icij.org/water/.

104. Public Citizen, "The Water Privatiziation 'Model': A Backgrounder on United Water's Atlanta Fiasco." Available at: http://www.citizen.org/documents/atlantafiasco.pdf.

105. See Public Citizen's "Water for All" campaign for details on communities fighting water privatization.

106. Hobbs, "Low Rates, Needed Repairs."

107. P. W. Singer, *Corporate Warriors: The Rise of the Privatized Military Industry* (Ithaca, N.Y.: Cornell University Press, 2003); William Hartung, *How Much Are You Making on the War, Daddy?* (New York: Nation Books, 2003); and "Making a Killing: The Business of War," Center for Public Integrity Report, 2002, available at http://store.publicintegrity.org/bow/.

CHAPTER 5

1. Jason Leopold, "Former Employee Says Enron Manipulated California Power Market," *Dow Jones*, February 20, 2002. Also see Senate Committee on Government Affairs, majority staff memo, November 12, 2002, available at http://govt-aff.senate.gov/_files/111202fercmemo. pdf.

2. John R. Wilke, "Enron Criminal Probe Focuses on Alleged Corruption Abroad," *Wall Street Journal*, August 5, 2002.

3. James V. Grimaldi, "Enron Pipeline Leaves Scar on South America," *Washington Post*, May 6, 2002.

4. Human Rights Watch, "The Enron Corporation: Complicity in Human Rights Violations," 1999, available at http://www.hrw.org/reports/1999/enron/.

5. The Conference Board Commission on Public Trust and Private Enterprise, "Findings and Recommendations, Part 1," September 17, 2002.

6. In 2000, for example, WorldCom paid a $3.5 million fine to settle charges that it switched customers' telephone carriers without permission. See "WorldCom Agrees to Pay $3.5 Million Fine," Associated Press, June 6, 2000.

7. AFL-CIO, "Death on the Job: The Toll of Neglect," April 2004. http://www.aflcio.org/yourjobeconomy/safety/memorial/upload/death_ 2004_intro.pdf.

8. Government Accountability Office, "Health Care Fraud: Information-Sharing Proposals to Improve Enforcement Efforts," GGCD-96-101, May 1, 1996. The GAO estimated that healthcare fraud costs between 3 and 10 percent of all healthcare expenditures. Malcolm Sparrow, author of *License to Steal: Why Fraud Plagues America's Health Care System* (Boulder, Colo.: Westview, 2000), says the cost of healthcare fraud is probably much higher, as much as 30 to 40 percent of all healthcare expenditures. See interview in *Corporate Crime Reporter*, June 1997.

9. F. T. Cullen et al., *Corporate Crime Under Attack: The Ford Pinto Case and Beyond* (Cincinnati: Anderson, 1987).

10. AFL-CIO, "Death on the Job."

11. Ralph Estes, *The Tyranny of the Bottom Line* (San Francisco: Berrett-Koehler, 1995), pp. 171–198.

12. DOJ/FBI, *Crime in the United States 2002*, available at http://www.fbi.gov/pressrel/pressrel03/ucr2002.htm.

13. In 2001, the national murder rate was 15,980. See FBI, *Crime in the United States 2001.* http://www.fbi.gov/ucr/01cius.htm.

14. U.S. Consumer Product Safety Commission, 2003 Budget Request and Performance Plan Overview Statement. As cited in CPSC Monitor, (Consumer Alert's update on the Consumer Product Safety Commission, Volume 7, Issue 4, April 2003).

15. Bureau of Labor Statistics, "National Census of Fatal Occupational Injuries in 2002," press release dated September 17, 2003.

16. AFL-CIO, "Death on the Job."

17. NRDC Particulate Pollution FAQ: http://www.nrdc.org/air/pollution/qbreath.asp.

18. An estimated 553,400 people in the United States died from cancer in 2001. See "Lifetime Risk of Being Diagnosed With Cancer" (StatBite) Journal of the National Cancer Institute, Vol. 93, No. 10, pp. 742. Using conservative estimates put forth by those who dismiss environmental causes of cancer as negligible (i.e., 2 percent of the total incidence of cancer deaths), we can calculate that at least 11,098 people died from cancers due to environmental causes (i.e., industrial pollution) in 2001. See Sandra Steingraber, *Living Downstream: An Ecologist Looks at Cancer and the Environment* (New York: Addison-Wesley, 1997), pp. 268–269.

19. Edward Sutherland, *White Collar Crime* (New Haven, Conn.: Yale University Press, 1983), p. 23.

20. *Unlawful Corporate Payments Act of 1977,* House of Representatives Report No. 95-610, September 28, 1977, available at http://www.usdoj.gov/criminal/fraud/fcpa/1977hse.htm.

21. Marshall B. Clinard et al., "Illegal Corporate Behavior," Report to the U.S. Department of Justice Law Enforcement Assistance Administration, October 1979.

22. Russell Mokhiber, "The Top 100 Corporate Criminals of the 1990s," *Multinational Monitor*, July–August, 1999.

23. Easterbrook and Fischel, "Antitrust Suits by Targets of Tender Offers," p. 1177 n. 57.

24. Clifton Leaf, "Send Them to Jail," *Fortune*, March 18, 2002.

25. Ibid. In December 2002, the Justice Department changed a long-standing policy of allowing many nonviolent first-time white-collar felons to serve their terms out in low-security halfway houses and community correction centers. The DOJ ordered the director of the U.S. Bureau of Prisons to move 125 white-collar felons to actual prisons at the end of 2002. See Dan Eggen, "White-Collar Crime Now Gets Real Time," *Washington Post*, January 7, 2003.

26. Michael Isikoff, "Hard Time for Corporate Perps," *Newsweek*, December 20, 2002.
27. Sarbanes-Oxley Act of 2002, Pub. L. No. 107-204, 116 Stat. 745 (2002).
28. Ibid.
29. Elisabeth Bumiller, "Corporate Conduct: The President," *New York Times*, July 31, 2002.
30. Christopher Stone, *Where the Law Ends* (New York: Harper & Row, 1975), p. 61.
31. Ibid.
32. Marshall B. Clinard and Peter C. Yeager, *Corporate Crime* (New York: Free Press; London: Collier Macmillan, 1980), pp. 170–171.
33. Canada Bill C-45 received royal assent in November 2003 and is expected to come into force sometime in 2004.
34. Government Response to the Fifteenth Report of Standing Committee on Justice and Human Rights, Corporate Liability, Canadian Justice Department, November 2002, available at http://www.uswa. ca/eng/westray/westray.htm.
35. Michelle Mann, "Corporate Criminals," *Canadian Business*, February 1, 2004.
36. California Penal Code Section 387, enacted in 1991.
37. Mokhiber, "Top 100 Corporate Criminals of the 1990s.
38. Ann Davis, "Treating On-the-Job Injuries as True Crimes," *Wall Street Journal*, February 26, 1997.
39. Henry Glasbeek, *Wealth by Stealth: Corporate Crime, Corporate Law, and the Perversion of Democracy* (Toronto: Between the Lines Press, 2002), p. 273.
40. Clinard and Yeager, *Corporate Crime* pp. 222; see also David Friedrichs, *Trusted Criminals: White Collar Crime in Contemporary Society* (Belmont, Calif.: Wadsworth/Thomson Learning, 1996).
41. Claire Cooper, "U.S. Grand Jury Indicts Energy Firm: Houston-Based Reliant Is Slapped with Six Counts of Defrauding California's Electricity Market," *Sacramento Bee*, April 9, 2004.
42. Larry D. Thompson, Deputy Attorney General, memo to heads of Department Components, U.S. Department of Justice, January 20, 2003, available at http://www.usdoj.gov/dag/cftf/business_organizations. pdf.
43. "Thompson Memo Opens the Door for Pre-Trial Diversions for Corporations," *Corporate Crime Reporter*, July 21, 2003.
44. Ibid.
45. By "independent," we mean free of any financial conflict of interest. Such directors should have no prior ties to the corporation as a stakeholder; should not be a shareholder, employee, contractor, director, or pensioner; and should have no business relationship or close personal relationship with other stakeholders. As such, the public director should strive to work within the corporation for the public good generally, even beyond the narrower interests of corporate participants. As Daniel Greenwood has suggested, "this broader conception of the managerial/director role is not an unmitigated good. Statesmanship is difficult . . . the public good is often controversial, and there is no reason whatsoever to think that unelected corporate managers or directors will reflect in their views the divisions of the citizenry as a whole." Yet public directors as proposed here are far more capable of representing the public interest than those appointed under the reigning share-centered ideology. See Daniel J. H. Greenwood, "Enronits: Why Good Corporations Go Bad," available at http://www. law.utah.edu/faculty/websites/greenwoodd/.

46. Stone, *Where the Law Ends*. See also Clinard et al., "Illegal Corporate Behavior."

47. Richard C. Breeden, "Restoring the Trust," Report to The Hon. Jed S. Rakoff, U.S. District Court for the Southern District of New York, August 2003.

48. "An Overview of the United States Sentencing Commission and the Organizational Guidelines," USSC, U.S. Sentencing Commission press release, October 8, 2003. The guidelines allow courts to impose a one- to five-year probationary period on any organization that commits a felony, has fifty or more employees, and "does not have an effective program to prevent and detect violations of law." Courts can "impose other conditions (1) that are reasonably related to the nature and circumstances of the offense or the history and characteristics of the organization."

49. John C. Coffee Jr., "Is Corporate Probation Worth the Cost? Guidelines Limit Discretion and Protect the Public Interest," *Manhattan Lawyer,* April 1990. Published in Manhattan Lawyer (American Lawyer Newspapers Group, Inc.), April 1990.

50. Robert Weissman, "Divide and Conquer: Restraining Vertical Integration and Cross-Industry Ownership," *Multinational Monitor,* October–November 2002.

51. Marshall Clinard et al., "Illegal Corporate Behavior."

52. Joe Thornton, *Pandora's Poison* (Cambridge, Mass.: MIT Press, 2000).

53. Marshall Clinard et al., "Illegal Corporate Behavior." p. 224.

54. During the height of the Vietnam War, John Kenneth Galbraith made a well-reasoned argument for public ownership of the weapons-manufacturing sector long before giant titans like Lockheed Martin and General Dynamics came to dominate certain weapons systems contracts. See John Kenneth Galbraith, "The Big Defense Firms Are Really Public Firms and Should Be Nationalized," *New York Times Magazine,* November 16, 1969.

55. Geov Parris, "Killing Corporations," *Seattle Weekly,* July 15, 1999. See also also the Congressional Progressive Caucus response to the State of the Union Address, 2003, Page 8. available at http://bernie.house. gov/pc/issues/AltSOUfinal-01-27-03.doc: "Progressives believe that corporations that repeatedly break the law or otherwise significantly violate the public trust should be placed under court-supervised probation until the company ceases operating in areas where it has shown repeated criminal conduct. In cases where such reform is not possible or the damage is greater than the company's ability to repay the victims, the corporation should have its charter revoked."

56. Interview with officials from the California State Tax Franchise Board, 2002. See Charlie Cray, "Chartering a New Course: Revoking Corporations' Right to Exist," *Multinational Monitor,* October–November 2002, p. 9.

57. "Commission Revokes Enron's Market-Based Rate Authority, Blanket Gas Certificates Terminated," June 25, 2003, available at http://www. ferc.gov.

58. Ohio Department of Agriculture press release, July 8, 2003. A hearing officer upheld the state's action after listening to hundreds of hours of testimony and researching the state's law. As in the case in Ohio, regulators have to provide for a reasonable closure plan and must remain vigilant to ensure that the company doesn't reorganize and reapply for permits under another corporate name.

59. http://www.essential.org/features/Clear_Channel_Objections.pdf.

60. Quoted in Robert McChesney and John Nichols, "Up in Flames: The Public Revolts Against Monopoly Media," *The Nation*, November 17, 2003. p. 11.
61. David Bollier, *Silent Theft* (New York: Routledge, 2002), p. 150.
62. Suspensions involve restricting a company from being eligible for further contracts until certain enforcement matters are resolved or certain changes are made within a the contracting corporation. Debarment is a form of suspension that usually lasts for a determined amount of time.
63. Statement of Stephen A. Perry, Administrator, General Services Administration, April 30, 2003, available at http://www.gsa.gov.
64. Project on Government Oversight, "Big Companies Break Law But Still Win Lucrative Government Contracts: $3.4 Billion in Settlements, Judgments, Fines and Penalties Since 1990," May 6, 2002, available at http://www.pogo.org.
65. 10 U.S.C. § 2305(b) (3) and (4) (C); 41 U.S.C. § 253b (c) and (d) (3).
66. FAR, 48 C.F.R § 9.103(a). For more information see, GAO-03-163, "Government Contracting: Adjudicated Violations of Certain Laws by Federal Contractors," November 2002.
67. Specifically, for federal contracts expected to exceed $100,000, prospective contractors were to certify whether, relative to these areas of law, they have been convicted of a felony (or have felony indictments pending against them), have had a federal court judgment in a civil case brought by the United States rendered against them, or have had an adverse decision by a federal administrative law judge, board, or commission indicating a willful violation of law. The FAR rule also provided guidance to agency contracting officers when considering a prospective contractor's compliance history.
68. The Contractors Accountability Act of 2003 (H.R. 2767) would establish a centralized, comprehensive database on judicial actions, consent decrees, administrative agreements, terminations, or settlements with respect to potential federal contractors or assistance participants. The law would prohibit a company from receiving federal contracts or assistance if it has had "rendered against it twice within any 3-year period a judgment or conviction for the same offense, or similar offenses, if each conviction constitutes a cause for debarment under the government-wide debarment system."
69. "Public Citizen Calls for Debarment of Reliant Energy from Federal Contracts Due to Company's Indictment for Role in California Energy Crisis," Public Citizen press release, May 26, 2004, available at: http://www.citizen.org/pressroom/release.cfm?ID=1718.
70. GSA #9930, "GSA Suspends Enron and Arthur Andersen and Former Officials," March 15, 2002. Note that in Enron and Arthur Andersen's cases, the GSA took action before the companies had even been charged with a crime.
71. Christopher Stern, "MCI to Begin Rebuilding of Iraqi Phones," *Washington Post*, May 15, 2003. Critics point out that WorldCom had no prior experience in establishing wireless service, and therefore there was no logical justification for extending the contract to the company.
72. Christopher Stern, "WorldCom Wins New Federal Contract," *Washington Post*, July 19, 2003.
73. Project on Government Oversight press release, January 8, 2004.

74. Robert Weissman, "Controlling Corporate Scofflaws or Blacklisting? The Clinton Administration's Proposed 'Responsible Contractor' Regulation," *Multinational Monitor*, July–August 1999.

75. "GSA's Deal with WorldCom: Bad Business for Taxpayers" Project on Government Oversight, press release, January 8, 2004 (available at http://www. pogo.org/p/contracts/ca-040101-worldcom.html). State and local governments can also adopt statutes and ordinances requiring greater scrutiny of bidders' records of compliance with the law. For model local ordinances, see the "Draft Municipal Ordinance to Provide for Corporate Accountability," available at http://www.stakeholderalliance.org; see also the Community Environmental Legal Defense Fund, http://www.celdf.org. The federal "Taxpayer Protection and Contractor Integrity Act," introduced in 2000, can also be viewed as a model for state legislation. For details on the Act, see: http://defazio.house.gov/ DEThreeStrikesSummary.htm.

76. Edwin H. Sutherland, *White Collar Crime* (New York: Dryden Press, 1949), p. 56.

77. Quoted in Morton Mintz and Jerry S. Cohen, *America, Inc.: Who Owns and Operates the United States?* (New York: Delta, 1971), p. 272.

78. Herbert C. Kelman and V. Lee Hamilton, *Crime of Obedience* (New Haven: Yale University Press, 1989).

79. Marshall Clinard et al., "Illegal Corporate Behavior."

80. Leaf et al., "Send Them to Jail."

81. Michael L. Benson and Francis T. Cullen, *Combating Corporate Crime* (Boston: Northeastern University Press, 1998), p. 241.

82. "Former Enron CEO Pays Attorneys $23 Million," Associated Press, March 18, 2004.

83. Russell Mokhiber, *Corporate Crime and Violence: Big Business Power and Abuse of the Public Trust* (San Francisco: Sierra Club Books, 1988), pp. 9 and 30.

84. Testimony of John C. Coffee Jr., Adolf A. Berle Professor of Law, Columbia University Law School, Senate Judiciary Committee hearings on White Collar Crime Penalties, July 10, 2002.

85. Marshall Clinard et al., "Illegal Corporate Behavior," p. 36. October, 1979.

86. David Burnham, *Above the Law: Secret Deals, Political Fixes, and Other Misadventures of the U.S. Department of Justice* (New York: Scribner, 1996), p. 218.

87. Leaf et al., "Send Them to Jail." p. 60.

88. Ibid. p. 60.

89. Executive Order 13271, available at http://www.usdoj.gov/dag/cftf/ execorder.htm. The task force's web page can be found at http://www.usdoj. gov:80/dag/cftf/.

90. Although one goal of the Corporate Fraud Task Force is to enhance cooperation between the SEC and the Department of Justice, the two agencies often act as rivals. In addition, the SEC's push for "real-time" enforcement (bringing cases to resolution quickly rather than taking years to pursue them) can also conflict with the tradition of giving criminal cases priority treatment.

91. David Johnston, "Big Names but No Authority to Prosecute," *New York Times*, July 10, 2002.

92. U.S. Department of Justice, Fiscal Year 2003 Performance Plan, section 2.4, available at http://www.usdoj.gov/ag/annualreports/pr2001/Section02. htm#SG2.4.
93. http://www.justice.gov/jmd/mps/strategic2001-2006/index.htm.
94. The growth of the Internet and the consequent importance of cybercrime should not be underestimated. But the point is that although the FBI established a new cybercrime division at its headquarters, as well as sixty specialized cybersquads in its field offices around the country, the bureau has no equivalent corporate crime division, instead leaving such matters to the Corporate Fraud Task Force, which has less permanent status and nowhere near the same budget.
95. S 2712, a bill to establish a Financial Services Crime Division in the Department of Justice, was introduced by Senators Bob Graham (D-FL) and John Kerry (D-MA) on June 7, 1990. It is available at http://www.thomas.loc.gov.
96. The Crime in America report is based on police reports from 17,000 law enforcement officials around the country. In late 2002, the GAO produced a report regarding violations of law by federal contractors, which provides some insight on what data would be available: at least six federal agencies maintain related databases of active or closed enforcement cases, including the EPA, the Department of Labor, the National Labor Relations Board (NLRB), the Federal Trade Commission (FTC), the Consumer Product Safety Commission (CPSC), and the Internal Revenue Service (IRS). See GAO-03-163, "Government Contracting: Adjudicated Violations of Certain Laws by Federal Contractors," available at http://www.gao.gov/new.items/ d03163.pdf. Few government agencies issue annual compliance reports, but such reports would be a constructive way to discipline federal agencies into paying close attention to corporate compliance with their laws and regulations. These rigorous annual reviews should be required as a way to strengthen the data-gathering process for the FBI's corporate crime report.
97. Lee Drutman, "Corporate Crime Acts like a Thief in the Night" *Los Angeles Times*, November 4, 2003.
98. The report language on the 2004 Commerce, Justice, State (CJS) appropriations bill (HR 2799) reads as follows: "The Committee is concerned that the Federal Bureau of Investigation [FBI] does not provide adequate information on corporate crime activities, such as pollution, accounting fraud, corruption, price fixing and tax evasion. While the FBI's Crime in the United States report provides information on street crime from 17,000 enforcement officials around the country, no similar report exists for corporate crime. The Committee expects the FBI to provide the Committee with information about the resources that it would take to produce a comprehensive report that includes all criminal, civil and administrative actions brought against a company, including resolution of the case. The report should also examine the trends and the number of civil cases referred by the Securities and Exchange Commission [SEC] and other agencies to U.S. Attorneys for criminal prosecution. Of these cases, the report should consider how many of those referrals were disposed, how many defendants were actually prosecuted, how many found guilty and how many were sent to jail."
99. Benson and Cullen, *Combating Corporate Crime,* p. 241.

100. For SEC budget history, see http://www.sec.gov/foia/docs/budgetact.htm; see also "SEC's Budget Indicator Is Up," *San Jose Mercury News,* January 17, 2003.
101. "The AM Law 100," *American Lawyer,* July 2002.
102. "Financial Oversight of Enron: The SEC and Private-Sector Watchdogs," Report of the Staff to the Senate Committee on Governmental Affairs, October 7, 2002, p. 10.
103. The SEC's 3,000-employee staff is barely half that of the Federal Deposit Insurance Corp., which oversees the activities of the nation's 13,000 FDIC-insured or -supervised banks. Yet at the height of the 1990s stock market bubble, the SEC was responsible for overseeing and safeguarding more than twice as much wealth as was held on deposit in all FDIC member banks combined. Congress passed a new law in June of 2003 that allowed the SEC to accelerate the hiring of new accountants, economists, and examiners by exempting them from civil service hiring requirements such as competitive exams, which can delay new hires by up to a year.
104. The SEC opened 598 cases in federal or administrative courts from October 2001 through September 2002, up 19 percent from the 12 months ending September 30, 2000.
105. "Interview with Jeff Ruch," *Multinational Monitor,* December 2003.
106. James L. Nash, "Lawmakers Press OSHA for Tougher Criminal Enforcement," *Occupational Hazards,* June 1, 2003.
107. AFL-CIO, "Death on the Job."
108. "Interview with Lisa Cullen," *Multinational Monitor,* September 2002.
109. "Interview with Margaret Seminario," *Multinational Monitor,* June 2003.
110. The proposal is encapsulated in a bill called the Wrongful Death Accountability Act, S. 1272 (108th Congress).
111. Joyce Rothschild and Terance D. Miethe, "Whistle-Blower Disclosures and Management Retaliation," *Work and Occupations* 26, no. 1 (February 1999):120.
112. "Blowing the Whistle on Corporate Wrongdoing: An Interview with Tom Devine," *Multinational Monitor,* October–November 2002.
113. For more information, see the Government Accountability Project and the National Whistleblowers Center, both at http://www.whistleblowers.org.
114. For more information, see Taxpayers Against Fraud, http://www.taf.org.
115. "Blowing the Whistle on Corporate Wrongdoing."
116. Ibid.
117. William L. Stringer, *The 1986 False Claims Act Amendments: An Assessment of Economic Impact* (Washington, D.C.: Taxpayers Against Fraud, The False Claims Act Legal Center 1996).
118. Joanne Doroshow, "Debunking the Myth of Frivolous Lawsuits," Letter to the Editor, *Washington Times,* May 25, 2001.
119. John C. Coffee Jr., "Guarding the Gatekeepers," *New York Times,* May 13, 2002.
120. *Reves v. Ernst & Young,* 507 U.S. 170 (1993).
121. *Central Bank of Denver v. First Interstate Bank of Denver,* 511 U.S. 164 (1994). Accountants, lawyers, and bankers have since used the *Central Bank* decision to get courts to dismiss shareholder litigation.
122. Twenty Democrats, including Senator Joe Lieberman, voted for the bill.
123. Private Securities Litigation Reform Act of 1995, Pub. L. No. 104-67.

124. Anthony Lewis, "Friends of Fraud?" *New York Times*, May 22, 1995.

125. Securities Litigation Uniform Standards Act of 1998, Pub. L. No. 105-353, 112 Stat. 3227 (1998).

126. For a full discussion, see "Plundering America: How American Investors Got Taken for Trillions by Corporate Insiders," by William S. Lerach, partner, Milberg Weiss Bershad Hynes & Lerach, available at http://www.milberg.com.

127. *Washington Post*, July 14, 2002.

128. Andrew Caffrey, "FBI Takes Up Heavy Load of Corporate Fraud Probes," *Boston Globe* May 6, 2003. Not all earnings restatements are an indication of fraud. Some restatements arise from honest mistakes or confusion over changing accounting rules. But the number of companies restating earnings is widely accepted as an overall indicator of the extent of accounting fraud. In 2003, the number of companies that restated their earnings dipped only slightly to 323. See Huron Consulting Group, "2003 Annual Review of Financial Reporting Matters." Available at: http://www.huronconsultinggroup.com/general01.asp?id=594&relatedNewsID=546&relatedProfessionalsID=563&relatedSolutionsID=333.

129. "Financial Oversight of Enron," p. 3.

130. "The Enron Debacle and Gatekeeper Liability: Why Would the Gatekeepers Remain Silent?" Testimony by Professor John C. Coffee before the Senate Committee on Commerce, Science and Transportation, December 18, 2001.

131. Government Response to the Fifteenth Report of Standing Committee on Justice and Human Rights, Corporate Liability, Canadian Justice Department, November 2002, available at http://www.uswa.ca/eng/westray/westray.htm.

CHAPTER 6

1. Judy Keen, "Bush, Lay Kept Emotional Distance," *USA Today*, February 26, 2002.

2. Ibid.

3. Hanna Rosin, "Bush-Lay Ties Based on Shared Priorities," *Washington Post*, March 24, 2002.

4. Minority Staff, House Committee on Government Reform, "Bush Administration and Contacts with Enron," report prepared for Rep. Henry A. Waxman (D-Calif.), May 2002.

5. Ibid. For a detailed history of Enron's involvement with the Bush Administration, see also "Enron's Shadow Government," a report by American Family Voices, available at http://www.americanfamilyvoices.com/pdf/shadowReport.pdf.

6. "How the White House Energy Plan Benefited Enron," report prepared for Rep. Henry A. Waxman by the Minority Staff of the Committee on Government Reform, U.S. House of Representatives, January 16, 2002, available at http://www.house.gov/reform/min.

7. Lowell Bergman and Jeff J. Gerth, "Power Trader Tied to Bush Finds Washington All Ears," *New York Times*, May 25, 2002.

8. Rep. Henry A. Waxman, letter to the Vice President, January 25, 2002; for background on the Dabhol plant, see "Enron's Pawns," by Jim Vallette, available

at http://www.seen.org, and "Power Play: A Study of the Enron Project," by Abhay Mehta. Available at http://www.seen.org/PDFs/pawns.PDF.

9. "Enron's Shadow Government," available at http://www.americasfami-lyvoices.org. Public Citizen's diagram of the relationships, available at http://www.citizen.org/documents/EnronTree.pdf.

10. For details on White's role at Enron and how he profited, see http://www.citizen.org/cmep/energy_enviro_nuclear/electricity/Enron/white/index.cfm.

11. Mark Green, *Selling Out: How Big Corporate Money Buys Elections, Rams Through Legislation, and Betrays Our Democracy* (New York: HarperCollins, 2002), p. 201.

12. Center for Responsive Politics, http://www.opensecrets.org.

13. Green, *Selling Out*, p. 199.

14. Michael Weisskopf, "Enron's Democrat Pals," *Time*, August 17, 2002. p. 20.

15. Minority Staff, House Committee on Government Reform, "Bush Administration and Contacts with Enron," report prepared for Rep. Henry Waxman (D-Calif.), May 2002.

16. Enron Political Action Committee, Inc., "Report of Receipts and Expenditures," July 21, 2001. See http://www.fec.gov.

17. Joe Stephens, "Hard Money, Strong Arms and 'Matrix': How Enron Dealt with Congress Bureaucracy," *Washington Post*, February 10, 2002.

18. FEC data, available at http://www.fec.gov.

19. Center for Responsive Politics: "Money is the Victor in 2002 Midterm Elections" November 6, 2002: http://www.opensecrets.org/pressreleases/Election2002Analysis.asp.

20. *Almanac of American Politics, National Journal*, 1998, 2000, 2002.

21. Center for Responsive Politics, "Business-Labor-Ideology Split in PAC, Soft and Individual Donations to Candidates and Parties," 2000 and 2002, available at http://www.opensecrets.org/.

22. Ibid.

23. Ibid.

24. Amy Keller, "Millionaires in Senate Top 40 for First Time," *Roll Call*, June 20, 2002.

25. Public Campaign, "Fueling Fears" *Ouch!* March 19, 2002.

26. Center for Responsive Politics, "Yucca Mountain: Did Money Influence the Senate Vote?" *Money in Politics Alert*, July 10, 2002.

27. For more comprehensive anecdotes on the influence of money in politics, see Public Campaign's *Ouch!* Newsletter as well as the Center for Responsive Politics.

28. Quoted in Ken Silverstein, *Washington on $10 Million a Day* (Monroe, Maine: Common Courage Press, 1998), p. 225.

29. Jeffrey H. Birnbaum, *The Lobbyists: How Influence Peddlers Get Their Way in Washington* (New York: Random House, 1992), p. 4.

30. Silverstein, *Washington on $10 Million a Day*, p. 23.

31. M. Asif Ismail, "The Clinton Top 100: Where Are They Now?" The Center for Public Integrity, available at http://www.publici.org/dtaweb/report.asp?ReportID=516&L1=10&L2=10&L3=0&L4=0&L5=0).

32. Chuck Neubauer, Judy Pasternak, and Richard T. Cooper, "The Senators' Sons: A Washington Bouquet: Hire a Lawmaker's Kid," *Los Angeles Times*, June 22, 2003.

33. Ibid.

34. Stephani Mencier, "Tom Daschle's Hillary Problem: If the Senate Majority Leader Runs for President What Will Voters Think of His Lobbyist Wife?" *Washington Monthly,* January–February 2002.

35. Silverstein, *Washington on $10 Million a Day*, p. 223.

36. Birnbaum, *The Lobbyists*, p. 6.

37. "Think Tanks for Sale," *TomPaine.Com*, op-ad, November 18, 2003.

38. Burdett Loomis and Michael Struemph, "Organized Interests, Lobbying and the Industry of Politics," paper prepared for presentation at the Midwest Political Science Association meeting, April 4–7, 2003, Chicago, Illinois.

39. Ibid.

40. Kevin Phillips, *Arrogant Capital* (New York: Little Brown and Company. 1994).

41. Loomis and Struemph, "Organized Interests, Lobbying and the Industry of Politics."

42. Dick Armey, "The Freedom and Fairness Restoration Act," available at http://flatax.house.gov/proposal/flat-sum.asp.

43. Phillips, *Arrogant Capital.*

44. William Greider, *Who Will Tell the People?* (New York: Touchstone, 1992), p. 106.

45. Bob Williams and Morgan Jindrich, "On the Road Again—and Again: FCC officials Rack Up $2.8 Million Travel Tab with Industries They Regulate," Center for Public Integrity, May 22, 2003. Also see Ralph Nader's letter to FCC inspector general William Feaster, May 29, 2003, available at http://www.citizenworks.org/corp/media/ralphletter.php.

46. Bob Williams, "Behind Closed Doors: Top Broadcasters Met 71 Times with FCC Officials," Center for Public Integrity, May 29, 2003.

47. Max Wigfield, "Bear Stearns Analyst Helps FCC Reshape Ownership Rules," *Wall Street Journal*, June 2, 2003.

48. See Chapter 2 for more about the Washington Legal Foundation.

49. Melody Petersen, "Who's Minding the Drugstore," *New York Times*, June 29, 2003.

50. "An FDA Q&A: How Does the First Amendment Limit Its Regulatory Power?" Washington Legal Foundation Legal Backgrounder, August 23, 2002; Phil Wallace, "Legal Foundation Praises First Amendment Review; Dietary Supplements," *Food Chemical News*, September 16, 2002.

51. Quoted in Petersen, "Who's Minding the Drugstore."

52. Anne C. Mulkern, "When advocates become regulators," Denver Post, May 23, 2004.

53. Ted Nace, *Gangs of America* (San Francisco: Barrett-Koehler, 2003), p. 148.

54. Ibid., p. 149.

55. *Buckley v. Valeo*, 424 U.S. 1 (1976).

56. Jamin B. Raskin and John Bonifaz , "The Wealth Primary: Campaign Fundraising and the Constitution," available at http://www.opensecrets. org/pubs/law_wp/wealthindex.htm.

57. US PIRG: Campaign Finance Reform Platform, available at http://pirg. org/democracy/democracy.asp?id2=5989&id3=CFR&.

58. See, for example, Public Campaign's *Ouch!* newsletter (which chronicles how money in politics hurts democracy) at http://www.publiccampaign.org. The

Center for Responsive Politics also puts out regular Money in Politics Alerts, available at http://www.opensecrets.org.

59. For a more thorough discussion of *First National Bank of Boston v. Bellotti*, see Chapter 2.

60. Phyllis S. McGrath, *Redefining Corporate-Federal Relations* (New York: Conference Board, 1979), p. 2.

61. Ibid., p. 58.

62. Ibid. p. 6.

63. David Vogel, "The Power of Business in America: A Re-appraisal," *British Journal of Political Science,* 13 (1983):30.

64. CBS News poll, January 15–17, 2002, as cited in Mark Green, *Selling Out*, p. 242.

65. ABC News/*Washington Post* poll, March 22–25, 2001, as cited in Mark Green, *Selling Out*, p. 242.

66. S. 1219, 104th Congress.

67. For a detailed narrative of McCain-Feingold, see Green, *Selling Out,* pp. 73–83.

68. Nick Anderson, "Campaign Reform Bill Passes Congress; Bush Says He'll Sign," *Los Angeles Times,* March 21, 2002.

69. "Soft Money: A Look at the Loopholes," *Washington Post* special report on Campaign Finance, September 4, 1998.

70. "Supreme Court Upholds Doubling of Hard Money Limits," U.S. PIRG press release, December 10, 2003.

71. Elisabeth Bumiller, "President Signs Bill on Campaign Gifts; Begins Money Tour," *New York Times*, March 28, 2002.

72. Don Van Natta Jr, "Soft Money Lives: Democrats Take In $12 Million (2 Gifts)," *New York Times*, March 22, 2002.

73. Public Citizen, "Cramming for the Midterm," November 1, 2002. Available at: http://www.citizen.org/congress/articles.cfm?ID=8495.

74. Derek Willis and Aaron Pilhofer, "Silent Partners: How Political Non-profits Work the System," Center for Public Integrity.

75. John Sents, "The New Soft Money: Gubernatorial Associations Skirt Campaign Finance Laws," Center for Public Integrity.

76. "Shays, Meehan Challenge FEC Regulations in Court," press release of Christopher Shays (R-Conn.), October 8, 2002.

77. Dan Christensen, "For Some Key Congressmen, Spring Break in the Keys," *Palm Beach Daily Business Review,* April 9, 2003.

78. John Bresnahan, "Texan Starts New Charity," *Roll Call,* November 13, 2003.

79. Michael Slackman, "Charity Tied to DeLay Cancels New York Convention Events" New York Times, May 20, 2004.

80. *McConnell vs. FEC*, No. 02.1674 (2003).

81. "Time to Rethink *Buckley v. Valeo*," *New York Times* editorial, November 12, 1998.

82. National Voting Rights Institute, "Reexamining *Buckley v. Valeo*," available at http://www.nvri.org/about/buckleyvvaleo.shtml.

83. *Nixon v. Shrink Missouri Government PAC*, 98-963 September 24, 2001.

84. *Austin v. Michigan State Chamber of Commerce*, 494 U.S. 652 (1990).

85. *Landall v. Sorrell*, U.S. Second Circuit, 2:99-cv146.

86. *Homans v. City of Albuquerque*, 264 F.3d 1240 (10th Circuit).

87. *Kruse v. City of Cincinnati*, 142 F.3d 907, 920 (6th Circuit), cert. denied, 525 U.S. 1001 (1998).

88. "Special Interests Take a Hit," *USA Today* editorial, March 28, 2002.

89. Public Campaign, "Clean Money Campaign Reform," available at http://www.publiccampaign.org.

90. Ibid.

91. Ibid.

92. Green, *Selling Out*, p. 250.

93. Ibid., p. 276.

94. Zach Polett, "Empower Citizens," in *Are Elections for Sale?* ed. Joshua Cohen and Joel Rogers (Boston: Beacon Press, 2001), p. 46.

95. For a good summary of the proposal, see Alliance for Better Campaigns, "The Case for Free Air Time," available at http://www.bettercampaigns. org/freeair-time/monograph.pdf.

96. Ibid.

97. "Broadcast Television: A Survivor in a Sea of Competition," FCC Working Paper, September 2002.

98. Center for Media and Public Affairs, "Campaign 2000 Final," *Media Monitor*, November–December 2000, available at http://www.cmpa.com/Mediamon/ mm111200.htm.

99. Ibid.

100. Alliance for Better Campaigns, "The Case for Free Air Time."

101. The Communications Act of 1934, available at http://www.fcc.gov/Reports/ 1934new.pdf.

102. Originally introduced as S. 3124 in the 107th Congress.

103. John McCain, "Free Air Time: The Continuing Reform Battle," *Election Law Journal*, available at http://www.freeairtime.org/docs/index. php?DocID=45.

104. Bob Edwards, "Fine Line Walked by Former Presidential Appointees When They Use Their Political Contacts in Post-Administration Jobs," *National Public Radio*, Morning Edition, February 23, 2001.

105. Ismail, "The Clinton Top 100."

106. "'Money in PoliTex' Offers the First Comprehensive Guide to a Texas Election," Texans for Public Justice news release, November 20, 2003, available at http://www.tpj.org/page_view.jsp?pageid=366&pubid= 208.

107. Diane Renzulli and the Center for Public Integrity, *Capitol Offenders: How Private Interests Govern Our States* (Washington, D.C.: Public Integrity Books, 2002), p. 18.

108. Ibid., p. 260.

109. National Resources Defense Council, "Corporate America's Trojan Horse in the States: The Untold Story Behind the American Legislative Exchange Council," available at http://www.alecwatch.org.

110. Ibid.

111. Ibid.

112. Ibid.

113. "Background About ALEC," available at http://www.alec.org.

114. Groups that do work on coordinating progressive state-level legislation include the New Rules Project (see http://www.newrules.org), the state Public Interest Research Groups (PIRGs, see http://www.pirg.org), the National Caucus of

Environmental Legislators (NCEL, see http://www.ncel.net/), and the Center for Law and Social Policy (CLASP, http://www.clasp.org).

115. For a more detailed look at state-level corporate influence, see Renzulli, *Capitol Offenders*.

116. Deborah Goldberg and Craig Holman, "The New Politics of Judicial Elections," Justice at Stake campaign, available at http://faircourts. org/files/JAS-MoneyReport.pdf.

117. Brent Kendall, "Chamber of Commerce Plans State Judicial-Race Campaigns," *Los Angeles Daily Journal*, January 8, 2004.

118. http://www.local.org.

119. John Browne, "Leading Toward a Better World? The Role of Multinational Corporations in Economic and Social Development of Poor Countries," April 3, 2002, speech at Harvard University. Available at: http://www.greenmoneyjournal.com/article.mpl?newsletterid=2&articleid=177.

CONCLUSION

1. The American Independent Business Alliance: http://www.amiba.net/.
2. The Living Wage Campaign: http://www.livingwagecampaign.org/.
3. Commercial Alert: http://www.commercialalert.org.
4. For more on cutting corporate welfare at the local level, see Good Jobs First: http://www.goodjobsfirst.org/.
5. http://www.citizen.org/cmep/Water/.
6. Randy Shaw, *Reclaiming America* (Berkeley: University of California Press, 1999), pp. 3–9.
7. Ibid.
8. Monica Wilson, "Dousing the Flames: Communities Unite Globally to Lock Out the Incinerator Industry," *Multinational Monitor*, January–February 2004. For more information, see http://www.no-burn.org.
9. Friends of the Constitution's website: http://www.i300.org.
10. New Rules Project, "Banning Corporate Ownership," available at http://www.newrules.org/agri/banning.html.
11. See Chapter 6 for a more thorough discussion of ALEC.
12. http://www.ncel.net/.
13. Institute for Local Self-Reliance, New Rules Project: http://www. newrules.org.
14. US PIRG: http://www.uspirg.org.
15. The Center for Policy Alternatives: http://www.cfpa.org/.
16. The American Legislative Issue Campaign Exchange: http://www. highroadnow.org/.
17. John Nichols, "ALEC Meets His Match: State Activists Are Learning How to Fight Back Against the Right's Powerhouse," *The Nation*, June 9, 2003. p. 14.
18. George Lakoff, "Framing the Dems: How Conservatives Control Political Debate and How Progressives Can Take It Back," *American Prospect*, September 1, 2003. p. 32.
19. Lawrence Goodwyn, *The Populist Moment: A Short History of the Agrarian Revolt in America* (Oxford: Oxford University Press, 1978), p. xviii.
20. Marc Cooper, "Teamsters and Turtles: They're Together at Last, WTO Summit: Seattle Is Only the Beginning as Activists from All Sides Come Together Against Growing Globalization," *Los Angeles Times*, December 2, 1999.

21. *What's Next for Organized Labor? The Report of the Century Foundation Task Force on the Future of Unions* (New York: The Century Foundation Press, 1999), p. 3.

22. Ibid., p. 22.

23. http://www.citiesforpeace.org.

24. At the giant protest against the IMF and World Bank in 2000, leaders of the Mobilization for Global Justice launched a boycott against World Bank Bonds, which has been joined by many cities, unions, investment funds, and other organizations. See http://www.econjustice.net.

25. John Sweeney, *America Needs a Raise* (New York: Houghton Mifflin, 1996), pp. 123–126.

26. Fair Taxes for All was formed to resist the Bush administration's series of legislative tax cuts (largely benefiting the rich and corporations), which are beginning to result in significant cutbacks in social services. See http://www.FTFA.org.

27. http://www.nicwj.org/index.html.

28. http://www.seiu.org/building/janitors/.

29. For a list of groups, see http://www.citizenworks.org/admin/press/unity-signons.php.

30. For the full text, see http://www.citizenworks.org/admin/press/unityplatform.php.

31. Carl Boggs, *The End of Politics* (New York: Guilford Press, 2000), pp. 6–7.

32. Mercedes M. Cardona, "Ad-Spending Soothsayers Optimistic on Year Ahead," *Advertising Age*, December 15, 2003.

33. Vincent P. Bzdek, "The Ad Subtractors, Making a Difference," *Washington Post*, July 29, 2003.

34. Robert J. Coen, "From Depression Depths to Bicentennial Booms, Ad Budgets Rose and Fell—Mostly Rose—with the Nation's Fortunes: Spending Spree," *Advertising Age*, March 29, 1999.

35. In 2001, for example, the Please Touch Museum in Philadelphia (a science museum) agreed to change its name to the "Please Touch Museum Presented by McDonald's Kids Charities" in exchange for a $5 million donation (though it neglected to give any mention to the state of Pennsylvania for a $15 million donation around the same time). As museum president Nancy D. Kolb explained, "we needed the money." See Lini S. Kadaba, "Museums Embrace Corporate Sponsorship," *Philadelphia Inquirer*, August 9, 2001.

36. National Public Radio (NPR) reports that "contributions and corporate underwriting totaled $40.5 million in FY 2002 and represented approximately 43% of NPR's total operating revenue for the year, a decline from 46.8% the previous year. Although NPR continues to maintain its traditional high standards, it has not been immune to the economic slowdown that began in 2000 and has since been exacerbated by terrorism and war. Such conditions have had an adverse and almost immediate effect on NPR's ability to secure contributed revenues." See http://www.npr.org/about/annualreports/npr2002.pdf for NPR's annual report.

37. In 2003, for example, the PTA came under fire for accepting a donation from Coca-Cola at a time when widespread placement of soft drink vending machines in schools was coming under increased attack. In defending the

decision to take Coca-Cola's money, PTA president Shirley Igo said, "We really need them. Our budget is very thin and if we didn't have them we wouldn't be able to develop new programs." Around the same time, the PTA also gave a seat on its board to John H. Downs Jr., Coca-Cola's senior vice president for public affairs and the company's chief lobbyist. But Coke isn't the PTA's only corporate donor. In the fall of 2002, Disney Interactive and Microsoft sponsored back-to-school programs designed to help parents see how technology could help their children with homework. The PTA has also taken money from AT&T Wireless and the National Football League. In announcing its intention to seek corporate money on its website, the PTA notes that companies can distribute material to more than 26,000 local PTAs using the "Proud Sponsor of National PTA" label on its packaging, getting the company logo on the PTA website, and being mentioned in the PTA newsletter. See Caroline E. Mayer, "PTA Turning to Corporate Sponsors for Funds," *Washington Post*, June 21, 2003.

38. George Farah, *No Debate: How the Republican and Democratic Parties Secretly Control the Presidential Debates* (New York: Seven Stories Press, 2004), p. 14.
39. James B. Twitchell, *Adcult USA* (New York: Columbia University Press, 1996), p. 2.
40. Amy Server, "The Malling of America," *Fortune*, October 13, 2003.
41. Juliet Schor, *The Overspent American* (New York: Basic Books, 1998), p. 107.
42. Booth Moore, "Heeding the Call—to Spend; Many Americans Consider It Their Patriotic Duty to Get Out and Shop," *Los Angeles Times*, October 8, 2001.
43. One narrow approach has been suggested by Rep. Pete Stark (D-Calif.), who in 2001 proposed denying "tax deductions for unbalanced direct to consumer (DTC) pharmaceutical advertising that places more emphasis on product benefits and dramatically minimizes product risks." See "Stark Introduces Fair Balance Prescription Drug Advertisement Act," Press release of Rep. Pete Stark (D-Calif.), June 27, 2001, available at http://www.house.gov/stark/documents/107th/dtcadpress.html.
44. David Bollier, *Silent Theft* (New York: Routledge, 2002), pp. 8–9.
45. Author interview with Richard Grossman, June 18, 2003.
46. David Wagner, *What's Love Got to Do with It?: A Critical Look at American Charity* (New York: The New Press, 2000). p. 161, 175.
47. Ralph Nader, *Crashing the Party: How to Tell the Truth and Still Run for President* (New York: St. Martin's Press, 2002), p. xi.
48. Ibid., p. xii.
49. Boggs, *The End of Politics*, p. 260.
50. Sue Branford and Bernardo Kucinski, *Lula and the Workers Party in Brazil* (New York: The New Press, 2003), p. 27.
51. Ibid., p. 31.
52. Ibid., p. 54.
53. Boggs, *The End of Politics*, p. 262.
54. For a detailed list and analysis of electoral reforms, see www.fairvote.org
55. Bill Moyers, Keynote Address to the National Conference on Media Reform, November 8, 2003, Madison, Wisconsin.
56. For more information, see http://www.mediareform.net.

57. "More than 1400 gather in Madison, WI for National Conference on Media Reform," Free Press press release, available at http://www. mediareform.net/news/release.php?id=7.

58. For a fuller treatment, see Robert McChesney: *The Problem of the Media: U.S. Communication Politics in the Twenty-First Century* (New York: Monthly Review Press, 2004), and Robert McChesney, *Rich Media, Poor Democracy: Communication Politics in Dubious Times* (New York: New Press, 1999).

59. Thomas Paine, "The Magazine in America." Published in Wheeler, Daniel Edwin (ed.) *Life and Writings of Thomas Paine*, Vincent Parle & Co, 1908.

60. Roughly ten transnational conglomerates with revenues ranging from roughly $8 to $35 billion a year thoroughly dominate the media landscape. The list includes Disney (ABC), AOL Time Warner (CNN), News Corporation (Fox), Viacom (CBS), Vivendi Universal, Sony, Liberty, Bertelsman, AT&T-Comcast, and General Electric (NBC). "The first tier owns all the commercial television networks, all the major Hollywood studios, four of the five firms that sell 90 percent of the music in the United States, a majority of the cable TV systems, all or part of most of the successful cable TV channels, and much, much, more. In the second tier are another roughly twelve to fifteen firms that do about $3 to $8 billion of business each year. Firms like Hearst, the New York Times Company, the Washington Post Company, Cox, Knight-Ridder, Tribune Company, and Gannett have holdings in only two or three media sectors. See Robert McChesney and John Nichols, *Our Media, Not Theirs* (New York: Seven Stories Press, 2002).

61. Buzz Bissinger, "The State of the American Newspaper: Feeling the Heat," *American Journalism Review,* December 1999.

62. Robert McChesney and John Nichols, "Up in Flames: The Public Revolts Against Monopoly Media," *The Nation,* November 17, 2003.

63. James McCartney and John Herbers, "State of the American Newspaper," *American Journalism Review,* April 1999. Available at: http://www.ajr. org/article_printable.asp?id=3269.

64. Quoted in David Shaw, "Foreign News Shrinks in Era of Globalization," *Los Angeles Times,* September 27, 2001.

65. Robert McChesney, *Rich Media, Poor Democracy* (Urbana: University of Illinois Press, 1999), p. 281.

66. http://www.pacifica.org.

67. Predictably, the proposal was opposed by the powerful National Association of Broadcasters, which claimed that LPFM would interfere with bigger stations. Three years after Congress slashed the number of frequencies available by about 80 percent, an FCC study revealed that the interference claim was essentially bogus, and in February 2004 the FCC recommended that Congress lift the industry-sponsored restrictions on lower power broadcasting. Congress has yet to respond. For details, see http://www.mediareform.net/lpfm/.

68. See http://www.ccbroadcasters.com/score-natl.htm for a breakdown by state.

69. http://www.indymedia.org.

70. *First National Bank of Boston v. Bellotti,* 435 U.S. 765 (1978). See also http://www.democraticmedia.org/issues/mediacrossroads.html.

71. David Stout, "Court Upholds Telemarketing Restrictions," *New York Times*, February 18, 2004.
72. For a detailed analysis of the Do-Not-Call case, see http://www.reclaimdemocracy.org/corporate_speech/ftc_call_list_legal_analysis.html.
73. The Antitrust Modernization Commission Act of 2002, also known as the "21st Century Department of Justice Appropriations Authorization Act" (Pub. L. No. 107-273, 116 Stat. 1758 [2002]), created a twelve-member bipartisan commission to determine whether a need exists to modernize antitrust laws. The law directs the commission to solicit the views of "all parties concerned with the operation of the antitrust laws" and to report to Congress and the president within three years after the commission's first meeting. Members of the commission were appointed in early 2004. Many of the appointees have worked on behalf of companies embroiled in antitrust disputes in recent years, including Microsoft.

RESOURCES AND BIBLIOGRAPHY

ORGANIZATIONS

AFL-CIO
815 16th Street, NW
Washington, DC 20006
http://www.afl-cio.org

Alliance for Democracy
760 Main Street
Waltham, MA 02451
(781) 894-1179
http://www.thealliancefordemocracy.org

Association of Community Organizations for Reform Now (ACORN)
739 8th Street, SE
Washington, DC 20003
http://www.acorn.org

The Association for Integrity in Accounting
(a project of Citizen Works)
PO Box 18478
Washington, DC 20036
(202) 265-6164
http://www.citizenworks.org/actions/aia.php

Center for Corporate Policy
PO Box 19405
Washington, DC 20036
(202) 387-8030
www.corporatepolicy.org

Center for Responsive Politics
1101 14th Street, NW, Suite 1030
Washington, DC 200005
http://www.opensecrets.org

Center for Public Integrity
910 17th Street, NW, Seventh Floor
Washington, DC 20006
(202) 466-1300
http://www.publicintegrity.org

Citizens for Tax Justice
(202) 626-3780
http://www.ctj.org

Citizen Works
PO Box 18478
Washington, DC 20036
(202) 265-6164
http://www.citizenworks.org

Commercial Alert
4110 SE Hawthorne Blvd. #123
Portland, OR 97214-5426
(503) 235-8012
http://www.commercialalert.org

Common Cause
(202) 833-1200
http://www.commoncause.org

Community Environmental Legal Defense Fund
2859 Scotland Road
Chambersburg, PA 17201
(717) 709-0457
http://www.celdf.org

Consumer Federation of America
(202) 387-6121
http://www.consumerfed.org

Consumer Project on Technology
PO Box 19367
Washington, DC 20036
(202) 387-8030
http://www.cptech.org

Corporate Accountability Project
http://www.corporations.org

Corporate Crime Reporter
http://www.corporatecrimereporter.com

The Corporate Library
45 Exchange Street, Suite 201
Portland, ME 04101
(207) 874-6921
http://www.thecorporatelibrary.org

Corporate Research Project
Good Jobs First
1311 L Street, NW
Washington, DC 20005
(202) 626-3780
http://www.corp-research.org.

CorpWatch
1611 Telegraph Avenue, #702
Oakland, CA 94612 (510) 271-8080
http://www.corpwatch.org

Derivatives Study Center
1660 L Street, NW, Suite 1200
Washington, DC 20036
(202) 533-2588
http://www.financialpolicy.org

The Foundation for Taxpayer and Consumer Rights
1750 Ocean Park Blvd., Suite 200
Santa Monica, CA 90405
(310) 392-0522
http://www.consumerwatchdog.org

Free Press
http://www.freepress.net
(413) 585-1533

Friends of the Earth
1025 Vermont Ave., NW
Washington, DC 20005
http://www.foe.org

Global Exchange
2017 Mission Street, Suite 303
San Francisco, CA 94110
(415) 255-7296
http://www.globalexchange.org

Government Accountability Project
1612 K Street, NW, Suite 400
Washington, DC 20006
(202) 408-0034
http://www.whistleblower.org

Greenpeace
702 H St. NW
Washington, DC 20001
http://www.greenpeaceusa.org

Infact
46 Plympton Street
Boston, MA 02118
(617) 695-2525

Institute for Local Self-Reliance
New Rules Project
1313 Fifth Street, SE
Minneapolis, MN 55414
http://www.ilsr.org

Institute for Policy Studies
733 15th Street, NW, Suite 1020
Washington, DC 20005
(202) 234-9382
http://www.ips-dc.org

International Forum on Globalization
1009 General Kennedy Ave., #2
San Francisco, CA 94129
(415) 561-7650
http://www.ifg.org

Jobs With Justice
501 Third Street, NW
Washington, DC 20001
(202) 434-1106
http://www.jwj.org

Multinational Monitor
PO Box 19405
Washington, DC 20035
http://www.multinationalmonitor.org

Pension Rights Center
Washington, DC
(202) 296-3776
http://www.pensionrights.org

Program on Corporations, Law and Democracy (POCLAD)
PO Box 246
S. Yarmouth, MA 02661-0246
http://www.poclad.org

Project on Government Oversight
666 11th Street, NW, Suite 500
Washington, DC 20001-4542
http://www.pogo.org

Public Campaign
1320 19th Street, NW, Suite M-1
Washington, DC 20036
(202) 293-0222
http://www.publiccampaign.org

Public Citizen
1600 20th Street, NW
Washington, DC 20009
(202) 588-1000
http://www.citizen.org

Public Information Network
PO Box 95316
Seattle, WA 98145-2316
(206) 723-4276
http://www.endgame.org

Reclaim Democracy
222 South Black Ave.
Bozeman, MT 59715
(406) 582-1224
http://www.reclaimdemocracy.org

Shareholder Action Network
1612 K Street, NW, Suite 650
Washington, DC 20006
(202) 872-5313
http://www.shareholderaction.org

Taxpayers for Common Sense
651 Pennsylvania Ave., SE
Washington, DC 20003
(202) 546-8500
http://www.taxpayer.net

Texans for Public Justice
609 W. 18th Street, Suite E
Austin, TX 78701
(512) 472-9770
http://www.tpj.org

United for a Fair Economy
37 Temple Place, 2nd Floor
Boston, MA 02111
(617) 423-2148
http://www.faireconomy.org

United Students Against Sweatshops
888 16th Street, NW, Suite 303
Washington, DC 20006
(202) NO SWEAT
http://www.usanet.org

U.S. Public Interest Research Group
218 D Street, SE
Washington, DC 20003
http://www.uspirg.org

Women's International League for Peace and Freedom
1213 Race Street
Philadelphia, PA 19107
(215) 563-7110
http://www.wilpf.org

SELECTED BIBLIOGRAPHY

Walter Adams and James W. Brock, *The Bigness Complex: Industry, Labor, and Government in the American Economy* (Stanford, CA: Stanford University Press, 2004).

Ben Bagdikian, *The Media Monopoly,* 6th ed. (Boston: Beacon Press, 2000).

Joel Bakan, *The Corporation* (New York: Free Press, 2004).

Michael L. Benson and Francis T. Cullen, *Combating Corporate Crime* (Boston: Northeastern University Press, 1998).

Robert Benson, *Challenging Corporate Rule: The Petition to Revoke Unocal's Charter as a Guide to Citizen Action* (New York: Apex Press, 1999).

Alex Berenson, *The Number: How the Drive for Quarterly Earnings Corrupted Wall Street and Corporate America* (New York: Random House, 2003).

Adolf A. Berle Jr. and Gardiner C. Means, *The Modern Corporation and Private Property* (New York: Macmillan, 1933).

Jeffrey H. Birnbaum, *The Lobbyists: How Influence Peddlers Work Their Way in Washington* (New York: Times Books, 1992).

Carl Boggs, *The End of Politics: Corporate Power and the Decline of the Public Sphere* (New York: Guilford Press, 2000).

David Bollier, *Silent Theft: The Private Plunder of Our Common Wealth* (New York: Routledge, 2002).

Robert A. Brady, *Business as a System of Power* (New York: Columbia University Press, 1943).

Sue Branford and Bernardo Kucinski, *Lula and the Workers Party in Brazil* (New York: The New Press, 2003).

Kate Bronfenbrenner et al., *Organizing to Win: New Research on Union Strategies* (Ithaca, N.Y.: Cornell University Press, 1998).

Jonathan Brown, *Financial Deregulation: The Need for Safeguards* (Washington, D.C.: Essential Information, 1993).

Robert Bryce, *Pipe Dreams: Greed, Ego, and the Death of Enron* (New York: Public Affairs/Perseus, 2002).

Michael Budde and Robert Brimlow, *Christianity Incorporated: How Big Business Is Buying the Church* (Grand Rapids, Mich.: Brazos Press, 2002).

David Burnham, *Above the Law: Secret Deals, Political Fixes, and Other Misadventures of the U.S. Department of Justice* (New York: Scribner, 1996).

John Cavanagh et al., *Alternatives to Economic Globalization* (San Francisco: Berrett-Koehler, 2002).

Noam Chomsky, *Understanding Power: The Indispensable Chomsky,* ed. Peter R. Mitchell and John Schoeffel (New York: New Press, 2002).

Marshall B. Clinard and Peter C. Yeager, *Corporate Crime* (New York: The Free Press, 1980).

Joe Conason, *Big Lies: The Right-Wing Propaganda Machine and How It Distorts the Truth* (New York: Thomas Dunne Books, 2003).

Jamie Court, *Corporateering: How Corporate Power Steals Your Personal Freedom and What You Can Do About It* (New York: Tarcher/Putnam, 2003).

Kevin Danaher and Jason Mark, *Insurrection: Citizen Challenges to Corporate Power* (New York: Routledge, 2003).

John P. Davis, *Corporations: A Study of the Origin and Development of Great Business Combinations and of Their Relation to the Authority of the State* (New York: Capricorn Books, 1961).

Michael Dawson, *The Consumer Trap: Big Business Marketing in American Life* (Champaign-Urbana: University of Illinois Press, 2003).

Charles Derber, *Corporation Nation* (New York: St. Martin's, 1998).

Charles Derber, *People Before Profit* (New York: St. Martin's, 2002).

George Draffan, *The Elite Consensus* (New York: Apex Press, 2003).

Richard B. DuBoff, *Accumulation and Power: An Economic History of the United States* (Armonk, N.Y.: M.E. Sharpe, 1989).

A. Larry Elliott and Richard J. Schroth, *How Companies Lie: Why Enron Is Just the Tip of the Iceberg* (New York: Crown, 2002).

Ralph Estes, *The Tyranny of the Bottom Line: Why Corporations Make Good People Do Bad Things* (San Francisco: Berrett-Koehler, 1996).

The ETC Group, *ETC Century: Erosion, Technological Transformation, and Corporate Concentration in the 21st Century,* available at www.etcgroup.org.

Thomas Frank, *One Market Under God: Extreme Capitalism, Market Populism, and the End of Economic Democracy* (New York: Anchor, 2001).

Peter C. Fusaro and Ross M. Miller, *What Went Wrong at Enron: Everyone's Guide to the Largest Bankruptcy in U.S. History* (Hoboken, N.J.: John Wiley & Sons, 2002).

Jeff Gates, *Democracy at Risk* (Cambridge, Mass.: Perseus, 2000).

Tom Geoghegan, *Which Side Are You On: Trying to Be for Labor When It's Flat on Its Back* (New York: Farrar, Straus & Giroux, 1991).

Harry Glasbeek, *Wealth by Stealth: Corporate Crime, Corporate Law, and the Perversion of Democracy* (Toronto: Between the Lines Press, 2002).

Lawrence Goodwyn, *The Populist Moment: A Short History of the Agrarian Revolt in America* (Oxford: Oxford University Press, 1978).

Mark Green, *Selling Out: How Big Corporate Money Buys Elections, Rams Through Legislation, and Betrays Our Democracy* (New York: HarperCollins, 2002).

William Greider, *Who Will Tell the People? The Betrayal of American Democracy* (New York: Touchstone, 1992).

Thom Hartmann, *Unequal Protection: The Rise of Corporate Dominance and the Theft of Human Rights* (Rodale, Pa.: Rodale Press, 2002).

Edward Herman, *Corporate Control, Corporate Power* (Cambridge: Cambridge University Press, 1982).

Edward Herman and Gerry O'Sullivan, *The "Terrorism" Industry: The Experts and Institutions That Shape Our View of Terror* (New York: Pantheon, 1989).

Noreena Hertz, *The Silent Takeover: Global Capitalism and the Death of Democracy* (New York: HarperBusiness, 2003).

Morton J. Horwitz. *The Transformation of American Law, 1870–1960* (Oxford: Oxford University Press, 1992).

Arianna Huffington, *Pigs at the Trough: How Corporate Greed and Political Corruption Are Undermining America* (New York: Crown, 2003).

David Cay Johnston, *Perfectly Legal: The Covert Campaign to Rig Our Tax System to Benefit the Super Rich—And Cheat Everyone Else* (New York: Portfolio/Penguin, 2003).

Josh Karliner, *The Corporate Planet: Ecology and Politics in the Age of Globalization* (San Francisco: Sierra Club Books, 1997).

Marjorie Kelly, *The Divine Right of Capital: Dethroning the Corporate Aristocracy* (San Francisco: Berrett-Koehler, 2001).

Allan A. Kennedy, *The End of Shareholder Value* (Cambridge, Mass.: Perseus, 2000).

David Kessler, *A Question of Intent* (New York: PublicAffairs, 2001).

Naomi Klein, *No Logo* (New York: Picador, 2002).

Scott Klinger with Holly Sklar, "Titans of the Enron Economy: The Ten Habits of Highly Defective Corporations," United for a Fair Economy, April 10, 2002. Available at: http://www.faireconomy.org/press/2002/Enron.pdf

David C. Korten, *When Corporations Rule the World* (West Hartford, Conn.: Kumarian Press and San Francisco: Berrett-Koehler, 1995).

David C. Korten, *The Post-Corporate World* (West Hartford, Conn.: Kumarian Press and San Francisco: Berrett-Koehler, 1999).

Paul Krugman, *The Great Unraveling* (New York: Norton, 2003).

Robert Kuttner, *Everything for Sale: The Virtues and Limits of Markets* (New York: Knopf, 1998).

Kalle Lasn, *Culture Jam: How to Reverse America's Suicidal Consumer Binge—and Why We Must* (New York: Quill, 2000).

William Lerach, "Plundering America: How American Investors Got Taken for Trillions by Corporate Insiders," available at http://www.milberg.com.

Arthur Levitt, *Take on the Street: What Wall Street and Corporate America Don't Want You to Know* (New York; Pantheon Books, 2002).

Nelson Lichtenstein, *State of the Union: A Century of American Labor* (Princeton University Press, 2003).

Charles Lindblom, *The Market System* (New Haven, Conn.: Yale University Press, 2001).

Jay W. Lorsch, *Pawns or Potentates: The Reality of America's Corporate Boards* (Boston: Harvard Business School Press, 1989).

Robert McChesney, *The Problem of the Media: U.S. Communication Politics in the 21st Cenury* (New York: Monthly Review, 2004).

Robert McChesney, *Rich Media, Poor Democracy* (Urbana, Ill.: University of Illinois Press, 1999).

Robert McChesney and John Nichols, *Our Media, Not Theirs* (New York: Seven Stories Press, 2002).

Bethany McLean and Peter Elkind, *The Smartest Guys in the Room: The Amazing Rise and Scandalous Fall of Enron* (New York: Portfolio, 2003).

Fred Magdoff et al., eds., *Hungry for Profit: The Agribusiness Threat to Farmers, Food, and the Environment* (New York: Monthly Review, 2000).

Jerry Mander, *The Case Against the Global Economy: And for a Turn Toward the Local* (San Francisco: Sierra Club Books, 1997).

Roland Marchand, *Creating the Corporate Soul: The Rise of Public Relations and Corporate Imagery in American Big Business* (Berkeley: University of California Press, 1998).

Carl Mayer, "Personalizing the Impersonal: Corporations and the Bill of Rights," *Hastings Law Review* 41, no. 3 (March 1990).

John Micklethwait and Adrian Wooldridge, *The Company: A Short History of a Revolutionary Idea* (New York: Random House, 2003).

Lawrence Mitchell, *Corporate Irresponsibility* (New Haven, Conn.: Yale University Press, 2001).

Russell Mokhiber, *Corporate Crime and Violence: Big Business Power and the Abuse of the Public Trust* (San Francisco: Sierra Club Books, 1988).

Russell Mokhiber and Robert Weissman, *Corporate Predators* (Monroe, Maine: Common Courage, 1999).

Robert Monks: *The New Global Investors: How Shareholders Can Unlock Sustainable Prosperity Worldwide* (Oxford, U.K.: Capstone, 2001).

Robert Monks and Nell Minow, *Power and Accountability* (New York: HarperCollins, 1991).

Michael E. Murphy, "Dispelling TINA's Ghost From the Post-Enron Corporate Governance Debate," *Santa Clara Law Review* 43:63.

Ted Nace, *Gangs of America: The Rise of Corporate Power and the Disabling of Democracy* (San Francisco: Berrett-Koehler, 2003).

Ralph Nader, *Crashing the Party* (New York: St. Martin's, 2002).

Ralph Nader, *Cutting Corporate Welfare* (New York: Seven Stories Press, 2000).

Ralph Nader, *The Ralph Nader Reader* (New York: Seven Stories Press, 2000).

Ralph Nader, Mark Green, and Joel Seligman, *Taming the Giant Corporation* (New York: Norton, 1976).

Ralph Nader and Mark Green, eds., *Corporate Power in America* (New York: Grossman, 1973).

Ralph Nader and Wesley J. Smith, *No Contest: Corporate Lawyers and the Perversion of Justice in America* (New York: Random House, 1996).

John R. Nofsinger and Kenneth A. Kim, *Infectious Greed: Restoring Confidence in America's Companies* (New York: Prentice Hall, 2003).

Greg Palast, Jerrold Oppenheim, and Theo MacGregror, *Democracy and Regulation: How the Public Can Govern Essential Services* (London: Pluto Press, 2003).

Frank Partnoy, *Infectious Greed: How Deceit and Risk Corrupted the Financial Markets* (New York: Times Books, 2003).

Kevin Phillips, *Arrogant Capital* (New York: Little, Brown and Company, 1994).

Kevin Phillips, *Wealth and Democracy* (New York: Broadway Books, 2003).

Frances Fox Piven and Richard Cloward, *Poor People's Movements: Why They Succeed, How They Fail* (New York: Vintage, 1978).

Robert Pollin and Stephanie Luce, *Living Wage: Building a Fair Economy* (New York: New Press, 1998).

Jeffrey Reiman, *The Rich Get Richer and the Poor Get Prison: Ideology, Class, and Criminal Justice* (Boston: Pearson Allyn & Bacon, 2001).

Dean Ritz and POCLAD, eds., *Defying Corporations, Defining Democracy: A Book of History and Strategy* (New York: Apex Press, 2001).

William D. Roy, *Socializing Capital* (Princeton, N.J.: Princeton University Press, 1999).

Henry Scammell, *Giant Killers: The Team and the Law That Help Whistle-Blowers Recover America's Stolen Billions* (New York: Atlantic Monthly Press, 2004).

Dan Schiller, *Digital Capitalism: Networking the Global Market System* (Cambridge: MIT Press, 1999).

Juliet Schor, *The Overspent American* (New York: Basic Books, 1998).

Juliet Schor, *The Overworked American* (New York: Basic Books, 1991).

Randy Shaw, *Reclaiming America: Nike, Clean Air, and the New National Activism* (Berkeley: University of California Press, 1999).

Michael Shuman, *Going Local: Creating Self-Reliant Communities in a Global Age* (New York: Routledge, 2000).

Ken Silverstein, *Washington on $10 Million a Day: How Lobbyists Plunder the Nation* (Monroe, Maine: Common Courage, 1998).

Tyson Slocum, "Blind Faith: How Deregulation and Enron's Influence over Government Looted Billions from Americans," Public Citizen, December 21, 2001, available at http://www.citizen.org/documents/Blind_Faith.PDF.

Lawrence Soley, *Censorship Inc.: The Corporate Threat to Free Speech in the United States* (New York: Monthly Review Press, 2002).

Lawrence C. Soley, *Leasing the Ivory Tower: The Corporate Takeover of Academia* (Boston: South End Press, 1995).

John Stauber and Sheldon Rampton, *Toxic Sludge Is Good for You: Lies, Damn Lies and the Public Relations Industry* (Monroe, Maine: Common Courage, 1995).

John Stauber and Sheldon Rampton, *Trust Us, We're Experts* (New York: Tarcher/Putnam, 2001).

Christopher Stone, *Where the Law Ends* (New York: Harper & Row, 1975).

James Surowiecki, ed., *The Best Business Crime Writing of the Year* (New York: Anchor Books, 2002).

Edwin H. Sutherland, *White Collar Crime* (New Haven, Conn.: Yale University Press, 1983).

Brian Tokar, *Earth for Sale: Reclaiming Ecology in the Age of Corporate Greenwash* (Boston: South End Press, 1997).

James B. Twitchell, *Adcult USA* (New York: Columbia University Press, 1996).

U.S. Congressional Joint Committee on Taxation, "Report of Investigation of Enron Corporation and Related Entities Regarding Federal Tax and Compensation Issues, and Policy Recommendations" (Staff Report), JCS-3-03 (Washington, D.C.: U.S. Government Printing Office, February 2003).

U.S. Senate Committee on Governmental Affairs, "Financial Oversight of Enron: The SEC and Private-Sector Watchdogs" (Staff Report), S. Prt. 107–75 (Washington, D.C.: U.S. Government Printing Office, 2002).

U.S. Senate Committee on Governmental Affairs, "The Role of the Board of Directors in Enron's Collapse" (Staff Report), S. Prt. 107–70 (Washington, D.C.: U.S. Government Printing Office, July 8, 2002).

Jim Vallette and Daphne Wysham, "Enron's Pawns: How Public Institutions Bankrolled Enron's Globalization Game," Sustainable Energy and Economy Network, Institute for Policy Studies, March 2002, available at www.seen.org.

Martin Weiss, "Crisis of Confidence on Wall Street: Brokerage Firm Abuses and the Worst Offenders," Weiss Ratings, Inc., 2002. See: www.weissratings.com

Robert Weissman, "Divide and Conquer: Restraining Vertical Integration and Cross-Industry Ownership," *Multinational Monitor*, October–November 2003.

Geoffry D. White, ed., *Campus, Inc.: Corporate Power in the Ivory Tower* (New York: Prometheus, 2000).

Chin-tao Wu, *Privatising Culture: Corporate Art Intervention Since the 1980s* (New York: Verso, 2002).

Gil Yaron, "The Corporation Inside & Out," The Aurora Institute, January 2002, available at http://www.aurora.ca.

INDEX

ABOUT CITIZEN WORKS

Citizen Works is a nonprofit, nonpartisan, 501 (c) (3) tax-exempt organization founded by Ralph Nader in April 2001 to advance justice by strengthening citizen participation in power. Citizen Works gives people the tools and opportunities to build democracy.

Citizen Works's strategy is to develop systemic means to advance the progressive citizen movement. It does this in three ways. First, it enhances the work of existing organizations by helping to share information, build coalitions, and institute improved mechanisms for banding activists together. Second, it brings new energy and support to the progressive movement by recruiting, training, and activating citizens. Third, it starts new groups and acts as a catalyst where there are too few public interest voices.

Citizen Works asks, "How can the citizen movement be more than the sum of its parts?" "Who is in the pipeline for advocacy that promotes the common good?" "What tools do we have to make it easier to train more people, fill the gaps in the many missing constituencies in the public interest movement, and help individuals and nonprofit groups have more voice and power in our communities and in the halls of our capitols?"

As part of Citizen Works's mission to help existing nonprofits work better together and to increase the numbers of public interest voices where there are too few, Citizen Works initiated a major effort toward coordinating and building the corporate reform movement in 2002. The goals of Citizen Works's Corporate Reform Campaign are to build and mobilize a national network of citizens, activists, and organizations that can educate the public about the current destructive course of our political economy and can facilitate a shift from market-driven, unsustainable values to life-affirming, sustainable values. The campaign's vision is to move our society from one in which corporations dominate virtually every aspect of the political economy to one in which people once again recognize their capacities as citizens to exert sovereign control over the behavior of corporations.

ABOUT THE AUTHORS

Lee Drutman is a member of the Citizen Works Corporate Reform Commission and the editor of Citizen Works's *Corporate Reform Weekly,* an e-mail newsletter detailing the latest in corporate reform and corporate scandal. His commentaries have been published in many outlets, including the *Los Angeles Times, New York Newsday,* and the *Providence Journal,* and online at TomPaine.com, Alternet.org, and CommonDreams.org, among other websites. He has critiqued corporate wrongdoing on National Public Radio, the BBC, and NBC's *Today Show* and is a regular commentator on Business Talk Radio's *Business Talk This Morning.* Lee is a former staff writer for both the *Philadelphia Inquirer* and the *Providence Journal.* He is also a 1999 graduate of Brown University, where he earned Phi Beta Kappa and magna cum laude honors.

Charlie Cray is a member of the Citizen Works Corporate Reform Commission and the director of the Center for Corporate Policy in Washington, D.C., a nonprofit public interest group working to make corporations publicly accountable. He is the former director of the Citizen Works Campaign for Corporate Reform. Between 1999 and 2002, he was associate editor of *Multinational Monitor* magazine, the only monthly magazine devoted exclusively to reporting on corporate abuses worldwide. Before moving to Washington, DC, from his hometown of Chicago, he campaigned for over ten years with Greenpeace against persistent toxic chemicals and waste incineration. He holds a B.A. in English and American studies from Amherst College.

Alternatives to Economic Globalization
A better World Is Possible

Editors: John Cavanagh and Jerry Mander

Written by a premier group of 21 thinkers from around the world, the revised and expanded edition of *Alternatives to Economic Globalization* lays out alternatives to the corporate globalization more fully, specifically, and thoughtfully than has ever been done before. It also includes a new chart showing the effects of globalization on the United States.

Paperback 11/04 • ISBN 1-57675-303-4 • Item #53034 $18.95

Regime Change Begins at Home
Freeing America from Corporate Rule

Charlie Derber

Since 1980, America has been run by a corporate regime that has co-opted both political parties and shifted sovereignty from "we the people," to transnational corporations. Charles Derber shows why the regime must be overturned, and lays out a vision of a new regime based on a political realignment that unites liberals and conservatives. Derber offers hope—and specific, sophisticated, often surprising advice—for defeating the regime and returning America to its citizens.

Hardcover • ISBN 1-57675-292-5 • Item #52925 $19.95

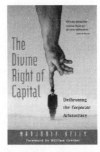

The Divine Right of Capital
Dethroning the Corporate Aristocracy

Marjorie Kelly

In *The Divine Right of Capital,* Marjorie Kelly argues that focusing on the interests of stockholders to the exclusion of everyone else's interests is a form of discrimination based on property or wealth. She shows that corporations are built on six aristocratic principles that work in the interests of wealth-holders, and against those of employees and the community. Most importantly, Kelly shows how to use democratic principles to build a new corporate order that serves the many, rather than the few.

Paperback • ISBN 1-57675-237-2 • Item #52372 $17.95

Berrett-Koehler Publishers
PO Box 565, Williston, VT 05495-9900
Call toll-free! **800-929-2929** 7 am-9 pm EST
Or fax your order to 1-802-864-7626
For fastest service order online: **www.bkconnection.com**

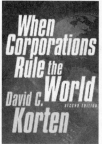

When Corporations Rule the World
Second Edition

David C. Korten

David Korten offers an alarming exposé of the devastating consequences of economic globalization and a passionate message of hope in this well-reasoned, extensively researched analysis. He documents the human and environmental conse-quences of economic globalization, and explains why human survival depends on a community-based, people-centered alternative.

Paperback • ISBN 1-887208-04-6 • Item #08046 $16.95

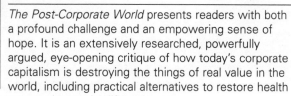

The Post-Corporate World
Life After Capitalism

David C. Korten

The Post-Corporate World presents readers with both a profound challenge and an empowering sense of hope. It is an extensively researched, powerfully argued, eye-opening critique of how today's corporate capitalism is destroying the things of real value in the world, including practical alternatives to restore health to markets, democracy, and everyday life.

Paperback • ISBN 1-887208-03-8 • Item #08038 $19.95

Hardcover • ISBN 1-88720-802-X • Item #0802X $27.95

Gangs of America
The Rise of Corporate Power
and the Disabling of Democracy

Ted Nace

Through a series of fascinating true stories populated by colorful personalities, *Gangs of America* details the rise of corporate power in America. Driven to answer the central question of how corporations got more rights than people, Ted Nace delves deep into the origins of this institution that has become a hallmark of the modern age. He also synthesizes the latest research with a compelling historical narrative.

Hardcover • ISBN 1-57675-260-7 • Item #52607 $24.95

Berrett-Koehler Publishers
PO Box 565, Williston, VT 05495-9900
Call toll-free! **800-929-2929** 7 am-9 pm EST

Or fax your order to 1-802-864-7626
For fastest service order online: **www.bkconnection.com**